DARK RIDE and OTHER PLAYS

DARK RIDE
and Other Plays

by
Len Jenkin

SUN &
MOON

CLASSICS
22

Sun & Moon Press
LOS ANGELES, CALIFORNIA

Sun & Moon Press
A Program of The Contemporary Arts Educational Project, Inc.
a nonprofit corporation
6026 Wilshire Boulevard, Los Angeles, California 90036

First published in paperback in 1993 by Sun & Moon Press
10 9 8 7 6 5 4 3 2 1
SUN & MOON EDITION
©Len Jenkin, 1993
Biographical information ©Sun & Moon Press, 1993

This book was made possible, in part, through a grant from the
Andrew W. Mellon Foundation, the National Endowment for the Arts,
and through contributions to The Contemporary Arts Educational Project, Inc.,
a nonprofit corporation.

Cover: *Pink Elephant,* by Reginald Marsh
Design: Katie Messborn
Book typography by Jim Cook

LIBRARY OF CONGRESS CATALOGING IN PUBLICATION DATA
Jenkin, Len
Dark Ride and Other Plays
p. cm. — (Sun & Moon Classics: 23)
ISBN: 1-55713-073-6
I. Title. II. Series.
811'.54—dc 20

Printed in the United States of America on acid-free paper

Contents

CURTAIN RAISER

Len Jenkin is one of the most fascinating, evocative, and important playwrights in America today. His work is overflowing with a highly charged theatrical life and imagination. Yet there's always a deep romantic, poetic current that informs and guides the verbal/visual fireworks. His insightful use and examination of the mythical aspects of American culture, and of the American psyche, is unique.

This book contains Len Jenkin's more recent plays for the stage. They exhibit an intense and spectacular creativity, and a growing sense of control and direction. The car is moving just as fast, the ride is no less exciting, but there's a firmer hand at the wheel. Jenkin knows better where he is taking us, and sometimes even gets us there in one piece.

These plays are searchlights in the darkness, explorations into the essence of how we live, what binds us and what makes us free.

—JOSEPH PAPP
New York Shakespeare
Festival Public Theatre
New York City, 1990

INTRODUCTION

The theatre came as an amazing surprise in my life. I was up at a friend's cabin in New Hampshire one fall long ago, trying to locate myself in the world, and/or the world in me, and it was 30 miles above Keene in the middle of nowhere. It was getting cold, and the wood stove didn't heat the place that well. I was doing pretty good though, and shaved in a cracked piece of mirror hung on a tree. I was a writer. I wrote poems and narrative prose. I had written, among other things, a novel called *High Speed Merge,* now resting peacefully in a drawer, that is so full of manic literary and spiritual energy that it tumbles over itself, roars out unintelligible blasts of language, and then stands there in the middle of the road, feets all tangled, not knowing which way to go.

For some reason, I put down whatever else I was trying to make up there in the woods, and I wrote a play. I think the solitude made me bring company into my head, and let them talk it out with each other.

I had read plays in college, but had never studied how to write them, and had never made any particular connection with the stage. I hadn't been an actor, or a theatre-goer. I was a writer, so I imagined a play, and since I didn't know better, I wasn't shy of flinging a huge dose of poetic language at it, along with impossible and glorious stage directions.

This first play, *Kitty Hawk,* is a story of two madmen who believe they are the "Wright" brothers and construct a huge plane on a deserted beach, using as material all the debris of Western Civilization. Other characters include a sea serpent, John Ringling North, John Ringling South, and the two end men from a minstrel show, Mr. Interlocketer and Mr. Bones.

It might have been the only play I ever made, except that its fate was different from that of all the novels and most of the poems I desperately sent off now and then to every kind of publisher. These were usually sent back to me, by the philistine establishment and lunatic downtown magazines alike, with the same message: Just forget it son, and good luck elsewhere. I was so unsure of the play I sent it to only one theatre. I got a letter back saying they would like to produce it. The world was calling. I left my cabin and hung out with this crowd of actors, actresses, designers, director etc. as they did my play. They were glad to have me there. I was crazy about the production. The actresses were beautiful. The actors were beautiful. The sea serpent was beautiful. I changed a few lines. They gave me a place to stay, and paid me a hundred dollars. I was hooked. Since that time, though I've also written two novels, and a number of films and television shows, I've consistently written for the stage.

There simply wasn't room in this book for "the complete plays," and I had to make some choices. You're holding only fairly recent work. Of the five plays in this collection, I've always thought of *Limbo Tales, Dark Ride,* and *My Uncle Sam* as a trilogy of a kind, in that order. In each succeeding play the search leads to more light, and more darkness falls away.

American Notes is the beginning for me of something new that I am still exploring. It's still multilayered, and tricky, and hiding behind itself. But I hope there is a directness, and an honesty that's not as present in the earlier plays. A little more heart, and less head. I believe this play is purer somehow, straight talk from America. I don't see it as an improvement over my previous work, but simply as a change. Maybe I'm learning to write for the theatre.

Poor Folk's Pleasure is the most recent play in this collection. It was developed in workshop, and the author/director owes a particular debt to its original company.

I was the first director of all the plays in this collection, either in a workshop *(Poor Folk's Pleasure, American Notes)*, or in the first full production *(Limbo Tales, Dark Ride, My Uncle Sam)*. Directing my own work demanded I make choices that kept creating the play I thought I'd finished. It taught me a helluva lot about what I'd done on the page, and what it means when thought and language is embodied, made flesh. Wonderful directors of my work have also taught me a lot about this process, and a lot about what I've written, as have actors and designers. I've learned from all of them, and some have shaped my words and pictures in ways that set the play on fire, lit up inside and out.

There are many extraordinary people in the theatre who've helped me enormously through their encouragement and their wonderful artistry. I can't list them all, but I want them to know how much working alongside them has meant to me. It's a great joy to me that we're in this world together. My heartfelt thanks, and my gratitude.

—LEN JENKIN

These plays are for Emily, and for Ramona

Limbo Tales

Limbo Tales was first presented by Pequod Productions at the Westbeth Theatre Center in New York, December 4, 1980, with the following cast:

MASTER OF CEREMONIES	John Nesci
DRIVER	Bill Sadler
MAN	Will Patton

The recorded voices were performed by: Richard Bright, Len Jenkin, Carol Kane, Gerald Marks, Nancy Mette, Charles Saaf, Dale Soules, and Richard Zobel.

Director: Len Jenkin
Set: John Arnone
Lights: Norman Coates
Costumes: Susan Denison
Stage Manger: Kate Costello

PRODUCTION NOTE

Staging *Limbo Tales* requires complex tracks of effects, music, and voice. All of this can be taped, the show then requiring only three "live" actors, and about eight others on tape. It is also possible to do all the voices in *Limbo Tales* live, either with the actors offstage on mike, or with an imaginative onstage placement of these actors.

The script for *Highway* is divided into two columns, TEXT and SET/SOUND, as the relationship and timing of words, sounds, and actions is meant to remain flexible, and to be subject to the individual set, actor, and new discoveries in production. For example, a "Radio on" cue here is not meant to be placed exactly between two spoken words of the DRIVER'S. That point needs to be found in production. In this text of *Highway*, visuals are achieved mainly through miniatures and their manipulation. The author also suggests that the text might be amenable to the use of projections, maps, etc., either alone or in combination with models.

Limbo Tales

1. HIGHWAY

2. INTERMEZZO

3. HOTEL

HIGHWAY

The MASTER OF CEREMONIES *enters. He wears a cheap
suit and tie. He talks directly to the audience, sinister and
slow.*

MC: Ladies and gentlemen, good evening. And welcome
to *Limbo Tales.* My associates, and I, wish you an
enjoyable evening. Good luck. And now, Limbo
Tales, Part One.

   [The MC *slowly puts on a pair of driving gloves. He
mimes driving. A look of sudden terror crosses his face.]*

MC: Highway

   [The MC *is gone. The lights go to black, come up to
reveal the highway set onstage, covered by a drop. The set
is a large table representing a miniature highway. It is a
two lane road, perfectly straight, perhaps in perspective.
The* DRIVER *will move about it as he talks. Structures,
vehicles etc. appear during the play as the* DRIVER
describes them. Events occur on set as the DRIVER
*describes them. Some occur which he does not describe.
Most of these visuals are created directly by the* DRIVER,
*by moving models by hand, or by mechanical or electric
switch. Some seem to occur by themselves. Lighting in-
dicates daylight. The* DRIVER *appears, with the surface of
the highway rolled up under his arm. He removes the
drop from the table. He rolls out the road, with its dotted
white line, sets it in place.]*

DRIVER: Highway. *[He places a small house on one end of the
set.]* This is Margaret's house. *[He places a small house
on the other end of the set.]* This is my house.

   *[Lights dim to night, as tiny lights inside the houses
on set come on. The* DRIVER *stands at one end of the highway, behind his house.]*

SET/SOUND   TEXT

DRIVER'S *car appears on the highway near his house.*

Car radio on (pop music).
Ignition sound, car take-off sound.

Car moves away from house.

Radio off.

DRIVER: I'm an assistant professor of anthropology at the State University here in Townsend. I hesitated tonight before taking my car out of the garage to make the two-hour drive to Bellingham. I've got an end-of-term lecture to deliver in the morning, and the call I received from Margaret was ambiguous to say the least. She seemed angry about something. I think she said she wanted to discuss our future, or the future, and that we had to get together right away. It was a bad connection and her voice was fuzzy, fading in and out. I remember asking if it could wait, and then either she hung up on me, or we were disconnected. I checked my watch. Ten fifteen exactly. I tried to call her back in Bellingham, but her line was busy. Either she'd taken the phone off the hook, which she's been known to do, or she was calling some bartender she met in the shopping mall.

Actually, I doubt that. Our relationship has been pretty

strong . . . Well, I have to admit its been strained a bit lately. My work's been piling up, and the two hour drive between us seems longer. . . .

DRIVER places his cassette player on set.

In any case, my lecture isn't till noon tomorrow, so I grabbed my cassette player with the tape of my notes, and jumped into the car. I started this drive at 10:19 P.M. There by midnight if I push it, we can talk, and I can be home by four. Or maybe I'll stay over in Bellingham, drive back in the morning. I hope this isn't going to be the kind of serious argument Margaret's been prone to lately. Hell, maybe the whole business is trivial—nothing. I'll get there and she'll wonder why I rushed over. . . .

Driving at night is strange, particularly over a route you're very familiar with. You see the landmarks you know come up out of the dark: Coppertone billboard, glow of a TV inside a certain house, diner, phone booth, factory, red exit lights on the landings, the quartet of gas stations on the four corners of one inter-

Some or all of these landmarks appear as spoken.

section: Exxon, Shell, Gulf, Mobil —luminous signs turn slowly in the air. At night the world is blanked out, except for these lit landmarks, and those few signals on which your life depends: white stripe on the blacktop, headlights, tailights, roadsigns. Ignore them for more than two or three seconds and you die. Pay attention to the lights in the dark . . . and yet, as all those other external signals disappear there's more and more room for internal signs to float up in the dark space the night makes in your mind. . . .

DRIVER *turns on his cassette player.*

Better prep that last lecture. Just get some of these ideas in my head, and I'll be able to wing it. . . .

CASSETTE TAPE: [DRIVER'S *voice.*] Yeah . . . uh . . . Final lecture notes, Anthropology 201, The Ancient Mayans. 12:48 a.m., and this is tape 2, side A., Father Diego Vasquez, *Indians of the Central Americas,* chapter three . . . ah, ah! O.K. Once the Mayans constructed their great pyramid at Uxmal, on top of it was stationed

Car moving. . . .

The first level of a Mayan pyramid is built near the midpoint of the highway.

a man chosen by lot, called the Illum Kinnal, the Time Watcher. His job is to protect the sequence of orderly time, to keep it running smoothly from past to future. He does this by guarding it with his eyes. If his attention weakens for one moment, there is a subtle break in the time line. Past, present and future mix. Work in the fields stops. People have visions, headaches, momentary hallucinations. The priests notice, and the Illum Kinnal is killed, his heart offered to the gods, and he's replaced by another time watcher. . . .

DRIVER: I don't think I'll mention it to Anthropology 201, but the truth is that the Mayans were nuts.

DRIVER looks at his watch.

Ten-thirty. Damn phone connection. Did I tell Margaret I was coming? I can't remember . . . and if I did I can't be sure she heard me. Knowing Margaret, if she doesn't know I'm on my way, she's likely to hop in her car and come rushing over to my house. . . . That's a possibility. Can't make out the cars, much less

Margaret's car appears on highway near her house, pointed toward his house.

who's at the wheel. If one of these sets of headlights coming at me is her, we'll arrive at each other's empty houses. . . . Jesus. That busy signal when I tried calling her back—she could've been trying to call me to tell me she's on her way. If she's coming this way, she'll just put the pedal to the floor. If she arrives at my place and I'm not there, she'll be furious . . . The last thing I need is a scene the night before my lecture . . . maybe I should turn around now, go home myself in case. . . .

Hell, I'm working myself up over nothing. She must know I'm coming. She's probably pacing the living room at her place right now, waiting for me.

Radio on: traffic and weather.

RADIO: *[Helicopter sounds.].* . . . This is Celeste from the WQEZ copter, and its a beautiful night up here, Bob, visibility unlimited. I can even see the planet Venus along the horizon, and not a traffic flow problem in sight. Bridges and tunnels are good, and the highway between Townsend and Bellingham is clear sailing. So to all you folks at home, and to those folks still on the road, this is your eye in the sky reminding you to drive safely. *[Music follows, rock and roll.]*

DRIVER: Uh oh. Low on gas. . . .
Gas station appears. I'm in luck. Station ahead.
[To station attendant.] Ten dol-
Car pulls in by the lars worth of regular please.
pump.

ATTENDANT'S VOICE: *[Offstage or tape.]* You got it.

DRIVER: Say, is there a pay phone around?

ATTENDANT'S VOICE: Yeah. It's out of order.

DRIVER: Look, I have a very important call I have to. . . .

ATTENDANT'S VOICE: Use the one in my office. Near the coffee shop.

Car to parking space DRIVER: Thanks.
near station, DRIVER
moves away from
highway to phone,
taking cassette

player. Sound of dialing, then phone ringing. The DRIVER *hangs up. Margaret's car moves forward on the highway.* DRIVER *sits at highway as counter. He has a cup of coffee. He turns on his cassette player.*

No answer. She must be in her car and on the way. All right. All I have to do is turn around and go home, meet her there. I can still get there a good half hour ahead of her. Might as well have a coffee here. I could use one.

Ah . . . let's see what else we've got for tomorrow.

CASSETTE TAPE: . . . Kornfeld's *Time and the Gods,* page 6 of the intro. . . . The Maya conceived of the divisions of time . . . days, hours, seconds, months, years, as weights carried on the backs of divine bearers. In our terms it's as if on, let's say April 26, 1993, there are five bearers in action: the god of number 26 with April on his back, the god of number one carrying the millenium, the god of number nine loaded with centuries, his twin shouldering the decades, and the god of three carrying the years. At the end of the day, as the date is changed, the gods change.

Ignition sound, etc.
Car onto highway,
heading back to
DRIVER'S *house.*

Radio on, then off.

Margaret's car makes
a U-turn, heading
back home.

U-turn, driving to
Margaret's house.

Margaret's car makes
another U, heading to
DRIVER'S *house.*

Both cars spin in
circles, end up
pointing in their
original directions. . .

DRIVER: Odd notion when you think about it, the gods all members of this gigantic relay team, marching on through eternity. Better hit the road, or Margaret'll get to my place before me. . . .

Uh oh. What if she stopped on the highway, like I did, and called my place. No answer. She'd figure I was on my way to see her, and she'd turn around to get back to her place before I got there. If that's true—right now we're racing away from each other in opposite directions, to end up exactly where we started. She's impulsive, but she's not dumb. She'd think to call. I better make a U. . . .

God. What if she's realized I'd stop on the road to call too, get no answer, figure she's coming, and go home myself. Then she'll make her U-turn, we pass each other in the night, she ends up at my house, I'm at hers. Nobody home. We turn, race back, pass each other again, and again, and again, and. . . .

This kind of thinking is pointless. All we have here is two people trying to find each other . . .

on a highway at night, true. I am going to stop making circles in my head and just go to her . . . *[sings]* Hit the road, Jack, and don't you come back no mo', no mo', no mo', no mo'. . . .

Radio on, static and pop music. . . .

You know, from within my Dodge Dart, the world is just pictures, a movie through the windshield. I can change the landscape's soundtrack with a simple flick of the wrist. . . .

DRIVER *changes radio stations . . . jazz music—lights change; country music—lights change. Then the mystery theatre:*

WBAZ. . . .
WQET. . . .
WKIT. . . .
WETC. . . .

RADIO: . . . London at midnight, a great city wrapped in a shroud of dense yellow fog. The streetlights, weird as elfin lamps, grow misty as something fashioned in a dream. Behind an ancient wall, a vast gloomy mansion crouches like an evil beast of prey. On the drawn shades, the shadow of a superman of incredible genius, possessing a brain like Shakespeare and a face like Satan. . . . *[Hysterical demonic laughter.]*

Changing radio station: One drum, slow beat.

DRIVER: I like that. Simple. Boom, boom, boom, . . . Hey? What the hell's that rattling around . . . sounds like something in the glove compartment.

DRIVER checks the "glove compartment" below the table—finds a bone flute.

What the hell is this thing? Who the hell's been driving this car besides me? Nobody, and I cleaned out this glove compartment last week. Some of my students must be playing some kind of practical joke. . . .

DRIVER plays flute, along with drum-beats.

Not bad.

DRIVER turns radio off, but drum continues, softer. Cassette on.

Well, back to work.

CASSETTE TAPE: The Mayans wanted badly to know which gods were marching on any day, because given this information they could define the combined influence of all the marchers of the day, for good or evil, on whatever they wanted to do. The priests did this figuring, but their calculations were far more intricate than you might imagine. Not only the gods of numbers, carrying years, minutes and cen-

Both cars rolling. . . . Second layer of the Mayan pyramid is built.

turies were marching. They had a cycle of nine nights, over each of which a god ruled. Each lunar phase and each revolution of Venus had its divinity. Then

Drum fades out. . . .

there were gods of the particular activity planned. If they were planting—the soil gods, rain

DRIVER *turns off cassette.*

gods, corn gods.

DRIVER: If they were driving, the tire gods, the god of the highway, the gasoline god, and the transmission gods, one for each gear. . . .

Cassette on.

CASSETTE TAPE: All these gods had to be taken into account, and their attributes, and their relationships to each other, before a prophecy about the probability of success of an action could be arrived at. Handling all these complex and shifting variables was a difficult business.

DRIVER: I bet. . . .
I just realized something about those crazy bastards. Like the mapmaker who wanted to make the most accurate map of the world, and kept making it bigger and bigger, and when his map

Drums begin, softly.

got a mile square, he realized the best map of the world was the world itself—so the job was done. A little tough to read, but that wasn't his trouble. Mayans work the same way. They figured every thing and every concept had its spirit, and they figured it in dee-tail. The world is nothing but a picture made by the combined activity of all the gods in action at this moment. No above, no below. Just here, and the gods are everywhere.

I don't even know if I'm coming or going, or Margaret's coming or going, but it doesn't seem *Radio on loud.* to matter too much at the moment. I'm driving. If I'm in luck I'll find her there. If not, I'll *Boy on bike appears* just drive back and forth be-*along roadside.* tween Bellingham and Town-*Drums louder.* send forever. Hey . . . there's a guy on a bike. Or a kid. What's he doing on the highway near midnight?
Boy on bike veers into Hey!
the path of DRIVER'S
car.   HEY KID!

Car hits boy on bike. [Searching with flashlight.]
Drums stop. Squeal
of brakes. Boy on bike
disappears. Silence.

God. Where the hell is he? I was sure I hit him. Can't even find the damn bike. Nothing anywhere. . . . Uh oh . . . seeing things. Or not seeing things.

Railroad crossing signal appears, center of set, alongside highway path.

Hell, this one's better in my head than splattered all over the road. Better take it easy. . . .

Crazy priests and their calculations, doping out the future. If the gods looked good, fine. If the situation looks lousy, the rules are simple. Gods need human blood to give them strength to do their work in the world . . . and they pay off devout donors in good fortune.

Ignition, car rolling again.
Margaret's car rolling. The cars are fairly close to each other.

Better take it easy. "Bellingham, sixty miles." Halfway. You know, this sounds crazy, but when I get there, I don't want to find Margaret home. If she's there—the argument, bitter and no doubt inconclusive. Then lukewarm sex, and sleep. No. What I want is for Margaret to have joined me on the road, racing toward me, and away, and to me again, her Chevy Chevette doing eighty, radio full blast. Both of us racing through the night, secretly hoping never to

Drums begin to build.

*Sound effects of car
driving fade, then
stop.
All lights on highway
set fade to black.*
DRIVER'S *car moves
toward RR tracks, the
highway midpoint.
RR signalgate
lowers, lights and
bells as if for
approaching train.
Drums continuing.
Top level of the
pyramid is built.*

catch up to each other, desires and doubts become flashes of passing light and steel.

Hey, that's funny. The mileage gauge is stuck. . . . or it's going too slow to see. I'm still doing sixty, the landscape is still passing the windows, but it seems static, featureless . . . as if I'm on a small circular track . . . and time is . . . time is. . . .

*RR signal sound out.
Light on pyramid.
Blood flows down the
sides of the pyramid.*

VOICE: Going to paradise is good, and to fall into hell is also a matter for congratulations.

DRIVER: Thou gods, lords of the mountains and valleys, I have given thee to drink. Tomorrow is again day, again light of the sun. I do not know where I shall then be. I am only a traveller. I pass beneath thy hands, beneath thy feet.

*Lights of the night
(bldgs., car, etc.) full
up. RR signalgate
rises.*

DRIVER *picks his car*
up in his hand,
climbs onto highway,
looks out. DRIVER
waves to her. All
lights bump to black.

Hey . . . where am I? My head feels like a bomb blew inside. Hey! Is that Margaret's car. There, across the tracks. I can pull over to the side of the road. Margaret! Here! I'm here! IIere!

John Nesci in *Limbo Tales*

INTERMEZZO

The MASTER OF CEREMONIES *enters, same cheap suit and tie. He holds up his hands for silence.*

MASTER OF CEREMONIES: Ladies and gentlemen. At this time, I'd like to mention to you those fabulous attractions who were unable to be with us this evening. My associates, and I, combed the fashionable boulevards and back alleys of this great nation, attempting not only to locate these stellar performers, but to lure them to this very stage. However, booking the great and near-great is difficult, not only because of their inflated and insane demands, but due to the fact that most of them have given up on the show business. Lack of appreciation and comprehension on the part of the public has caused them to lapse into a life of aimless musing and despair. We were also hampered, as you might imagine, by our lack of funds, and the condition of this shabby venue. Hard luck dogged our footsteps. Our failure was complete.

We contacted Baron Capiletto, the Italian midget who is not only no taller than the average cigar, but can, and will, open his mouth, and for the pleasure of the viewers, jump down his own throat. He was insulted when we proposed he appear on this program. The little bastard was insulted. Couldn't move him.

We planned to negotiate with Doctor Wu, the Oriental dental artiste. The doctor's act is to painlessly extract the teeth of any member of the audience, shake them up in a bag, load them in a little cannon of his own invention, which he then fires at the head of the volunteer, who miraculously finds all his teeth in place again, whiter and brighter than ever. We finally got the Doctor's unlisted number, only to discover his phone had been disconnected. Couldn't reach him.

We tracked Art Hubble to his trailer camp in Florida. He turned us down flat. He wanted big bucks, the pig. A genius, however. Hubble is known in the trade as the Human Balloon. He just lies down onstage, and swallows the business end of a tire pump. Then a member of the audience pumps, and pumps, and pumps, and Art's belly swells, and swells, until you're sure he's gonna explode, and the crowd is screaming "Stop! Stop!" and Art is saying "Keep pumping you bastard. . . . " Well, you're not gonna see that one.

I personally met with the great Count Orloff, in his room in the Hotel Rio, in the heart of New York's theatre district. The count is ossified and transparent. You can watch his blood circulate, and a copy of the *Daily News*, held across his back, can be read through his chest. Old man now. He was born in Budapest. When he was in his teens he collapsed one day, bones so soft he couldn't stand. They got him into a chair, and he never left it. The Count has always been in pain, smokes opium constantly to relieve his suffering. Showed himself around the world for sixty years. I begged him to make his comeback in this very show. No luck. Permanently retired.

We also failed to obtain the services of the Bold Grimace Boy. It's a shame you won't see him. He has a tongue about a foot long, can turn one eye out and the other in at the same time, make his face about as small as an apple, then push his mouth out about six inches and shape it like a bird's beak, with his eyes like an owl's. To end the act he twists his face up in some kinda way, that damned if he doesn't look like a corpse that's been buried fifty years. Nice guy, too.

Then we thought of adding some kind of interesting scientific exhibit to the evening—giant spider display—freak baby show—or a waxworks. We saw one of those that was something special. Guy has it in a barn up in New Hampshire. He bought it from a Chink who made it back in the thirties. A brass plate in front reads "Mukden, 1937." That's in China. It's a street scene after a Japanese bombing. Regular blood show, but the modeling is really fine. Those statues even have nostril hairs. About ten figures, all wounded and in agony, a pregnant woman, a child, an old man, one guy with his guts bursting out of him, all of them lying there like broken rubble. They just lie there in this barn, and the cows wander in and moo into the dusty Chinese faces, all twisted up with pain. The owner wouldn't rent, and he wouldn't sell.

However, we did manage to obtain one fascinating historical exhibit. See this box?

[He holds up a small box.]

Inside this box rests the iron fly of John Molitor, greatest work of art of this or any age. He was a watchmaker from Bremen. That's in Germany. He's dead now. He made this fly for fun. When he let it out, it just buzzed around the room like the real thing, but if it landed on your hand you knew something was funny. It's heavy. This very fly flew to meet the Emperor Maximilian on his arrival in Bremen on June the seventh, 1840. Molitor figured he'd surprise the Emperor with something special. The Emperor just reached out and swatted it with his left hand. He wore a yellow glove.

The fly's been busted ever since. It looks like a dead fly in a box. Not worth showing to you, really.

[He slips the box into his pocket.]

Thank you. Thank you all very much. Intermission.

INTERMISSION

Will Patton in "Hotel" from *Limbo Tales*

HOTEL

The MASTER OF CEREMONIES *returns. He wears a hat, and is carrying a shabby suitcase. He lights a cigarette, sinister and slow.*

MASTER OF CEREMONIES: Ladies and gentlemen, welcome back. And now, my associates, and I, present, *Limbo Tales*, Part Three: Hotel.

The MC *is gone, and the Hotel set is revealed onstage. A* MAN *is in the cheap hotel room. The room is filthy, and very small. On the far side of each of the walls that enclose the room and its occupant is a large audio speaker. These two speakers provide the sound from the rooms on either side of the one we see. The* MAN *hears these sounds through the walls. The basic set structure is therefore:*

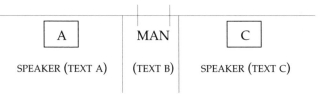

The MAN *is reading the Gideon Bible. A window shade is drawn down over a window behind him. There is a suitcase. A circular fluorescent overhead lights the room harshly. There is a telephone. A wilted plant is on the windowsill. The* MAN *is dressed in a rumpled suit and tie. Disco music, street sounds, dim and far away. The* MAN *closes his book, looks out at the audience.*

TEXT B

MAN: The toilet's down the hall, and the landlady's got a padlock on it. She won't gimme the key. So I'm forced, you understand. I am not an animal, but I piss in her goddamn hallway just the same. I'd piss in here if I still didn't have a little while to go. I paid a week when I moved in. Time was up today at noon. Check out time. I'm still here, for the moment. I can't pay any more cause I don't got it. What I got is the clothes I'm wearing, my sample suitcase, one plant from Woolworth's, and three dollars fifty cents ready cash, which is gonna go as soon as the delivery guy from Wong Lo's Chinese take-out place gets here with my food. I gotta eat something. . . . It ain't like she's got a big crowd waiting for this room. "What am I supposed to do," I tell her, "sleep in the street?" "Yeah," she says, "My ex-husband, for one, does it every night, and he's a better man than you." I thought maybe if I came on to her— she's about fifty, wears this filthy pink housedress all the time and fat, but I figured I could do it, and then she'd let me stay till I figured out where to go.

SPEAKER A: [TEXT A] *Sound of light snoring begins, fades, begins again, continuing. . . .*

MAN: . . . and then I thought: how am I gonna figure where to go? What's the difference. Nothing to figure. I don't need any time. Just waiting a little bit, and then I walk out the door. I don't want to get thrown out of here by the cops. I am not an animal. I'm a man, spelled M,A,N. Man. I tell you this cause I don't know if you'd know by looking.

It goes to show you. If you don't have the

smooth tongue of a clever man, or the beauty of a successful whore, its hard to get away with it in this generation. Hard work and dumb love won't do you, my friends, and that's a fact. I don't like to say it, but it's so.

You sign in to this hotel, you sign your name on water. "You got a name?" she says to me at the desk. "Damn right I do," I told her. "I not only got one, I know it by heart." "Sign it then," she says, "but it don't get you nothing. Name or no name you pay in advance. I deal with transients only." "Fine with me," I tell her, "I'm just here temporarily." "That's what they all say," she says. So I'm starved, stalled, and stranded, only this is not the depression so there's no excuse. This is modern times. . . .

SPEAKER A: *[Snoring louder for a moment, then subsides. . . .]*

MAN: However, I'm not alone. I got neighbors, and these walls are made of low-grade cardboard. *[The* MAN *gestures toward* SPEAKER A.] One crazy writer who talks to the furniture—sleeping at the moment—and the other one—*[*MAN *gestures toward* SPEAKER C.]*—a girl. I never saw either of them. Only hear them through the walls. *[The* MAN *listens.]*

SPEAKER C: *[Sounds of steps. Then they stop. Coughing, very harsh. Then the voice of* SHELLEY. *She's eighteen.]*

SHELLEY [C]: Shit. *[She coughs again, then silence.]*

[Street noise rises, then falls away. . . . Shadow of a pigeon on the shade behind him, and then its gone.]

MAN: My mother died when I was ten. My father never married again, brought me up himself. Five years ago he died. Some kind of blood clot on the brain. I never understood, really. He was coming home from work, and he fell down, and he never got up. Fifty-five years old. So, then I got lonely, and I married Eileen. Had a baby boy, and then I got this selling job, and I was away a lot. I heard she met some guy in the shopping mall who was real good-looking, or funny, or something. I don't know, really. I was sending money home all the time, so Eileen must have liked the other guy a lot, cause that money must have made her feel bad. . . .

SPEAKER C: [Humming of a little song, coughing, very soft . . . continuing and fading . . .]

MAN: . . . She should have, too, cause all I thought of on the road was her and the kid.

I'd been away two months one time. When I came back, they were gone. I heard about the guy from the neighbors—got an address too, and I kept sending money for the kid. But I never went there, cause I was scared to. Then I asked in one letter if I could visit. I never got an answer, but the checks kept getting cashed. I guess she didn't want to cash 'em but she had to. Then one of my letters came back with the money still in it. Return to sender, address unknown. So now I don't know where they are or even if they're alive. That was two years ago. So, this is it. This is no song and dance about a hotel room. This is a hotel room.

[A knock on the door. The MAN opens it. A hand extends through the door holding a brown paper bag. The MAN takes the bag, puts money in the hand. The hand withdraws. The MAN closes the door, opens the bag: two egg rolls, wonton soup, a fortune cookie. He begins to eat.]

[NOTE: During all material from SPEAKERS A and/or C, the MAN in the room, though he may be occupied with what he's doing, is also listening carefully.]

SPEAKER A: [*Sound of snoring rises, and then stops. Noises of someone getting up out of bed. The voice we hear from this speaker is that of an older man, strong and melodious: the* WRITER.]

WRITER: [A] My god! It's all there! Floating perfect inside my head! I see it all. Am I awake? I've dreamed poems before, but this is extraordinary. I remember every word of it. It may even be good. Good? Genius! Stately pleasure dome! Caves of ice! This one will hit the anthologies for sure! . . . Uh oh. . . . What if I forget it? What am I thinking? I'm a writer. I'll write it down. [*Sound of typing begins and continues, interrupted by the* WRITER'S *exclamations.*] Sunless sea! Nicely turned . . . decree, sea. . . . This is fabulous—I don't even have to think! . . . Mazy motion . . . ah! . . . A miracle of rare device! I love it, and there's more. [*Sound of typing continues, softer, fading in and out. . . .*]

MAN: [*He is almost finished eating. He takes out an address book, finds a number, picks up the phone.*] Operator? [*The operator's voice is amplified, but out of a hidden speaker (as with street sounds, etc.), not from* SPEAKER A *or* C.]

OPERATOR'S VOICE: Hello there, handsome. [*Sings.*] What can I do, do do—For you, you youuuuuuu?

MAN: Could you try 444-7701 for me, please.

OPERATOR'S VOICE: Try? I'll simply ring the damn thing. Here you go, sweetheart. [*Phone rings. No answer. The man hangs up.*]

MAN: Girl I used to know in this town. Long ago. Must be out. Or maybe she's moved away. *[The* MAN *opens his fortune cookie. Reading.]* "You are intelligent and sincere. You will go far in life." Yeah. Let me tell you, when you start losing your grip on some things, if you get nervous and your hands get sweaty—then everything slides out and away. I can remember hanging on strong to all kinds of things. . . . You know, it is possible to devote your life to relieving other people's misery. People do it. It is also possible to devote your life to certain ideas. People do it. It is possible to devote your life to cultivating certain internal vibrations. People do it. It's also possible to just stand on the corner and take what comes.

I thought I could never love enough, never shout loud enough, never be quiet enough, never go deep enough, or fast enough, or enough times to suit me. It's a wide highway, and you're following it and somehow it turns into a narrow alley, the houses crowding in on both sides. Surrounded. The earth quakes. Wells have gone dry. Piles of corpses are stacked up against the walls. We who are left split bones, and dig for the marrow. *[There is a knock on the door. Loud aggressive voice from the hallway, the* LIGHTNING ROD SALESMAN.*]*

VOICE OF THE LIGHTNING ROD SALESMAN: Sir or Madam! Better safe than sorry! BETTER SAFE THAN SORRY! Lightning rods for sale! All shapes, all sizes! Better safe than sorry? *[Knocking.]* Anybody home?

[The MAN *does not answer.]*

LIGHTNING ROD SALESMAN [O.S.]: Free brochure. *[The brochure flies in over the transom—a paper plane. The man grabs it, glances at it, shows it to the audience, crumples it up and tosses it away. Steps of the salesman fading away down the hall.]*

MAN: Insane.

SPEAKER C: *[Sound of a rhythmic knock on the door, soft.]*

SHELLEY: [C] Who is it? *[GAIL is SHELLEY'S age, 19 or so, and COUNTRYBOY is a few years older. The sound of their voices should be more mature than SHELLEY'S.]*

GAIL: [C] It's us, Shelley. Open up. *[Sound of door opening, people entering.]*

SHELLEY: [C] Am I glad to see you guys. I been calling and calling. . . .

GAIL: [C] They cut the phone off. We don't need the damn thing anyway. Jimmy around?

SHELLEY: [C] I been sick, Gail.

COUNTRYBOY: [C] Where's Jimmy?

SHELLEY: [C] I don't know. He hasn't been here for a week. Gail, I'm trying to tell you. . . .

COUNTRYBOY: [C] Shelley, you got a Dr. Pepper or something. . . . You got some M&Ms for the Country Boy? Anything sweet.

SHELLEY: [C] I haven't been out. There's just water down the hall in the bathroom. You want some?

COUNTRYBOY: [C] Yeah. I want some.

SHELLEY: [C] O.K. I'll be right back.

[Sounds of door opening. SHELLEY'S footsteps fading as she walks down the hall.]

GAIL: [C] Will you stop being so damn ugly?

COUNTRYBOY: [C] You don't get it. She's gonna be sick for a long time. She's got nothing.

GAIL: [C] I told you. Her mother sends her something every month. . . . *[Sound of* SHELLEY *returning, door opening.]*

SHELLEY: [C] I got you the. . . . *[*SHELLEY *coughs harshly. Sound of her falling, glass breaking.]*

GAIL: [C] Jesus. Country, get her up on the bed, hah. . . .
      *[*SHELLEY'S *crying, sobbing.]*

SHELLEY: [C] You guys can find me something.

COUNTRYBOY: [C] This drugstore is closed, darling. I am carrying nothing.

SHELLEY: [C] Pretty please, Country. Jimmy took everything when he split. I even had a taste I was saving in this little perfume bottle. He took that too.
      [The MAN, *who was at first indifferent to the overheard conversation, now listens intently.]*

GAIL: [C] Baby, you're like ice. You got another blanket in here?

SHELLEY: [C] You can get me something. Country, you got some cottons in your shirt pocket. I know you do. . . .

COUNTRYBOY: [C] If I could find you something, what am I gonna pay with, darling? I'm broke. Even if you had the bread, nobody's holding. Downtown, anyway. I ain't about to get myself killed on Lenox cause you got the shakes.

SHELLEY: [C] . . . there's a twenty in that top drawer . . . under the sweater. . . . Country, take it, please.

COUNTRYBOY: [C] All right. I'll do what I can. Maybe I can find some yellows, something to take the edge off.

SHELLEY: [C] I love yellows. I'd like to go to sleep.

COUNTRYBOY: [C] Gail, you coming?

GAIL: [C] Shelley, you eat anything today?

SHELLEY: [C] Yeah. I ate soup.

COUNTRYBOY: [C] Gail, I'm out the door here.

GAIL: [C] Lemme get my shoes on, dammit.

COUNTRYBOY: [C] Don't worry, darling. The Countryboy always comes back with something.

[Sound of door slamming as GAIL and COUNTRYBOY leave Shelley's room.]

MAN: Oh Lord. If they come back to her, I'm Elmer Fudd. *[His phone rings. As it rings, the dim shadow of an old man appears on the window shade behind him. He picks up.]*

OPERATOR'S VOICE: It's for you, sweetface. Hold a moment, while I patch you in. This one's long distance, to say the least.

MAN: I'm holding.

PHONE: *[Voice of MAN'S father.]* Hello, son?

MAN: Dad? Is that you?

PHONE: Who else would bother?

MAN: But you're dead.

PHONE: What are you, prejudiced? Listen, there's a message for you. Came while you were out, from one of your girlfriends, I think. Let me find it here. Your mother must have put it on the. . . . Ah. I got it. "Call Linda."

MAN: That's it? That's the message?

PHONE: Yeah. "Call Linda."

MAN: Who's Linda?

PHONE: How should I know?

MAN: Dad, when did you get that message?

PHONE: Don't ask about whens. I'm dead, remember. And another thing. I don't want you wasting your life. It's not only stupid—I don't like it, understand. Do what's right, and don't get crazy. Understand?

[The shadow on the shade begins to fade away . . .]

MAN: Yeah, but Dad, listen. I seem to have messed up a little here. Maybe you can. . . . Dad? Dad?

> *[The* MAN *jiggles the button, but its clear the phone's gone dead. He calls the* OPERATOR.*]*

MAN: Operator?

OPERATOR'S VOICE: Sock it to me, dreamboat.

MAN: That call I just got, the connection. . . . I got cut off. Do you have the number or anything?

OPERATOR'S VOICE: That call was from Deadland, sweetheart, and the connections never last long. I'll see if I can buzz the party. Uno momentito, slugger. *[Buzzings and clickings from the phone.]* No luck, big shoulders. Trying to reach anyone over there is a hassle. They've got one switchboard for the entire joint, and sometimes no one's on duty. You're just ringing the air, blue eyes.

MAN: My eyes are green.

OPERATOR'S VOICE: You keep making these fine distinctions, buster, its gonna cost you. *[Click as the phone line goes dead. The* MAN *hangs up.]*

SPEAKER A: *[Sound of feverish typing, interrupted by exclamations of delight.]*

WRITER: [A] Ah! Perfect! Damsel with a dulcimer!

> *[Sounds from* SPEAKER A *continue very softly.]*

MAN: *[Gesturing toward* SPEAKER A.*]* He's found something to do. Keeps him happy sometimes. I used to be a salesman. Like that madman who was in the hallway. I guess I still am, if my company still exists. Door to door worker, selling *Feldman's Original Books of Knowledge,* a set in twenty-two volumes. Help you to the world's wisdom. Help your kid through school. Gonna deny your child this invaluable opportunity for learning? *[Taking a volume out of suitcase.]*

The damn thing is actually a blurry photo-offset job on cheap paper, of the 1892 edition of the *Encyclopedia Britannica*, with every other article missing. Actually, not bad. I sold the damn thing in every little town along the route of the Canadian Pacific—Montreal to Vancouver. Train, hotel, do the town, back on the train. If they bought, I gave 'em one book, took a down payment, then filed their order with Feldman in the main office. The company was supposed to do the rest, mail a book a month and collect their money. The people I sold were poor, and thought the books would help their kids. In the end, they could never afford the whole set, so they'd stop paying, and the books would stop coming. I don't think Feldman even had any volumes beyond S. . . . Border towns in Canada are deficient in the knowledge of things like Tasmania, and Utopias, and Velvet, and Weathervanes, and Xenophobia, and Yuletide, and Zinc . . . *[Holding up the volume.]* A. *[He begins to read. . . .]*

SPEAKER A: *[Sound of typing rises. Sharp knock on the door, followed by the voice of the* LIGHTNING ROD SALESMAN *from the hallway.]*

LIGHTNING ROD SALESMAN [O.S.]: Sir or madam? Sir or madam? A moment of your time! Better safe than sorry! *[Repeated knocking. Typing stops. Sound of door opening.]*

WRITER: [A] What is it, dammit?

LIGHTNING ROD SALESMAN [O.S.]: Thank you, sir. My demonstration will only take a moment. *[Sound of closing door.]*

WRITER: [A] I don't recall inviting you in.

LIGHTNING ROD SALESMAN [O.S.]: You need not make excuses, sir. In my business rudeness is commonplace. I represent the Porlock Lightning Rod Company. Save yourself from nature's white flash of death.

WRITER: [A] Please. I'm in the middle of the most wonderful piece of work of my life. I'm really not inter—

LIGHTNING ROD SALESMAN [O.S.]: SIR! Lightning is far more common than you suppose. At this very moment, a thundercloud boils with a negative charge, building in potential till that probing lance of massed electrons sets out in quest of the victim below. Sir, there is even a type of lightning that concerns itself with direct attacks on the human brain. Comes right at your head. To make it shit simple for you, sir—next storm, you end up fried meat. Now a simple personal lightning rod that can be worn directly on the body can insure that you and your loved ones are guarded against the ravages of wild electricity. The rods are made of genuine copper plated plastic, and come with a velcro clip to attach them securely to your person. Every rod is prepared under rabbinical supervision, and has been blessed by the pope. Let me demonstrate how comfortable—

WRITER: [A] GET OUT!!

LIGHTNING ROD SALESMAN [O.S.]: Pardon me?

WRITER: [A] Get out of my hotel room, NOW! Before I smash your face, sir!

LIGHTNING ROD SALESMAN [O.S.]: Disgusting. A fellow human being offers to help you save yourself from natural disaster, to preserve your life and sanity, and you treat him like an animal.

WRITER: [A] GET OUT!!

[Slamming of a door. Footsteps of the LIGHTNING ROD SALESMAN *fade down the hallway. Sound of typing beginning again, hesitating, then stopping. The* MAN *is listening intently now.]*

WRITER: [A] My god. It's gone. That idiot drove the poem out of my head. . . . Nothing. I remember nothing. My head's as empty as a balloon. Shit. And the damn thing's not finished. It just stops in the middle. Hell, maybe it can just end there. . . . *[Reads.]*

>Beware! Beware!
>His flashing eyes, his floating hair!
>Weave a circle round him thrice,
>And close your eyes with holy dread,
>For he on honey-dew hath fed,
>And drunk the milk of Paradise.

MAN: Not bad. *[He puts volume A of the Book of Knowledge back in his sample case.]* I quit. I tried to call Feldman at the office to tell him to get another boy, but the phone's been disconnected.

My last sale. There was this very sunny morning, really supernaturally bright sunshine, and everything in the world looked lit. And I was going door to door, and the people who opened them that one morning looked radiant and fine somehow—a man with a towel over his shoulder, half-shaved, blinking in the sunlight, little girl with a doll under her arm, a woman with her hair in curlers, smell of coffee floating out of kitchens, lawns getting mowed, and this sparkle on everything, like I was in a crystal world. And it was a sure thing to me that morning that these people had in them all the light in the world, and intelligence and humor and peace glowed in their eyes. All this was in a town called Bent Fork, in Alberta. So, it looked to me like selling a *Book of Knowledge* to these godlike creatures with their families and chores and work and play and children and earth and sky, would be just like selling the old refrigerator to the Eskimos, like teaching monkeys to climb trees, like looking for water by brushing away the waves. . . .

SPEAKER C: *[SHELLEY coughs, then moans as if in pain. She is sobbing, then manages to stop herself. She sings, in a little child's voice. . . .]*

SHELLEY: [C] *[Singing.]*

> Uncle John is very sick, what shall we send him?
> Three good wishes, three good kisses, and a slice of ginger
> Who shall we send it by, by the ferryman's daughter
> Take her by her lily-white hand and lead her over the water. . . .

[She is sobbing, and then the sound fades . . .]

MAN: Oh God . . .

So, I was saying, I stood there in the middle of town like a man from Mars, holding my sample case full of books under one arm, and I figured I'd try one more house. I knock. This woman comes to the door, and I don't think she's more than twenty-five, and she's got a dustpan in one hand, and her hair's tied up on her head some way, and she's got freckles running across her nose, and she's beautiful. She says come in, and I can see her ass moving under this thin dress she's wearing, and she wants to hear all about Feldman's *Book of Knowledge,* and before you know it we're in bed upstairs, banging away. She's real excited and having a great time, and I'm doing O.K. myself, but sort of wondering what's happening since this wasn't particularly my idea. So all the rubbing and oohing and ahhing is over, and she gets up, and it's early afternoon, and she pulls her dress back on, and she says don't you think you better get out of here. We're in the bedroom and her husband's stuff is lying all around. In fact, I trip over one of his shoes climbing out of bed, a dark brown loafer. I ask her if she wants to buy *Feldman's Book of Knowledge* and she says are you kidding and get out of here dammit the kids'll be home from school any minute. I put my clothes on all right, but I don't leave. I'm happy there. She's angry, and after all that loving she sure enough hates me now, but I don't leave, and the kids come home, and their names are Ellie and Daniel, and they look like good kids to me, and she tells them I'm a man selling books and they look at them and the house feels comfortable all around me and I can hear some birds chirping in the backyard and I sit in a chair in the living room. She's fixing dinner, putting a roast beef in the oven and I go in and watch her, and she looks over at me and says you're crazy you know, but I don't feel crazy one bit. Soon her husband comes home from work, and he's got this little moustache and he works in a sporting goods store, and they hug each other, and he shakes my hand, and invites me to dinner and the food's great, and I'm telling 'em about my travels, and after dinner I'm playing a game called Submarine Chase with Daniel and I can hear them arguing in the kitchen about me and who I am, and I can see I'm bringing fear and lying and no love here, and so I say excuse me, Daniel, and I pick up my sample case and go out on the porch. It's night, and a dog barks somewhere, and the Canadian Pacific through train to Vancouver whistles, pulling out of Bent Fork. I walk down to the station. I lie down on a bench. There'll be another train in the morning. . . .

That was my last day on the job. If anyone here wants a set of *Feldman's Book of Knowledge,* I'm sorry but I no longer sell them. Find Feldman, if you can. You know, it's a fact, and it goes to show you. You work at it, and work at it, and you get a little older and you figure out what you've bought with all that effort. You bought death. Somehow you got it backwards. It's life you been trying to buy. Death you're supposed to get for free.

SPEAKER C: *[Sharp knocking on* SHELLEY'S *door.]*

SHELLEY: [C] Country? Country? Gail? Is that you? *[Knocking again.]* Who is it?

LIGHTNING ROD SALESMAN [O.S.]: It's the lightning rod man! Is your Mommy home?

SHELLEY: [C] No.

LIGHTNING ROD SALESMAN [O.S.]: Open the door and let me in!

SHELLEY: [C] No!

LIGHTNING ROD SALESMAN [O.S.]: Safe and sound. Last

chance at this price. Shelley, let me in, or I'll pick up my sample case, walk down the stairs and out, into the street, where I'll be hidden from you forever. [SHELLEY *does not answer.*] Goodbye. [*Sound of the* LIGHTNING ROD SALESMAN'S *footsteps going down the stairs, fading. . . .*]

SHELLEY: [C] [*Singing, slowly.*] Oh Mary Mack, Mack, Mack,

>All dressed in black, black, black,
>
>With silver buttons, buttons, buttons,
>
>All down her back, back, back.
>
>She asked her mother, mother . . .

[SHELLEY *stops singing. We hear her talking now, in a very small voice. . . .*] . . . Oh, Mom, I'm so sick . . . can I stay home from school today . . . please . . . I'm sorry, I'm so sorry. . . .

MAN: [*To himself.*] Shelley, please stop crying. The man on the other side of the wall is checking out, and I'm hoping someday I'll look back over my shoulder and you'll be running to catch up to me, and I'll wait there in the road for you. . . . [*The* MAN'S *phone rings. He picks up.*]

OPERATOR'S VOICE: Hello handsome. One moment for Madame!

LANDLADY'S VOICE: [*On phone.*] Listen you cheap chiseler! Pack your shit and get out of my room! Now! You hear me?

MAN: I hear you. I'm going.

LANDLADY: And another thing! If you're jerking off in the room, that's three bucks extra! You hear me!

MAN: I have ears.

LANDLADY: You're going now?

MAN: Yeah.

LANDLADY: The world's a wonderful place. I remember it. Stay sober. There's no need to check out. I'm crossing you off the book right now. There. You're gone. *[Click of the* LANDLADY *hanging up the phone. The* MAN *hangs up.]*

MAN: It goes to show you. You can spend the time you're given playing around in the shallows, or you can dive deep and swim with the fishes. I am gonna disappear now, a spot of snow floating down into the fire. If you blink just once in your coffin you'll miss me. You won't even see me go.

Cow shit becomes tomatoes, piss becomes rain, petals of roses turn to black soil, comets into sparklers that burn away in the air, young girls into old women, ink into dust, dead trees to diamonds, and stones into sand on the shore. My turn now.

[He stands, straightens his tie, picks up his suitcase, then drops it onto the floor. He puts his toothbrush in his pocket. He picks up the plant on the windowsill, touches its dirt—dry. He looks around for water—none. He spits into the plant pot, watering it with his saliva. He places it back on the sill. He picks up the Gideon Bible, goes to put it in its drawer, stops. He sticks his finger into the book at random, opens it to that page. Reading.]

MAN: "For ye shall go out with joy, and be led forth with peace: the mountains and the hills shall break forth before you into singing, and all the trees of the field shall clap their hands." Yeah.

[He puts the Bible in its drawer, leaves the room. Strong light coming through the windowshade. The

shadow of a pigeon appears, is there a moment, and is gone.]

SPEAKER A: [Sound of typing begins, hesitant at first, then consistent and strong. This sound fades slowly. All lights, including the circular fluorescent on set, fade to black.]

END PLAY

Dark Ride

Dark Ride was first presented by the Soho Repertory Theatre, in New York City, on November 12, 1981. The cast was as follows:

TRANSLATOR	David Brisbin
MARGO	Melissa Hurst
JEWELER	Bill Sadler
THIEF	Will Patton
WAITRESS	Betty LaRoe
GENERAL	Eric Loeb
ED	Walter Hadler
EDNA	Saun Ellis
MRS. LAMMLE	Joanne Akalaitis
MR. ZENDAVESTA	John Nesci

Director: Len Jenkin
Set: John Arnone
Lights: Bruce Porter
Visual Projections: Gerald Marks
Costumes: David Woolard
Sound Design: Kathleen King
Stage Manager: Joanne McEntire

PRODUCTION NOTE

The text of *Dark Ride* includes a minimum of stage direction, and a minimum of description of set and costume. My hope is that all the necessary information as to set, movement of actors, gesture, necessary props, etc., can be inferred from the dialogue and the stage directions given.

I would like, despite my desire for anyone working on a production of *Dark Ride* to allow their visual and theatrical imaginations full rein, to make some suggestions.

The idea of a "dark ride," or a carnival spook or ghost ride through a funhouse, where images and scenes appear suddenly out of darkness and just as suddenly disappear, is helpful to keep in mind: lights in the dark.

A cinematic approach, where scenes dissolve into one another, or are cut to rapidly, would also be helpful to think about, and in the blunter style of B movies. The lighting should be hard, colorful, and jarring, like that of a seedy carnival: lights to look at, as well as lights to light the scene.

Settings can be simple. Place can be indicated by props or small set units that can easily be moved on/offstage. The use of slides, film, and sound to establish place and mood is also possible. The text offers within itself many visual suggestions. At times, all that is necessary to establish place is the language alone.

It is also of interest, in a piece like *Dark Ride*, to stage certain moments of thought or memory as well as, or as an overlay to, the present time-place of the action.

The director and performers should be aware that
Dark Ride is a weave of tales, of scenes within scenes,
like the facets of the diamond. That a scene is within a
book, or a picture, or in someone's mind makes it no
less "real" in terms of staging. The "real" point of view
is a shifting one.

The following scene list may be helpful as well.

ACT I

1. The Dark Ride begins/introduction
2. The TRANSLATOR at home
3. MARGO at home/at the clinic in her mind/with the
   JEWELLER, HEAD NURSE
4. The THIEF at the Embers Cafe/with WAITRESS and
   DEEP SEA ED as cook
5. The GENERAL on TV
6. The TRANSLATOR again
7. THIEF at the Embers/DEEP SEA ED and ticket
   windows/WAITRESS
8. The JEWELLER in his office/with THIEF
9. The THIEF at DEEP SEA EDNA'S motel
10. MRS. LAMMLE at a lecture hall/ALL as audience and
    demonstrators
11. The TRANSLATOR and the THIEF at MR. ZENDAVESTA'S
    oculist shop–occult bookstore/with MRS. LAMMLE
12. The JEWELLER and the GENERAL at the JEWELLER'S
    office
13. MARGO at home, with JEWELLER and GENERAL

ACT II

DARK RIDE

– I –

1.

Ride in: light, sound.

VOICE: Listen lady. If he's old enough to enjoy the ride, he's old enough to need a ticket. . . .

2.

TRANSLATOR: My translation of the *Book of the Yellow Ancestor* is progressing very poorly. Ever since I began the work for this publisher of occult esoterica, I've suspected that something was seriously wrong. Possibilities: the text submitted to me was claimed to be a xerox copy of a parchment recently discovered in a cave in Szechuan Province, near Foo-Chow. How this document came into the possession of Mr. Zendavesta of Sublime Publications he did not say. His response, when queried, is a genial grin. It is possible, then, that this text is fraudulent, or, if genuine, extremely corrupt. Either one of these theories is true, or—I'm somehow no longer able to make modern English sense out of ancient Chinese. In all honesty, with this text, it sometimes seems that I can no longer even read the language—brush-strokes seem like chicken scratchings in the sand.

Yet the *Book of the Yellow Ancestor* is definitely not composed of the kind of subtle or paradoxical discourse that could trouble the translator: Still, my tentative drafts all feel wrong—not nonsense, but *off* somewhere, at some angle. . . .

I better explain. Actually, this *Book of the Yellow Ancestor* is not a book. It consists of one hundred and one fragments, which I assumed at first to be pithy phrases about life, or a set of directions for spiritual practices. Now I am not sure but that it is actually the journal of a housewife, equivalent to a laundry list, or the pointless travel diary of a garrulous lunatic, or a series of instructions for operating some partially biological machine that no longer exists.

The work of translation, as you might imagine, is confusingly dependent on my changing notions of these contexts.

Well, whatever the cause, there seem to be major blocks in the way of progress.

That's an understatement. The truth is that certain sections of the manuscript make me almost sure that either it's a modern forgery, or that I'm going crazy. There's even one fragment . . . let me find it here . . . Ah—I've worked this passage over a dozen times, and it persists in coming out the same way. It seems to be describing a young woman reading some sort of popular novel. I quote. "Margo lies back on the couch in her apartment, and opens a book. She turns the pages slowly, until she finds her place. Her lips move slightly with the words she reads, like a child. . . ."

3.

MARGO: Chapter Nine. At the Clinic. The man in bandages stands up slowly and walks over to the window. The sunlight is bright, and perhaps a ghost of it filters in through the layers of gauze that cover his face. But there's no need to speculate. Actually the light is felt by the man in bandages as heat . . . non-specific. He translates it into whatever suits him: this morning, a certain theatre in flames. Once his facial parts are sufficiently warm, he speaks to his visitor, a figure in white.

JEWELLER: I'm Ravensburg. I remember you, your voice, the smell of your hair—from long ago—or from a dream. I've dreamed every night since they brought me here. Who are you?

MARGO: The figure does not answer.

JEWELLER: He has robbed and beaten me. These bandages come off tomorrow, and then . . . WHO ARE YOU?

MARGO: Ravensburg says suddenly, with an unusual amount of emotion. The man in the next bed groans.

MAN: Unnnhh!

MARGO: Ravensburg continues.

JEWELLER: Here at the clinic they've treated me well. After the operation, they offered to spice my recuperation with all sorts of improvements. They offered plastic surgery, a new face—but I wanted to keep the scars. But you? What about you?

DOCTOR: Ah, there you are, number ten. You know you're not allowed out of the ward. Nurse—is anyone else disturbing the others?

MARGO: Enough book. Record player. *[Music.]* Stories

David Brisbin and Melissa Hurst in *Dark Ride*

about mental illness make me nervous. I keep thinking I'm a nurse at this clinic. It's actually a small
sanitarium in the mountains. I'm a minor character
who has her own little life . . . a boyfriend, a bicycle,
a little house in the village . . . and I receive the
major dramatic events, not in a direct and concerned way, but from a distance, like I'm overhearing two people I'll never see again, while I'm doing
something else. Crazy, hah?

I've been jumpy since my boyfriend disappeared. Three weeks ago, he went out to sell something he found on the street—he finds things all the
time—but he never came back. I thought he was
dead or something, and I called every precinct, and
then I called the hospitals.

Nobody ever heard of him. So I'm like a war
bride or something, and then I get this postcard
with a picture of some guy I don't even know on it.
Can you believe it? "Dear Margo, I can't say where I
am cause there's some people probably looking for
me."

THIEF: I ran into some good luck and some trouble. I'll
send for you.

MARGO: Send for me. He didn't even sign it, and I'm
supposed to give up my job and go someplace? I
can hardly stand living with him here where I got
people I know. So now he's gonna write me from
Cloud Cuckoo Land and say come on out the
weather's fine. Pack your ermines, Margo. I love
him but it's stupid, you know, like we have no idea
how to love each other but we love each other anyway so we try but it comes out stupid.

Well, I've been nervous. I've been feeling that wherever I am, a certain someone else has been there just before me. Crazy, hah?

This card is postmarked, Indianapolis, Indiana. You know what I think of when I think of Indianapolis, Indiana? . . . It's like it reminds me of something that's not it . . . some other place that I don't particularly want to dream about . . . outskirts of some city, for miles alongside highways, feeding out into suburban streets. . . .

4.

THIEF: Outskirts of some city, for miles alongside highways, feeding out into suburban streets, and I'm walking, and I keep looking over my shoulder to see if anyone's behind me. I have the damn thing in a leather bag around my neck, and I'm heading south, and I figured I better . . . after three days on the road, I figured I better get inside somewhere, I figured I better eat something. I'm in America, coming into town. There's these long stretches of seedy apartment houses. Some people on the steps of one of them with a baby, and they're drinking beer, and they say hello out of the dark, and they don't even know who they're talking to, you know, but I say hello back anyway, and that seems to be it cause I just keep walking and they don't say anything else. O.K. Now I'm really hungry but it's a long way between neon, and then I see one coming, a red blur in the distance, and I squint at it, wanting it to say

Café or *Eat Here* or something, but it ends up saying Tri-City Furniture or Red Robin Autos—Used But Not Abused—and finally I see another one, and it's a revolve, turning and turning, and it says THE EMBERS. We Never Close. So I go in. I'm here. Jukebox.

WAITRESS: Please wait to be seated.

THIEF: I'm seated. I'm in a chair at this table with this sugar and salt and pepper and a napkin and silverware and—I make sure the bag is hidden under my shirt. I got a menu, and I'm reading the section entitled: Burgers. Embers Burger—bacon cheese and tomato with our special sauce. Burger Hawaiian with zesty pineapple. Burger Royale. . . .

WAITRESS: You know what you want?

THIEF: Uh . . . yeah. A Burger Royale.

WAITRESS: Anything to drink?

THIEF: Yeah.

WAITRESS: What?

THIEF: Coffee.

WAITRESS: *[To kitchen]* Burger Royal.

DEEP SEA ED [COOK]: Burger Royale.

THIEF: I'm still reading the menu to see if I made a mistake—Baked meatloaf Viennese, mashed potatoes, mushroom sauce. Vegetables du jour: carrots and peas, cauliflower, creamed corn . . . and this guy comes out of the kitchen wearing this white apron, and he slides into the seat across from me.

ED: Hello, Slick.

THIEF: He says.

ED: Got a cigarette?

THIEF: I give him one and he says

ED: Thanks. You new here?

THIEF: Then I just look at him, and he looks back at me, and then he goes away. I can see the TV, over the bar alongside the dining room. The waitress flips it on. It's in funny color like the tint knob's twisted, and she's tuned in to Outer Limits. O.K. I like that. Then she changes the channel.

Desert wind, billows of sand, straggly barbed wire. Zoom in past a dead camel covered with flies . . . on to a tattered tent. Inside, at a table covered with maps, sits this man in some kinda uniform, and he looks right at me. . . .

5.

GENERAL: Serving as field commander for a senile and capricious ruler is a thankless task. You are blamed for everything, though you simply follow orders. If you fail to develop the psychic strength necessary to deal with the intense and often obscure demands of the situation, you end up in the bird barracks, training seagulls to shit on the periscopes of enemy submarines. But you didn't come here to listen to me complain about my station in the service. No. You came to learn. I need not remind you that you'll require every bit of your knowledge out here. Simply to survive. Our position is hopeless. The enemy is everywhere. He has the material, the momentum, the cooperation of the natives, and time is on his side. We have only our brain power. Pay attention. Your life depends on it.

The reliability of incoming intelligence depends on two factors: the probable truth of the information itself, and the credibility of its source. Information that contradicts known facts has a low "probability of truth" rating. Think of an example.

Information coming from a notoriously unreliable source has a very low probability rating. Think of an example.

Or from a source that could not conceivably have come into possession of the information. Think of an example.

Now. Even with a mass of scrupulously assessed information—where there is an enemy whose moves you must anticipate, decision making is complex. The Basic Rule: The *more* likely the enemy's action *seems* the *less* likely it *becomes*—as he will forsee that you will forsee it. He's clever. He'll change his plans—try to fool you. Therefore, the *less* likely the enemy's action becomes, the *more* likely it is that he'll resort to exactly that strategem. If it seems impossible—it's certain. Think of an example.

We are moving out at dawn to attack point B. I am presently sending out false information that we intend to attack point A. I am also giving out information that we will attempt to convince the enemy that we are going to attack point B. If the enemy should intercept any of our real communiques in regard to our target B, rather than the false ones concerning A, they will think that those actually genuine pieces of information are only part of the attempt to deceive them.

I receive many intelligence reports on the

enemy daily. I cross file them carefully in my *Book of Intelligence.* I attempt to assess their relevance and truth. However, I have not seen the enemy themselves for quite some time—years. But I understand their strategy in this. They wish to convince me that this is all some kind of game. Once this speculation has hold of my mind, and I relax my vigilance, they'll be on me like sewer rats, ripping at my throat. But, of course. . . .

6.

TRANSLATOR: You see. You torture your mind to find modern equivalents for what seems to be ancient wisdom, and you end up revealing the seemingly obscure conversations of military officers, or peasants, hotel-keepers, fisherman, senile nuns at roadside shrines. It's indicative of the fate of serious scholarship in our time that, for the pittance Mr. Zendavesta pays me, I continue to struggle with this impossibly recalcitrant text.

However, there is one dim light. Structure. I'm fairly sure this book presupposes, as a frame device, the existence of a group of companions, who were originally ten in number. Whether these characters relate to actual people, or are pure inventions, I have no idea. The author seems obsessed with their moving from place to place like peripatetic shadows.

The Chinese setting itself is also subject to debate: I've come to believe it may well be a fiction. I'm almost certain that the book relies on geographical information about China plagiarized from a certain *Child's Picture Atlas of the World* . . . though at times the author seems to have either misread this source, or is deliberately inventing locations which never existed.

Yet this *Book of the Yellow Ancestor* remains somehow fascinating. I understate the case. I have been up all night with it for days. I think of nothing else. It's even crossed my mind that this text may be identical to one or more of the fabled "hidden" books: *The Book of the Black Pilgrimage*—or the *Book of Brightness of Rabbi Isaac the Blind,* or even—the legendary *Epistle of Illusion and Caution.* It's even crossed my mind that Chinese may not be its original language . . . that this work in front of me is itself a translation, or a translation of a translation . . . of a translation. . . .

7.

WAITRESS: Will that be all?

THIEF: What?

WAITRESS: You having dessert?

THIEF: Uh, yeah. Gimmee some pie.

WAITRESS: Apple, cherry, lemon meringue? Key lime, rhubarb, pecan, peach, pumpkin? Boston cream?

ED: I quit.

WAITRESS: You're breaking my heart. Where you going?

ED: I'm southbound. *[ED is dragging what looks like the body of a man wrapped in brown paper and string. Ticket windows appear.]*

TICKET SELLER: What's the situation?

ED: Through the sharp hawthorn blows the cold wind.

TICKET SELLER: Too bad. What are you doing about it?

ED: Going south.

TICKET SELLER: How many?

ED: Party of one.

SELLER: If that thing's gonna ride, it needs a ticket.

ED: It'll fit on my lap.

SELLER: The hell it will. Pay or walk. [ED *checks his money. Not enough.*]

ED: They used to let John ride the hound for free. Travelled everywhere with him. But this is sweet goodbye. You people are in luck. Deep Sea Ed is caught short here, so I gotta unload my prize possession: the genuine preserved and mummified body of John Wilkes Booth, the most famous assassin of all time. I got the papers and everything. Affidavits from doctors. Got 'em framed—some of 'em. I got an X-ray photo of the fractured leg where he hit the stage floor. Even got a ring. You can mention that he swallowed it while attempting to disguise himself as he ran. You found it in the mummy's stomach. Even got a B on it. Get it? B for Booth.

Look, you can make it over Egyptian if you want. Rig it with a battery so it wiggles. Jesus. You people don't know what you're looking at. This attraction took in five hundred dollars a day last season. You do that good with what you're showing? John Wilkes here makes money when everything else on the lot is dead. I built the fucker, and I'd run him all winter in a goddamn storefront if I didn't have to go back to Canada. My mother's in a fucking clinic in fucking Winnipeg, and you people are hassling me.

Look, I don't know what kind of trade you got, but if it ain't fun and fulfilling, try the show business. Hey, I'm begging you. Take him off my hands.

All right. I made my offer, you turned me down. I ain't saying you won't regret it, cause you will. *[To* TICKET SELLER.*]* Gimme one.

SELLER: Winnipeg?

ED: Hell, no. Look, can I leave something in the baggage claim? I'll be back to pick it up in a few days. . . .

WAITRESS: Will that be all?

THIEF: What else you got?

WAITRESS: Jello. *[Music.]*

THIEF: I'll have some of that jello.

WAITRESS: Red? Or green? Red? Or green?

THIEF: I was telling you, I'm running away, cause I went over my head, you know. I mean I grabbed something good, real good—and I don't know what to do with it. It's the kind of thing—you had it and somebody took it—you'd kill people to get it back.

See, I had a ring I found somewhere, so I'm looking to sell it, and I hear about a guy in an office building . . . I'm in this corridor, see . . . wandering around, somebody's playing a radio behind one of these doors. . . .

8.

JEWELLER: I am a dealer in precious stones. This particular favorite of mine first turned up in India in 1712. Supposedly, the raw stone was ripped from the forehead of an Indian idol, and came into the hands of a trader from Sumatra, who was promptly torn to pieces by a pack of rabid dogs. But that, of course, is hearsay.

Louis the Fourteenth is said to have given it to the lovely Mme. Montespan as a mark of royal favor, which she lost soon afterwards. She became a nun at a Spanish convent, where she is rumored to have been badly mistreated by the sisters . . . It appeared again in London in 1847 as the stickpin of Prince Ivan Kanitovsky, who was murdered by a bellboy at the Connaught Hotel. Abdul Hamid of Turkey possessed it briefly until he was dethroned, and it was sold to Simon Montharides, whose carriage was dragged over a cliff by shying horses near the Borgo Pass, killing him, his wife, and two children. What a coincidence.

The stone was then placed by his executors in the Green Vaults of Dresden, which will be mentioned more than once this evening. The American actress who purchased it in 1930 was burned to death in the tragic fire at the Bijou theatre in Los Angeles. I bought it from her attorneys in 1971.

When I came into possession, the stone had its original Indian design. An idiotic waste. This first cutting and faceting had been done in Venice by Joseph Asscher. The months of tension preceding

Bill Sadler in *Dark Ride*

his botch of the job caused him to be hospitalized for a nervous disability . . . a small sanitarium near the Grand Canal. Still there, I believe. . . .

The decision of how to cleave and cut the stone so as to reveal its full power was the most difficult of my life. My final decision was the right one. The stone is now a triple cut brilliant, with one hundred and one facets around its table. I did this.

I have possessed this stone for ten years now. I spend each night alone with it.

THIEF: So I'm in this corridor, see, wandering around this office building. I know the guy's name, but I don't remember the office number. I try one.

JEWELLER: Yes?

THIEF: Mr. Ravensburg?

JEWELLER: Yes, I am Ravensburg.

THIEF: I'm here to sell something. A ring. It's a family heirloom.

JEWELLER: I buy nothing.

THIEF: But I was told you could help me out.

JEWELLER: I do not buy anything.

THIEF: You don't buy anything *tonight?*

JEWELLER: Not tonight, not ever.

THIEF: It's my mother's wedding ring. This guy Bernard, he sent me. You know Bernard?

JEWELLER: I do not have the honor.

THIEF: Then I guess there's a mistake here. I'm looking for a Mr. Ravensburg.

JEWELLER: I am Mr. Ravensburg.

THIEF: But you don't buy anything.

JEWELLER: No. Here we do cutting and shaping.

THIEF: Hey, maybe there's someone else in this building named Ravensburg.

JEWELLER: No doubt. In this building, it's a very common name. [JEWELLER *turns away,* THIEF *grabs him from behind, knocks him down. A scream. The* THIEF *steals the diamond. Blackout. Music of distant Motel. NO VACANCY sign.*]

9.

DEEP SEA EDNA: You know how to read? Words?

THIEF: I can read—but there's nothing else for miles, and I thought I'd ask you personally . . . [EDNA *looks him over, changes sign so that the NO is gone.*]

EDNA: I happen to have one room I always leave empty. Room ten. The last guy I put in there—pool hustler from Grand Forks, North Dakota—died in his sleep. He died of a dream.

THIEF: Well, that's too bad, but I'll lie down anywhere. Besides, I didn't know him. His ghost won't trouble me.

EDNA: Good enough. [*Hands key.*] You woke me up, so tell me some lies. What are you doing here?

THIEF: Well . . . there's a man in town that won't be happy till he sells me a dog. I gotta see him.

EDNA: Good.

THIEF: Thanks. Uh, I don't like to bother you, but you got something to eat? A sandwich and a beer or something . . . I can pay you. . . .

EDNA: Sorry. Usta have a coffee shop. "24 hours. We never close." My husband ran it. Cook, and a good one too. But every time he gets twenty bucks in his pocket he thinks it's time to see the world. Bastard's been gone for six months this time. He'll come back—but I don't suggest you wait up for him. Everything's in the room—towels, magazines. And if you get lonely, don't ring my bell. [EDNA *is gone.*]

THIEF: But I want you people to understand that running scared isn't my full-time occupation. I mean, your mind keeps working too. I'm a writer. I write Margo postcards. And I read—magazines. You can read a lot of interesting things in magazines. This one here is the *UFO Review,* published by Sublime Publications, and it's got articles like "I Was Transported to Venus," and "PLATILLO VOLADOR . . . Saucer Over Brazil."

   [*By the end of this speech the* THIEF *is seated, and* EDNA *appears to sit alongside him—two lawn chairs.*]

EDNA: Fascinating. Listen, I know you're running. Why don't you run with me. I got a little sideline I take out on the road. Deep Sea Edna's Shooting Gallery and Marine Museum. You'll do for setup and takedown. You can feed the fish.

THIEF: Well, I might be better off on my own. I could bring trouble.

EDNA: Trouble's a friend of mine. Stay in your tracks, whoever's looking for you'll find you sure. Probably stab you in your sleep behind a billboard. Go down my road for a while, you'll disappear. Besides, you can help me look around.

THIEF: For what?

EDNA: For Ed.

THIEF: But I don't know anything about fish.

EDNA: Don't worry. I have an eye for talent. And if people are looking for you, get a disguise . . . pair of glasses or something. We can leave in the morning. Southbound. [EDNA *exits.*]

THIEF: But in case you people think I'm only interested in the sensational—there's another article in this magazine that's different. I been thinking about it—reading it over and over. It's by a Mrs. Carl Lammle, who is someone I'd like to talk to sometime. It's called:

ALL: THE WORLD OF COINCIDENCE.

                              10.

MRS. LAMMLE: All of you are, I'm sure, familiar with what I term the WORLD OF COINCIDENCE. In this world, events seem to be more connected . . . than they are in our everyday world, where they most often seem, random, absurd—if not perniciously unrelated to each other. In the world of coincidence, however, the most common expression is:

ALL: What a coincidence!

MRS. LAMMLE: For example:

MAN: Excuse me, sweetheart, you dropped your fish . . . I mean . . . scarf.

WOMAN: Thanks, mister . . . [To herself] . . . Odd he should say that. Last night I dreamed of a fish.

MRS. LAMMLE: Or. . . .

MAN: Excuse me, sweetheart, you dropped your scarf . . . I mean . . . fish.

WOMAN: Thanks, mister. Odd he should say that. Last night I dreamed of a scarf.

MRS. LAMMLE: Of course.

OTHER MAN #1: I was in the middle of writing my chapter on wind-force, when a sudden breeze blew my papers all over the room.

OTHER MAN #2: Remarkable. *[To himself.]* Odd that he should say that. Last night I dreamed of papers, blowing all around me. . . .

MRS. LAMMLE: Yes. Our common idea of cause and effect is succinctly illustrated in the common expression: "Just one thing after another." This notion is linked to our childish ideas of the nature of space and time. In the World of Coincidence, these ideas are null, and void. In man's original mind, as we find it among primitive peoples, space and time have a very precarious existence. They become fixed concepts only in the course of our mental development. Actually, the truth is, that in themselves, space and time consist of nothing. They are only concepts born of the discriminating activity of the conscious mind. They do, however, form the indispensable coordinates for describing bodies in motion. Think of an example. A ball rolling down an incline, a man travelling south along a certain highway. . . .

Let's get on with it, shall we. I have been keeping a personal journal of coincidence for thirty years. After a very fruitful year or two, the question arises forcefully in the seeking mind . . . was I simply more aware of coincidences by keeping this journal—or was I . . . making them . . . happen?

In any case, some convincing examples from the

collection: You ask me, what were the names of the three men who murdered Doctor Berry at Green Hill? Ed Green, Fred Berry and Ted Hill. FACT. John McCabe of Fulham Road in the Bronx, New York, was listening to a record of "Cry of the Wild Goose" by Frankie Laine . . .

[The song plays. "My heart goes where the wild goose goes, And I must go where the wild goose goes . . . etc.]

. . . when a Canadian goose crashed through his bedroom window. FACT.

As the Danforth family of Peru, Indiana was watching the sinking of the Titanic on a TV movie of the week, just as the iceberg hits the ship, a large block of ice falls through the roof of their ranch style home, smashes the TV to smithereens. FACT.

Alphonso Bedoya was crossing Prince's Canal in Amsterdam. He was struck and killed by a green taxi carrying a passenger named Ravensburg. His brother, Armando Bedoya, was also struck and killed, in Amsterdam, while crossing Prince's Canal, by a green taxi—carrying a passenger named Ravensburg—ten years later. FACT.

At times an expert witness has coincidentally been present at the scene of the coincidental . . . as when Dr. A.D. Bajkov, the noted ichthyologist, visiting the United States, was bombarded with fish from the sky, shortly after breakfast in Biloxi, Mississippi. FACT.

But let's take a more ordinary example. Let's say you decide to go to the oculist to get a pair of glasses. You walk into the shop, past the displays of glasses and frames in the window. A bell rings. Once inside, you notice that the oculist's shop seems also to be an outlet for the books of a company called Sublime Publications. . . .

11.

TRANSLATOR: Introducing Mr. Zendavesta, my employer in this suspect venture. He should have just finished his usual breakfast: quail eggs in which the blebs of fertilization are kept raw, lace cake, jompoo juice, and jello. As the fisherman can infer the presence of the great whale from a single bubble on the sea—so Mr. Zendavesta claims to be able to discern the . . .

ZENDAVESTA: *The Book of the Yellow Ancestor!* The translation! You've finished!

TRANSLATOR: Are you joking?

ZENDAVESTA: The wisdom of the Yellow Ancestor is no joking matter. You're almost finished?

TRANSLATOR: I've made some headway. But this text still seems extremely unreliable.

ZENDAVESTA: Unreliable to you—perhaps. A rock of sanity to me. Forge ahead. Translate! What have you got so far?

TRANSLATOR: Well, there are some completed sections, but they're really . . . odd.

ZENDAVESTA: My ears are yours.

TRANSLATOR: O.K. . . . I'm fairly sure about this one— "The Genii's Pharmacy—prescription ten. Feed a small duckling on rose petals, mixed with oil and blood. When the bird is grown and its feathers come out red, kill it, dry it, crush it, feathers and all, and take a teaspoon of this powder every day for three hundred days."

ZENDAVESTA: That's it?

TRANSLATOR: That section, yeah.

ZENDAVESTA: And for what condition is this the cure?

TRANSLATOR: It doesn't say.

ZENDAVESTA: Of course.

TRANSLATOR: I might be mistaken about the characters for prescription. Perhaps "document" or "dispatch" . . . I also had trouble with. . . .

ZENDAVESTA: Please. Sublime Publications owes you a debt it can never repay. Your photo on the jacket? A certainty. Tell me, are there any passages that seem to be *directions* to a place?

TRANSLATOR: Not yet.

ZENDAVESTA: Keep at it. Don't fail me. I'm leaving shortly for the Oculists Convention near Mexico City. I'm sure you'll be kind enough to meet me there. We'll work together by the pool. A change of scene might calm your fevered brain. Your ticket. *[Hands* TRANSLATOR *a ticket. A bell rings.]*

THIEF: Anybody here?

ZENDAVESTA: *[To* TRANSLATOR*.]* Excuse me. A customer. Wait here. Browse. *[To* THIEF*.]* Yes?

THIEF: I want to get a pair of clear glasses with just glass in them, you know.

ZENDAVESTA: I know. Read the top line please.

THIEF: I can't make any sense of that.

ZENDAVESTA: Fine. Lie down. This will only take a moment.

TRANSLATOR: *[As* MR. ZENDAVESTA *examines the* THIEF*.]*

Zendavesta used to be an optical lens grinder in Chicago. He lived in a small room at the Diamond Hotel. He was a bachelor. He thought a lot about the nature of this life we lead, and his own particular destiny. He often lay awake nights, turning these two questions over in his mind like dice in a cage.

One day he was walking down West Madison Street after work, when he saw a man wearing a sandwich board sign, which read: *We live inside.* The man was selling a pamphlet for ten cents, also titled *We Live Inside.* The lens-grinder bought a copy. Years later he could be heard to remark:

ZENDAVESTA: I read it in bed, and before I fell asleep that night, I was inside.

THIEF: What'd you say?

ZENDAVESTA: *[To* THIEF.*]* Ah! Just as I suspected. The green quinsy. Invariably leads to blindness and insanity. This condition requires an immediate surgical procedure.

THIEF: Hey, look. I just. . . .

ZENDAVESTA: Stop. I know what you think. I can anticipate your query. The answer is: would I tell you you needed an operation if you didn't?

THIEF: I'll take my chances. Gimme the glasses and I'll get out of here.

ZENDAVESTA: Perhaps you'd like to purchase a new face, something so attractive that social graces will become unnecessary? You'll be able to get away with it, if you follow me. . . .

THIEF: No thanks. I'll be going now.

ZENDAVESTA: Just a moment. You seem like a malleable young man, who's in trouble. I'm preparing an expedition, and am currently attempting to hire a muscular assistant who's not bright enough to cause any harm.

I have sent every senator and representative in the Congress of our United States a registered letter, on the letterhead of Sublime Publications, appealing for immediate financing to equip us for *the adventure.* As soon as these funds arrive, we depart.

I'll take you where jewellers and policemen will never find you. We'll even send for Margo.

THIEF: Margo? How do you know . . .

ZENDAVESTA: Where are we going, you ask? Young man, the new cosmogony has been revealed to me. The key is simple. We live inside the earth. Modern astronomers are perfectly correct, except that they have everything inside out. The entire cosmos is like an egg. We live on the inner surface of a hollow shell, and inside the hollow are the sun, the moon, the stars, the planets, and the comets in their courses. What, you ask, is outside the shell? Nothing. Absolutely nothing. The inside is all there is.

However, at a certain point in the shell, there is a hole. A tiny hole, through which a man could enter that endless effluvium of endless absence, to annihilate himself in bliss. I'm talking to you about the resurrection, with a difference.

THIEF: Yeah. . . .

ZENDAVESTA: As soon as the exact location of this hole is revealed, the funds assembled—we set out! We have, of course, been subjected to insolent ridicule in our attempts to bring this knowledge before the public.

THIEF: You ever think about UFOs?

ZENDAVESTA: The things you call unidentified flying objects are neither objects, nor flying, nor unidentified. We know very well who they are. *[A bell rings.]*

ZENDAVESTA: Wait here. Browse.

THIEF: *[To* TRANSLATOR.*]* You . . . read these books?

TRANSLATOR: Some of them.

THIEF: They interesting?

TRANSLATOR: Some of them.

THIEF: Tell him I couldn't stay, hah. And good luck with your expedition.

TRANSLATOR: I doubt I'll be going . . . Hey! What's your name? *[The* THIEF *is gone.]*

ZENDAVESTA: *[To* MRS. LAMMLE.*]* Yes?

MRS. LAMMLE: I'm not interested in your philosophy. I want to pick up a pair of glasses.

ZENDAVESTA: Name?

MRS. LAMMLE: Mrs. Carl Lammle.

TRANSLATOR: Mr. Zendavesta claims to have the world's most complete library of the occult, excepting only the collection stored in the Green Vaults of Dresden. Maybe there's a manuscript copy of the *Book of Brightness,* or the *Epistle of Illusion and Caution* . . . Hmmm . . . *Nine Holes of Jade,* by Soo Ling, "the candid memoirs of a Hong Kong call girl." . . . Here's one called V*enus in India,* by a Captain Ernest Devereaux, "the amorous adventures of a gallant soldier" . . .

  This one's got an odd frontispiece. . . . Looks like an engraving of a long corridor, anonymous office building. One door is partly open, and I can see a small room within. A man sits at a table, a safe behind him, diamond dust and oil coat his fingers.

12.

JEWELLER: I am the dealer in precious stones. I know them, their sounds, their crystal hums.

GENERAL: *[Writing.]* Crystal hums. . . .

JEWELLER: I am a patient man. I studied in Amsterdam for ten years to learn to mark the stones for the chisel. Ten more years to cleave. Place the chisel, kiss it, and the stone falls into its parts. Like men. One tap, and into parts invisible. Now the stone I love has been stolen from me, and I will have it back, and I will wash it clean in the thief's blood.

I'll explain myself, if you don't mind. I met a girl once. She was a Dutch girl, and she worked in a bookstore in Amsterdam, on Prince's Canal. Children's books. She also played the flute in an amateur orchestra. I came to buy a book in English for my brother's son in America. For his birthday. She helped me choose. I chose one about a monkey. . . .

GENERAL: . . . a monkey. . . .

JEWELLER: I stared at her the whole time. She was not embarrassed. We had coffee.

She loved me. When I tell it to you now it is difficult, even for me who lived it, to believe. For one year, she brought me into the world. We went to cafes, the theatre, even to the countryside. At home, she would watch as I marked the stones. She was quiet, and asked for nothing. I thought I was reborn under a new sun.

One night she met the conductor of the state symphony at a party at the university. One week

later she went to live with him in a house in a suburb of Amsterdam. For a month, I could not believe
this simple truth. Her smell was everywhere.

After she moved away, I cut the stone. It had
arrived a year ago, and I had spent months delay-
ing, staring at it as she watched me. I always felt
that my mark was wrong, and if I cut—the stone
would fall into worthless fragments. That night, I
opened the *Zohar* to the *Book of Brightness,* and
though I read it without understanding, it calmed
me. I erased my mark. And then I bled from my
nose and mouth, and the blood flowed down onto
the stone, a transluscent coat of my blood, and the
stone shone clearer than ever. I remember the open
Zohar, the blood, the light, the diamond dust from
the polisher, the view out over the canals, the passing boats of the tourists. Then, almost without my
noticing—the tap of the hammer on the blade.

Once I spent my nights looking into the facets of
the stone to see the past, the future, and the roads
between. Now I can only look into my mind's picture of it. The blue glow fills my skull. I can't find
the thief, but I see something he'll follow as I follow
the stone. Do you see it, general? See it.

GENERAL: *[Aside.]* This private work can be distressing to
a professional soldier. *[To* JEWELLER.*]* Right, sir. Just
give me the information. We'll screw the enemy to
the wall.

JEWELLER: Into the tenth facet! An apartment in this city!
She's dreaming, and she thinks my eye is something
in her dream. She wakes, opens a novel . . . odd
book, must read it sometime. She closes the book.

She turns on the TV. Perfect. General, get your hat and stick. We have work to do.

13.

MARGO: My Sony is a one-way communication system, sending me words and pictures that never end. They're always changing, and despite this, I always understand them. My TV can communicate with me, if I'm awake, and watching. To communicate with me means to say stuff, or show me stuff I understand. If you say something to me I don't understand, we're not communicating, are we? If I say something to you and you don't understand, we're not communicating. Are we? But we're communicating right now.

 If we keep communicating like this—so we understand each other— it'll only lead to little ripples in our context, this world of common words and pictures that allows us to communicate in the first place. Like me and my TV—it never does much more than give a little shuffle to the cards I've already got. It's pleasant, but now I'm turning it off. I need a new deck.

JEWELLER: General, do something. I'm not interested in her philosophy.

GENERAL: Why don't you forget everything you know about all that and let us get on with it.

MARGO: If you step out of this pleasant sensation of understanding, and the world that makes it possible, you stop communicating. These postcards from my lover are perfect: notes from somewhere else, torn up and delivered by the wind.

GENERAL: Why don't you forget everything you know about all that and let us get on with it. . . .

MARGO: I miss the crazy bastard. I did book—I did TV—now record player. [*Music.*]

GENERAL AND JEWELER: Gotcha. [MARGO *screams.*]

INTERMISSION

– II –

14.

MRS. LAMMLE, MARGO, DEEP SEA EDNA, MARCELLA

MRS. LAMMLE: Yes. Our Bible is a deep mine of treasure for the student of coincidence. The Book of Revelation lists ten plagues, ten seals, and ten archangels: Michael, Gabriel, Zakiel, Uriel, Jamalel, Nuriel, Samael, Raziel, Ariel and last, but not least, Fleuriel. And how many heads has Babylon, the mother of harlots? Ten. FACT.

One particular jewel in this mine is the story of Jonah. The prophet's dark ride in the belly of the whale—three days. Christ's tenure in the tomb before his resurrection—three days. FACT.

And now, from my journal. Twenty years ago, when she was four years old, a young woman, who shall remain anonymous, stood quietly outside a gypsy fortune telling parlor in Chicago, while her mother had her palm read. The gypsy, a certain

Madame Edna, . . . Marcella, would you bring out the model, please. [MARCELLA *brings out a Charlotte Russe.*] Thank you, Marcella. The gypsy, a certain Madame Edna, gave the girl a Charlotte Russe, insisting that she try it.

EDNA: Try it.

MRS. LAMMLE: She loved it. Recently, the girl saw her second Charlotte Russe, in the window of an expensive restaurant. When she entered and ordered it, she found that the Charlotte Russe was reserved for a special customer—Madame Edna, looking exactly the same after all these years. They shared the Charlotte Russe, and both seemed astonished at meeting once again over the same confection.

At some time in the future, this young woman attends a formal banquet near Mexico City. To her surprise it features Charlotte Russe as dessert. Meanwhile, Madame Edna herself has been invited to another, rather less formal affair in the basement of the same hotel. She loses her way in the maze of the building's corridors, knocks on a door to ask for directions. Our young woman, holding a Charlotte Russe in her hand, opens it. They stare at each other. What a coincidence.

I still tell these stories, but I'm no longer sure what they signify. Perhaps I'm tired. I want to get away for a while— from Carl—that's my husband— and my life here. Lately, I've been dreaming of trains—little locomotives, with pleasant curls of smoke twirling into blue skies, crossing little child's maps of the continent, heading south to some resting place under a new sun. I need a vacation.

15.

GENERAL: Hmmm. A dispatch from the front. Thank you, Marcella. Perhaps a notice of a promotion. Recognition of my efforts at our particularly exposed station is long overdue.

However, it's possible that the news enclosed will take a grimmer turn. Battle statistics. The valor of my second in command has long been suspect. . . . The truth is that I left the station in charge of my waterboy, whose command of English is far from . . . but why speculate? The applicable rule in these complex situations: never assume you know where you're going, till you've gotten there. In other words, you've got to suck it and see. [Opens envelope.]

Hmmmm. It seems that in my absence our position has been overrun by the enemy, the remainder of our unit, destroyed, and my personal possessions burnt to ashes. I have been reassigned to the bird barracks. "Report immediately."

I refuse. As you've seen, I am already embarked on a new career. I am a kidnapper. However, this is not as tawdry as it sounds. Margo actually behaves as if we're taking her on holiday. In any case, as Mussolini said to the British ambassador when their limousine ran over a child in the streets of Naples. . . . "Never look back."

This adventure will also serve as a snazzy final fillip to my memoirs. Memoirs with a difference. Not only my actual experience in the service, but my dreams, fantasies—the inner man. And I have developed a compositional technique. Among all the methods of writing, I may not be certain my own way is the best, but I am absolutely sure it is the most religious. I begin by writing the first sentence, and trust to almighty God for the second.

But let's be frank for a moment. This jeweller is a madman. When he returned from this private clinic in the mountains, his imagination was diseased. However, he's paying me. His plan? Now that we've kidnapped the girl, we follow the postcards she receives from this thief to track him down. Then we use her as bait to draw him into our figurative maw. We get train tickets . . .

We head south.

We cross over the border into Mexico.

We race through the desert, its stark beauty interrupted by an occasional panorama of local business: Panchito's Tacos, Valdez auto-repair. The jeweller is abstracted. Margo is resigned . . . or pleased. She knows we're taking her to him. She cannot imagine what this jeweller plans to do to her lover, once we find him.

CONDUCTOR: Tickets? Tickets?

JEWELLER: Why don't you ask the engineers in the locomotive for their tickets?

CONDUCTOR: Because they're driving the train.

JEWELLER: So are we.

MARGO: Right.

JEWELLER: She's a quick study.

GENERAL: I examine the final postcard for clues. Seems to be a souvenir card from some seedy roadside attraction. The thief must be gone from there. Postmark is ten days old . . . We rush on toward the posh hotel outside Mexico City, where the Jeweller has engaged a number of ballrooms to bait our trap.

MARGO: So this is Mexico.

JEWELLER: Yes.

MARGO: It's just what I thought it would be. I've seen it on TV. . . . Dead cows.

JEWELLER: Do you love me?

MARGO: Love you? You're kidnapping me. Besides, I don't even know you. I mean maybe if I knew you for years or something. . . . I doubt it. No.

JEWELLER: You may change your mind. You may discover that love is not so much a feeling . . . as it is a situation.

GENERAL: Though this thief seems both dangerous and resourceful, my jeweller is confident he'll rise to the bait, like a great whale coming up from the bottom of the sea.

JEWELLER: Confident? No. Certain. I had the stone, and it brought me the evil fate to lose it. Now I pursue, but he has the stone, and the weight of its power slows him, his legs grow heavy, his alertness dwindles, and we have him! Only a man of learning and restraint can possess the stone without it leading him to his doom.

GENERAL: Right. Hmmm. The picture on this latest postcard is curious. In it is a badly lettered sign, that clearly once said DEEP SEA ED'S WORLD OF WONDERS, but two new letters—NA—have been squeezed in after ED. . . .

16.

EDNA: You curious about love?

THIEF: Yeah.

EDNA: Psst. Here's the secret. It's a mystery. The truth is that loving Ed is just something I do, you know. I don't think about it anymore.

He was the original owner of this popgun palace and marine museum. When I met him he specialized in window sleeps, went into trances in store windows to advertise furniture sales. "Suspended animation. Hasn't eaten for two weeks!" He was doing it at Watson Discount. After Mom was asleep, one, two in the morning—I'd go down there and slip food to him, bags fulla greasy tacos, sneaking down Main Street like a thief. I was seventeen. . . . When he left town. I left with him.

You still don't know what the hell to do, do you?

THIEF: Well, I'm still trying to hide. . . .

EDNA: Get a straight job. That'll hide you. Nobody looks at working people. My brother's got a body shop in Las Cruces. That's on the border. Means the crosses.

THIEF: I don't know anything about the insides of cars. I don't really know how to do anything.

EDNA: Then go into show business. Take that girl along. She could do the parachuting, which is easy for women and they enjoy it too. Gives 'em a thrill. I used to do it with Ed. Last time was a state fair in Jackson, Mississippi. I lost myself up there, landed in an empty gondola heading east. I stopped jumping after that, and Ed was scared to, so we got a

Mexican kid named Eduardo. Lot of style. Made himself up a batman suit. He did one season with us. Next year some circus picked him up. Took him to Europe. His luck didn't hold. He was doing his batman jump in Venice when his shrouds tangled and that was it. Never had a chance. Batman into the Grand Canal.

For a while, me and Ed were big time. Owned a carnival on the Canadian circuit, even did the Winnipeg Provincial Fair. Had a Hall of History, all kinds of figures in dramatic tableaus. Looked realer than hell. Ed made them all himself. Papier mâché and spit.

And then Ed got religion. He invented a new ride for the midway, his idea being that its motion would provide a spiritual experience for the clientele. It was called the Ezekial, and that's what it looked like: wheel in a wheel, way in the middle of the air. The little wheel run by faith, and the big wheel run by the grace of God. . . . Well, on its first run with live customers some drunk teenager flies out of the damn thing. Ed is sued by these lawyers, and he loses everything—his carnival, the Ezekial ride, everything. Then he disappeared. When I found him again he was a fry cook at a place called the Embers.

ED: Here's your two over light, I got a burger royale working. . . .

EDNA: It was back then that we started doing the casket of death. Ten sticks of dynamite, lead shielding, some cotton in your ears, a bag of stage blood, and they faint in the seats. When we were testing—I learned something. Best thing I can teach you. We'd light the fuse and walk away. It'd burn down in about five minutes, but sometimes it seemed like an hour waiting for the charge to go off. That's what kills people. Time seems stretched. They figure the fuse has gone out, they go back to check, and are right on top of it when she blows. I learned to give it plenty of time. . . .

MAN: I'm not interested in philosophy. We want to see the fish. One, please.

EDNA: Hey, Mister. If she's old enough to enjoy the show, she's old enough to need a ticket. Take 'em in. *[The* THIEF *is gone with the customers.]*

ZENDAVESTA: Are you showing people to these fish, or vice-versa.

EDNA: Cute. Think it over. You're the one who paid at the door.

ZENDAVESTA: Yes, indeed. Should I be amused, or is this somehow educational?

EDNA: Educational. These fish are quiet, and besides, they know the secrets of the deep.

ZENDAVESTA: Do you mind if I sit down a moment, the better to contemplate these marvels.

EDNA: Help yourself.

ZENDAVESTA: I am Mr. Zendavesta, a humble explorer of the etheric borderlands. I'd appreciate it if you'd examine this small pamphlet, entitled *We Live Inside.* You might find it instructive.

EDNA: Tell me if I have this right. You are a harmless crank.

ZENDAVESTA: Crank? Madam, I deplore cranks. The discoverer of the corpuscular theory of sounds, of kine-

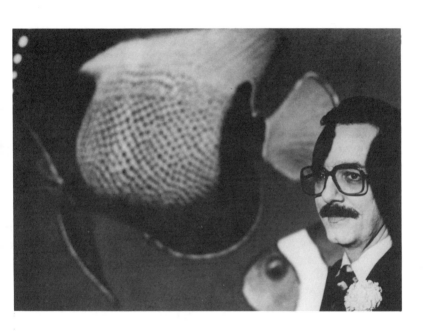

John Nesci in *Dark Ride*

matic relativity, of the cosmic donut, where are they now? Already dead, and buried alongside the Mad Hatter. I am a scientist.

EDNA: I'm proud of you. But I'm closing up now.

ZENDAVESTA: Please. I know what you think.

EDNA: Do you now?

ZENDAVESTA: Of course. There are two sides to every argument, and both of them are mine. You see, I was once a common voluptuary like yourself. Yet I soon realized that the ordinary mines of enjoyment are easily exhausted. I perceived that these twisted paths of pleasure turned back on themselves in diminishing spirals of decreasing delight. Once I had escaped the toils of the serpent of desire, my mind opened. Ideas descended on me like a flight of vultures on a dying antelope.

You're quite a handsome woman, you know. I've been looking for a group of brave companions to set out on a certain expedition I have in mind. . . .

EDNA: Sorry. I gotta babysit that night.

ZENDAVESTA: Then perhaps something less total in its implications. I am also the entertainment coordinator at the upcoming World Oculists' convention at the extraordinary Hacienda Ramón on the outskirts of Mexico City. Perhaps you'd consent, for a fee, of course, to display these fish in some suitable. . . .

17.

JEWELLER: Margo—you are now the hostess for the annual World Oculists' Convention near Mexico City. We've published your photograph in all the newspapers.

GENERAL: Congratulations.

MARGO: Thank you.

JEWELLER: As usual, the oculists' affair is held at the legendary Hacienda Ramón. Your friend is in the neighborhood. He'll see your photo. He will come. He won't leave the stone behind, and I'll hear it singing in his pocket. It belongs in my forehead, a dim glow in the darkness of the temple, the incense spirals upward. . . . Pardon my enthusiasm. Hmmm. It seems my new associate is late—or perhaps. . . .

TRANSLATOR: Café con leche, por favor.

WAITRESS: Got it. Anything else?

TRANSLATOR: Yes. Some jello, please.

WAITRESS: Red? Or green?

JEWELLER: [To TRANSLATOR.] Are you the taxidermist?

TRANSLATOR: No . . . I'm the translator.

JEWELLER: Who?

TRANSLATOR: I mean, no. I just stopped in for a drink on my way to . . .

JEWELLER: Thank you. Margo, you look lovely in this light. You remind me of someone. . . .

MARGO: Really? How interesting.

JEWELLER: Do you play the flute?

MARGO: No.

JEWELLER: You could learn.

MARGO: Can I get another coco-loco?

JEWELLER: Of course. . . . You know, I'd planned to im-
mure you forever, along with your clever boyfriend,
in the Green Vaults of Dresden. I even brought my
trowel along. But I've had a better idea.

GENERAL: O God. I would hesitate to present you raw
recruits with my informed speculation as to the
nature of this jeweller's revenge. However, familiar
as I am with illegal conduct in the line of duty, I
have begun to prepare my abili.

TRANSLATOR: "'When the fog is heavy on the road to the
Emperor's Jewelled Garden, you hear voices all
around you, shouting directions. Go South. When
the fog burns away, no sign of travellers—no
horses, no carriages, no tracks in the dust.' The man
in bandages stopped talking, stood up slowly and
walked over to the window. . . ."

WAITRESS: Anything else?

TRANSLATOR: Uh . . . say, Miss . . . I'm a stranger here,
and I thought you might . . . have a drink with me
after work.

WAITRESS: I'd love to, cowboy, but we never close.

TRANSLATOR: What? But you can't mean that you . . .

WAITRESS: Will that be all?

GENERAL: [To MARGO.] You're thinking about him, aren't
you?

MARGO: I think about him all the time.

GENERAL: I was married once. I loved my wife. Loved
the children.

> One day, after we'd been married for ten years,
when I came home from work my wife kissed me
with surprising passion. She'd bought me a present—some kind of aftershave. That night, in bed,

she was heaven. She did everything I liked best, and that woman knew me. I fell asleep full of renewed hope for our future.

The next morning before I left for work, she wrapped her arms around me, as if she never wanted me to go. Finally I got to the garage, got in my car, turned the key in the ignition, and the world exploded. She'd had her boyfriend wire a bomb behind the dashboard. I almost died. I had so much glass in my face it took the doctors two weeks to get it out of me.

MARGO: Why are you telling me this?

GENERAL: So you'll understand.

MARGO: Understand what?

WAITRESS: What'll it be, folks? [DEEP SEA ED *comes out of the kitchen, goes to the* TRANSLATOR'S *table.*]

ED: Hello, Slick. Got a cigarette?

TRANSLATOR: Sorry. I don't smoke.

ED: You new in town?

TRANSLATOR: Well, I . . .

WAITRESS: A Blue Plate Special, heavy on the gravy, Enchilada combination, and a coco-loco.

ED: I quit.

WAITRESS: Don't tell me. Tell your mother. Tell those nice folks at table ten.

ED: The hell with them. I gotta get my ticket.

    [*Ticket Windows.*]

TICKET SELLER: How many?

ED: I'm a first-class grill man, a soldier of fortune, and a doctor of medicine. You happen to be looking at the inventor and sole distributor of Deep Sea Ed's anal-gesic balm, an unfailing cure for mumps, measles, malaria and all other diseases beginning with the letter M.

I am also an artiste—sole inspiration and executor of Deep Sea Ed's Hall of History, a faithful and three dimensional panorama, a solemn reminder of the grandeur of bygone days, including a diorama of the glacial age of the cave man, constructed under the supervision of college professors; a tableau of the hideous murder of Prince Kanitovsky by a bellboy at the Connaught Hotel; a complete model of Ford's theatre, featuring the great President Lincoln, and his vile assassin, John Wilkes Booth!

I made all these figures that you see before you, in poses taken from the life. Lessons to be learned! Not only entertaining, but educational as well!

Hell, that show is what you call defunct.

It's a moving world, my masters, and the sands are forever shifting.

The Central Labor Service down on Avenida Juarez got me something near Mexico City. World tells you something, you go along.

TICKET SELLER: I'm not interested in philosophy. I'm interested in selling tickets. What's the situation?

ED: Through the sharp hawthorn blows the cold wind.

TICKET SELLER: Too bad. What are you doing about it?

ED: Going south.

TICKET SELLER: How many?

ED: One, please. [MARGO *to the* TRANSLATOR'S *table.]*

MARGO: Hi.

TRANSLATOR: Hi.

MARGO: You know, there's only really two ideas about

the things people believe. One is—only the stuff *everyone* believes is true, like the sun is wonderful, and there's probably some kind of God inside, and hurting people isn't nice . . . that stuff. The alternate choice is: If every one believes it, how *could* it be true? I mean, it's obvious that everyone else is not too bright, and that only the stuff *I* believe is true. I mean, if anyone agrees with me about something, I start thinking my idea must be pretty stupid. Do you agree?

TRANSLATOR: I . . .

MARGO: Shhh. I'm being kidnapped.

TRANSLATOR: That's, uh . . . too bad.

MARGO: They want my boyfriend to come for me.

TRANSLATOR: Where are they taking you?

MARGO: They didn't say. Oh, yeah—a hotel in Mexico. The Hacienda Ramón.

TRANSLATOR: What a coincidence. That's exactly where I. . . .

JEWELLER: Ah. Here's the taxidermist now.

TAXIDERMIST: Listen carefully, so that when you bring me the skin you won't have marred all. In preparing lifesize mounts of men, a cut should be made from the throat to the crotch in the underbelly. They cut in from the center of each palm to this main cut. Peel this thief's skin back, and off completely. Skin the feet out to the last joint in his toes. Proceed in the face area as for antlered animals.

MARGO: He isn't antlered.

TAXIDERMIST: Wash any blood off with cold water. Salt the skin thoroughly. Let drain, salt again. Regular table salt will do. Diamond Crystal, for example, is fine.

JEWELLER: General, write that down. Diamond Crystal.

GENERAL: Diamond Crystal. . . .

TAXIDERMIST: Do all this, bleach out the bones. I will articulate and mount him with pleasure. Half now, half on delivery.

JEWELLER: Nothing now. I need to see the work. It's going to be complex. He won't be complete.

MARGO: You'll need to improvise.

TAXIDERMIST: Who's plaything is that? What is she saying?

JEWELLER: She has been refusing to accept her . . . situation. Her mind is playing tricks on her.

GENERAL: She's the bait.

MARGO: I'm a nurse in this clinic. There. How easily we communicate when we're in the same context. We understood each other, just for a moment. Isn't that fun. *[To herself.]* I'm beginning to think these patients are making sense. A bad sign.

DOCTOR: Nurse, relax. You've had a long day. *[Pointing to a small silver box.]* Have a cigarette while I check the ward. The box is full.

MARGO: *[Picking up silver box.]* The darn thing's a paperweight.

JEWELLER: That's exactly what it is.

MARGO: Oh God. I miss my playmate. Did I tell you about him? The Unseen Playmate. You have one of those? You know what I remember about love? When She is disfigured, He blinds himself. And vice-versa. When He is disfigured, She blinds her-

self. Uh oh. I better read my book. It calms me
down. It's a silly adventure story.

JEWELLER: In the *Book of Brightness,* Rabbi Isaac the Blind
mentions the two causations: horizontal or "one
thing after another" . . . and vertical. There are no
accidents, says Rabbi Isaac the Blind.

MARGO: I'm off duty now.

TAXIDERMIST: She's delightful. When you're done with
her, perhaps I could. . . .

MARGO: You. Go home. Sort the bones.

JEWELLER: The man in the next bed to mine has these
dreams where he is in a dark place, red and green
lights in the distance . . .

GENERAL: Ah! Service!

> [WAITRESS *is heading toward them. Music. They're
> gone, and she is the barmaid,* TERESA.]

18.

THIEF: I'm in this bar in Hermosillo. I couldn't stay with
Deep Sea Edna forever, but I took her advice.

EDNA: Buy a butterfly net, and go to Mexico.

THIEF: Yeah. No one would think that a crazy gringo is
wandering around with a ball of fire around his
neck. . . . You know I go through these little Mex
towns and sometimes I think that these people
sitting around the Zócalo can see my thoughts
'cause the stone is shining in my head and they can
look right in and see it . . . and one of them is gonna
say. . . .

MAN: Beer, Señor? I myself am very interested in red and
green butterflies. . . .

THIEF: . . . and lead me down this alley and a coupla guys with pigstickers are gonna emerge from a pink door while Marty Robbins sings "El Paso" and I'm gonna be in a big puddle of blood, and I'm not only gonna be there, I'm gonna stay there. So I'm a careful traveller . . . down through Ensenada, Guaymas. Here in Hermosillo, I got nervous. I hired ten guys to dress up like me, gave 'em butterfly nets, told 'em to go to the public library and carry books around town, so my image would drift confusingly around these dusty streets, past the statues of generals. . . . Or did I dream that? . . .

I'm in this bar in Hermosillo, the PLATILLO VOLADOR. Sitting at the bar next to me is a guy from America, and it seems to me I've seen him somewhere before. He looks like a pool hustler from Indianapolis and I'm not far wrong as he's from Grand Forks, North Dakota. I open the conversation. How you doin'?

DEEP SEA ED: Behaving.

THIEF: And I gotta think about that one. I figure he wants me to know that right now he is not in a Mexican whorehouse, or chasing the waitress around the tables while his wife sits in North Dakota screaming at the kids. But he wants to imply that he could be going wild if he wasn't exercising control. He's got the potential.

DEEP SEA ED: Hey—Teresa, gimme another, will you.

TERESA: You got it.

THIEF: Then I understand what he meant. He just wants to tell me he's 'behaving' like exhibiting behavior, like at the zoo—and implying that I should watch

this with some attention and I might learn something. Just see him lift his glass, slide his elbow forward on the bar, sit back and breathe. Just breathe.

DEEP SEA ED: They could put me in jail for what I'm
thinking about doing to Teresa, but they won't.
They can't find out. It's inside my head.

THIEF: Yeah.

DEEP SEA ED: What's your line of work, Mr. . . .

THIEF: "Mr. Raven" I tell him. I'm a dealer in precious
stones. He'd look at me like I was crazy, but he
don't, cause he isn't listening. *He* wants to tell *me*
something.

DEEP SEA ED: I been around the world. Three years in
Thailand, two in Japan, all over the USA. I been in
France, England, all those places, and you know
what? This town we're in right now, this is the best
damn place in the world.

THIEF: I think that one over. Well, I don't know, I mean,
I'd like to be somewhere else. I have this girlfriend
and I find this place a little scary.

DEEP SEA ED: You're wrong. I been around. I know, This
is it. Best damn place in the world.

TERESA: Teresa brings him another.

THIEF: He tosses it down, leaves a pile of pesos on the
bar, and stalks out, all before I have a chance to
agree with him.

TERESA: Teresa hands the Thief a newspaper.

THIEF: Hey . . . Margo's picture. It's her. I quote. "The
Oculists' annual trade fair and exhibition will be
held, as usual, at the exclusive Hacienda Ramón.
Miss Margo Lamont will present the Oculist of the

Year award at seven in ballroom E. Party at eight.
There's more . . .

[Arrivals at Hacienda Ramón: DEEP SEA EDNA, GEN-
ERAL, JEWELLER, MARGO, *and then the* TRANSLATOR.*]*

The Hacienda's electric garden is open to the
public between 3 and 6 P.M. At this moment, on the
terrace adjacent to the main dining room, two men
are deep in conversation. Continued p. 101, column
10.

TERESA: Will that be all?

THIEF: No. There's more. I gotta bring something somewhere. I gotta meet someone. *[*THIEF *is gone.]*

TERESA: HEY—you forgot your butterfly net.

19.

[The electric garden and/or the Hacienda Ramón]

ZENDAVESTA: Have you taken the tour?

TRANSLATOR: Mr. Zendavesta, you said there'd be peace
and quiet down here, that we'd have time to work
on the translation. You've done nothing but dance
with the wives of oculists from Detroit till dawn.
You're never in your room. Look, I have to be honest with you. This text is either so corrupt with
modern emendations that further work on it is
pointless, or I am simply incapable of—

ZENDAVESTA: Have you taken the tour?

TRANSLATOR: No. . . .

ZENDAVESTA: Take the tour.

TRANSLATOR: I don't think you understand. This supposedly third century B.C. text has a fragment in it in

which a jeweller and some companions take a train ride. It's like translating some kind of grade-B adventure story. This can't be the *Book of the Yellow Ancestor.* Yet, there's something about it that . . .

ZENDAVESTA: These oculists, all around us . . . don't they seem to you to be somehow—wonderful?

TRANSLATOR: Look, I've been trans. . . .

ZENDAVESTA: No doubt you're an intelligent young man, and I appreciate your efforts . . . but I'm no longer concerned with how they—end. Keep the manuscript. Translate it if you wish. Its secrets no longer matter to me.

I'll be frank. For most of my life I assumed that those men and women I saw around me were . . . contraptions, not people with feelings like my own. I planned to escape them by creating a separate universe and moving there.

But this convention has opened my eyes. I was sitting in the Tropical Lounge, in this very hotel, the night I arrived, alone. Upstairs, at the desk, the first oculists were checking in. The bartender was missing two of his front teeth. I had a stomach ache. Then suddenly, I understood the truth. That evening, in the Tropical Lounge at the Hacienda Ramón, by divine miracle, nerves of God had been projected into my body. God's semen, you see, in the form of divine white nerves, has extended down from heaven and pierced my form. Impregnation has taken place. There is no longer anything I want to know, or any place I want to go.

I have enemies, however. Plans are being made at this very moment to abort the sacred seed, by pumping out my spinal cord. This they intend to do by means of so-called little men, placed in my feet.

TRANSLATOR: You are totally out of your fucking mind.

ZENDAVESTA: Take the tour. I think you'll find it instructive.

TRANSLATOR: What tour? Where are you going?

20.

MRS. LAMMLE: Do you mind if I sit down? I couldn't help overhearing your conversation. My name is Mrs. Carl Lammle. I'm not interested in philosophy. I used to be, but now I think it's a lot of shit. I just want to talk to someone.

TRANSLATOR: I'm someone.

MRS. LAMMLE: Good. I'm here with my husband—Carl. He's a professor of the retina or something. Very disciplined, Carl. We've been married for twenty-seven years. Carl's a member of the Rotary Club, hasn't missed a weekly meeting for those twenty-seven years. He went to a meeting yesterday in Mexico City, doesn't speak a word of Spanish, and there were all these Mexican Rotarians saying things he didn't understand, and shaking his hand. He came back very pleased.

We have a son. His name is Fred, and I don't tell you this to make you feel bad for me. He was born with brain damage. He's 26 years old now. Carl goes to this clinic in the mountains every weekend, to shave him. Fred never recognizes him. I stopped going years ago.

You know, people say I look all right, but
inside, I'm a basket case. Last night I woke up about
2 a.m., thought I was sick. I was covered with sweat,
racing inside like a car engine when the accelera-
tor's stuck. I even got dressed and went down to the
Tropical Lounge. Nobody around but the bartender.
Some Mexican song was on the jukebox. It made me
cry. Sometimes I think that nothing's happened for
the past thirty years, except inside my head, and
that's always repeating itself. I used to write articles
for magazines, and believed I knew things other
people didn't know, and that they should find them
out from me. That's a lot of shit—don't you think?

TRANSLATOR: I don't know. . . . The most amazing thing
about this place is that even when I close my eyes,
and then open them again, it doesn't go away.

MRS. LAMMLE: You think that's amazing?

TRANSLATOR: Well . . . yes.

MRS. LAMMLE: Fine. Ah. Room Service. I want to tell you a
story. There's no point, really. It's part of my life and
very simple. When I was a young girl, I got a job
demonstrating gas stoves for the Magic Chef stove
company. This was in the depression, and people
didn't have much money to buy food, much less gas
stoves, and I was selling them in Oklahoma, which
was worse off than most. But it was the time of the
oil and gas boom down there. Lots of people whose
land was crossed by pipeline were allowed by the
companies to tap into the gaspipe for free. So they
were a pretty good market for the Magic Chef range.

I had a driver, who also did my grocery shopping and rented the town theatre, where I'd put on

this cooking show. I memorized certain recipes and had practiced, so I did 'em just right on the Magic Chef. I'd pass the results around the hall on paper plates. Those people would figure a pretty young thing like me couldn't cook that well, so the stove must have done it. And they'd buy. I'd do all this cooking dressed in a gypsy costume. I'd do a few simple tricks too—color changing scarves mostly. After all, it was Magic Chef. I did that for two years.

     What do you do?

TRANSLATOR: I'm a sort of writer.

MRS. LAMMLE: Are you going to put me in a story?

TRANSLATOR: Don't worry. I'd never put you in a story in a way you wouldn't like.

MRS. LAMMLE: What way wouldn't I like? It's all the same to me.

21.

JEWELLER: General, the ballroom is ready. The party begins. When the Thief appears, searching for Margo, approach him cautiously. Some casual conversation. . . .

GENERAL: Good idea.

MARGO: Yeah. Let's talk to him. I've got a few things to tell him myself.

JEWELLER: Soon, I'll meet him. I'm no longer sure what I will do. A man may wander, unaware, into murky windings underground, from which he may never emerge. The Zohar tells of three men who determined to explore this realm of darkness. They descended. One still clings in terror to the wall near the entrance, too fearful to move. One went mad, and disappeared among the pathways of the black maze. Only the third, Rabbi Isaac the Blind, returned safely. He claims to have met himself, and led himself back to the upper world. *[Music.]*

22.

[The Ballroom. Music. All characters except the THIEF *appear.* COOK *emerges from his cage.]*

DEEP SEA ED: Edna!

DEEP SEA EDNA: Ed! *[A stately dance, during which the* THIEF *arrives, and places the diamond on a pedestal among the dancers. The dancers stop their movement.]*

23.

MRS. LAMMLE: Just how I like it.

EDNA: Right in the sight lines.

MARGO: Very up-tempo.

MRS. LAMMLE: Under control.

GENERAL: And on the level.

JEWELLER: Just how I like it.

ZENDAVESTA: Perfect. Just going through the motions.

MARGO: Exactly. I want my life to be so pure I'll get death threats from the public.

ED: You got anything worth safe-keeping, leave it with the Fat Boy. He never leaves his chair.

THIEF: I like to spend my money on things that disappear—liquor, food, drugs.

TRANSLATOR: Things that come and go.

GENERAL: Sex is barely worth dropping my pants for.

ZENDAVESTA: Just going through the motions.

MRS. LAMMLE: Up tempo.

ED: Under control.

WAITRESS: And on the level.

THIFF: Just how I like it.

ZENDAVESTA: Have you taken the tour?

MRS. LAMMLE: The flying figure of a mutilated man? Yes,
    last night. . . .

JEWELLER: What a coincidence.

MARGO: Leave it with the Fat Boy.

WAITRESS: Is the guest of honor here yet?

GENERAL: Who is he?

JEWELLER: I don't remember.

THIEF: I just feel good.

MARGO: Why?

THIEF: I don't know why.

EDNA: Good feeling from nowhere, that's a sign of death.

ED: Right . . . things that come and go.

TRANSLATOR: . . . The flying figure of a mutilated man.
    Last night . . .

EDNA: Perfect. Just going through the motions.

MRS. LAMMLE: That's right. Certain portions of my brain
    are being held hostage.

WAITRESS: Red or green?

TRANSLATOR: At this moment, a limping Persian is pass-
    ing by the wharf.

MRS. LAMMLE: At this moment, a plate of food is being
    soiled by the shit of two rats.

ZENDAVESTA: At this moment, one hundred and one
    emaciated monks are holding up their broken fans.

JEWELLER: At this moment, the black turtle climbs up the
    candlestick.

Joanne Akalaitis with the company of *Dark Ride*

EDNA: At this moment, the bride is facing her husband, the old man is feeding his grandchild. The bottle is warm in his hand.

GENERAL: What a coincidence.

THIEF: Things that come and go.

MARGO: Just how I like it.

ED: Leave it with the Fat Boy.

GENERAL: I'm not interested in philosophy. Just tell me how it ends.

EDNA: I'm not interested in philosophy. Just tell me how it ends.

WAITRESS: I'm not interested in philosophy. Just tell me how it ends.

ZENDAVESTA: I'm not interested in philosophy. Just tell me how it ends.

MARGO: I'm not interested in philosophy. Just tell me how it ends.

ED: I'm not interested in philosophy. Just tell me how it ends.

MRS. LAMMLE: I'm not interested in philosophy. Just tell me how it ends.

JEWELLER: I'm not interested in philosophy. Just tell me how it ends.

THIEF: I'm not interested in philosophy. Just tell me how it ends.

TRANSLATOR: I'm not interested in philosophy. Just tell me how it ends. *[Ride out. Sound out. End ride.]*

VOICE: Those who wish to ride again, stay in your seats. A man'll be around to take your tickets. Those getting off, step lively. Exit to your left or to your right.

END SHOW

My Uncle Sam

My Uncle Sam was first presented by the New York Shakespeare Festival Public Theatre on October 7, 1983, with the following cast:

DARLENE/LITTLE PERSON	Laura Innes
THE BOTTLER	Olek Krupa
LILA	Kathleen Layman
OLD SAM	Mark Margolis
JAKE/PROFESSOR FINLEY/ GOLF MANAGER	John Nesci
SACRISTAN/ASSISTANT TRAVEL AGENT	Kristine Nielsen
CAPABILITY BROWN/ MEXICAN DOCTOR	Rocco Sisto
AUTHOR/TRAVEL AGENT	Scott Wentworth
MISS SIMMONS/STELLA	Margaret Whitton
YOUNG SAM	R. Hamilton Wright
MR. FLEAGLE/LIGHTHOUSE KEEPER	Ray Xifo

Director: Len Jenkin
Set: John Arnone
Lights: Frances Aronson
Costumes: Kurt Wilhelm
Sound: Len Jenkin
Stage Manager: Jane Hubbard

ACT I

INTERMISSION

ACT II

PRODUCTION NOTE

The Narrators should not be consistent reappearing characters. They are always different, and visually conform to the setting in which they appear *[nautical in Lighthouse, etc.]*. They can appear briefly to say their lines, or be present longer during the scene, or even be offstage on mike—this to depend on the style and requirements of each individual production.

The author's thanks to Thomas Peacock and William Gaines for the misquotations.

ACT I

1

The AUTHOR, *alone. In another area, a nightclub* DUO *[man and woman]. They are lip-synching badly to a record, with exaggerated romantic gestures. An elderly man in a suit and tie listens to them.*

DUO: This is my story, I have no song
      But a lone and broken heart—
      Because I fell in love, in love with you—
      I pray that you'll come back to me
      Just to hear you say you love me,
          and we'll never never part
      Never never part—oooh oooooh, oooh oooh—
      [They fade, as the figure of MY UNCLE SAM, *the elderly listener, rises. He is as described by the* AUTHOR. *He stands quietly.]*

AUTHOR: I saw my Uncle Sam once a year. He was my grandfather's brother, my great-Uncle Sam actually. He was exotic. Points of exoticism: ONE: He lived in Pittsburgh, which may not be exotic if you're from Pittsburgh, but if you're seven years old and have never been anywhere, and don't know anybody who's ever been anywhere, Pittsburgh means a complete other place, with its own other kind of people and cars and houses which I could only imagine at the very edge of my consciousness . . . a parallel world full of stuff made up in your head, and Uncle Sam would walk through the door with the smell of Pittsburgh in his thinning hair—dust of that impossible place on his shoulders. Point of

Mark Margolis, Rocco Sisto, and Kristine Nielsen in *My Uncle Sam*
Martha Swope Associates/Susan Cook

Exoticism TWO: He lived in a hotel. I had never even *seen* a hotel, except in a movie, where a hotel was a place only for adults, featuring sex and adventure. THREE: He was a bachelor. I knew that meant he wasn't married, but that special name for it, and the way it was said about him, was a label I couldn't read. I knew it meant he lived some other way from us—different, and not quite respectable. FOUR: He had a moustache, which he waxed. FIVE: He wore expensive cashmere coats. SIX: He smoked cigars. *[The figure lights a cigar.]*

The simple truth, which I can now understand as I am no longer seven, is that my great Uncle Sam was a traveling salesman in Pennsylvania. I understand bachelor and hotel and Pittsburgh very well. I've even been there, and yet a certain mystery never leaves his image in my mind. He would give me five dollar bills. That was so much money I never knew what to do with it but hide it. He gave me a Viewmaster, with circles of Asia, and Peru, and the U.S.A. I can almost dismiss it—pretend I can understand him without that sense of strangeness I always felt in his presence . . . but now I know that My Uncle Sam stepped aside, in some extraordinary way, from everything around him, and made that stepping aside his life.

He died alone. When he died he left me all the money he had. Four hundred and ten dollars. I hadn't seen him for thirty years. When I was little he never told me a story. I'm telling myself one, for him. Now.

UNCLE SAM SOLD NOVELTIES!!

[*The company, as* SALESMAN, *including the* AUTHOR, MY UNCLE SAM, *and a* YOUNG MAN *with a moustache who we will discover to be* MY UNCLE SAM *in his youth.* OLD *and* YOUNG SAM *speak together at times. They are linked by similarities in costume. All are in the postures of forties salesmen. The* SALESMEN *take these lines by turn, and demonstrate as they speak. One has a View-master.*]

SALESMEN: French batmask, pert and saucy! There's a certain spice to this style.

Ubangi lady and gentleman masks, 100 percent rubber!

Religious items! The luminous crucifix.

Jumbo chicken feet! Yellow molded plastic!

Hairy gorilla feet! Genuine black rubber, imbedded with black plastic hair!

OLD SAM: Unusual costume accessories: jungle drums boudoir set, a daringly designed two-piecer, inspired by darkest Africa, with frou-frou fringe!

ALL: OOOOOH!

OLD SAM: Leaves barely enough to the imagination to be legal.

ALL: OOOOOOH!

SALESMEN: Genuine imitation platinum French ring with views.

Bathing beauties! The Panama Canal!

OLD SAM: You say you want more for your money?

YOUNG SAM: You say what you've already heard just ain't enough? Tell you what I'm gonna do. Devil tail! Old Switch himself would be proud to wear this three foot long beauty!

ALL: OOOOOOOH!

YOUNG SAM: Frenchman kit!

SALESMEN: Beret, moustache, beard, cigarette holder!

ALL: OOOOOOH!

AUTHOR: Chinky Chinaman kit: a genuine thinking cap, a pair of foo-yong goggles with slit eyes, a pair of special protruding plastic teeth.

YOUNG SAM: Pussy-cat kit. Purrfect! Wear with a black bikini. Plush cat ears, pom-pom cattail, jumbo eyelashes, black gloves!

ALL: OOOOOHH!

OLD SAM: Goozelum Goggles!

ALL: OOOOOHH!

YOUNG SAM: The poo-poo cushion!

ALL: OOOH!

OLD SAM: The joy buzzer!

ALL: OOOOOOHH!

YOUNG SAM: The X-ray specs!

ALL: OOOOH!

OLD SAM: I AM MY UNCLE SAM. Next time you meet me, you're gonna thank me.

> *[The group gathers around him curiously. A* MAN *narrates]*

MAN: *[As others listen attentively.]* After a certain period in his life, he contrived, or rather he . . . happened . . . to sever himself from the world—to vanish—

ALL: Aaaah!

MAN: —to give up his place and privileges with living men, without being admitted among the dead.

> *[They slowly back away, staring at* OLD SAM. YOUNG SAM *is the last to leave. They're gone. Three* SECRETARIES *remain, in a row, pencils poised.]*

OLD SAM: I am My Uncle Sam. *[*OLD SAM *settles in to speak.*

He is in his hotel room in Pittsburgh. Old armchair. Standing ashtray. The three SECRETARIES *cross their legs. When* OLD SAM *speaks they start writing, taking dictation. He does not notice them.]*

I am a bachelor. I live in this hotel. Sherman Arms, Pittsburgh. I came into this world seventy years ago without a dime, and I've about held my own to date.

I'm not feeling well. I'm home from work today. Called in sick, but they know there's no action on my route this time of year. Allentown across to East Stroudsburg. . . . So I'm here at my window—and out there, the Monongahela, as usual, Jones and Laughlin steel on the river, plumes of fire off the stacks. My stars at night. See 'em from my window. Sherman Arms. Not night yet, but I'm waiting. I like the dusk. I like to watch the lights go on in people's apartment windows in the evening. And off, late at night. The only times you're really certain somebody's *there.*

I'm sitting in Market Square yesterday, and this young guy with a Pirates cap on sits next to me and opens his lunch. Peanut butter. I'm thinking his mommy made it for him now that's sweet, and then this gorgeous blonde who's all of eighteen comes toward us and I'm thinking whatever you want darlin' it's eight to five I'll do it. She's getting closer, and I'm watching every move. She waltzes up and sits down on the kid's lap, like I'm not there. They walk away, holding hands. And I'm full of envy for him up to the top of my head and beyond. And then I see them together in ten years screaming at each other in the kitchen, and he picks up a wine glass and throws it through a window and I remember that it's not envy that's for the living. It's pity. Envy is for the dead.

I'm too smart to keep thinking that young girls ask me for directions downtown cause they think I'm an interesting guy, moustache and all, like I'm somebody in a movie—like I'm a *character*. . . . I am no longer more interesting to good looking young women than a lamp post. I love secretaries. . . .

[SECRETARIES *cross legs, continue taking his "dictation."*]

I am no longer more interesting to Pittsburgh secretarial talent than a well.

SECRETARY 1: [*To* SECRETARY 2.] A well?

SECRETARY 2: Well.

OLD SAM: Now let's say you're in Pittsburgh. A tourist in Market Square. Center of the universe. You're lost. Transparent as I am, you spot me, like seeing a shadow. I am quasi-neutered by age. I am unlikely to stab you or rape you, so if you want neither of those things to happen to you on this gray morning I am a good person to ask directions. I'm moving slow. You catch up to me. I'm not busy . . . tell you what I know. Listen. You got time. . . . What's your life anyway? A few winters waiting for spring. A few summers waiting for the first clean chill of fall. A few bottles of whiskey, and three or four women you remember—if you're lucky. You might as well die now as later. Dust to dust, a fine darkness drifting with the dust of every other thing into a perpetual night. Even the names are dust. Names of the dead . . . last to go. Just as well. We got a way out of this world that's wide open. [*The* AUTHOR *appears behind his* SECRETARIES.]

Directions. I know Pittsburgh perfect. Purrfect. I used to sell punchboards on the south side. Drugstores. Candy stores. I drove every turn of those streets in a Buick Roadmaster.

SECRETARY 1: A what?

SECRETARY 2: It's a car.

OLD SAM: However, it is possible my information is no longer current. I could tell you how to get out to Medvink's Drugs on Howland, told the desk man to head out there to buy his granddaughter something for her birthday. He came up here. Only time he ever did that. Opened my damn door with his key. He yells—

DESKMAN'S VOICE: NO SUCH PLACE!

OLD SAM: No such place. I had directed him to 1948. . . . I missed something back there. My own damn fault. Been looking ever since, but you get so you know you won't find it. Hell, you don't even know what it was, passed by so quick—but you keep looking out of habit—or else you'd have to say, well, what I am now, what I'm doing now, this is my life. What man wants to say that? 1948. I had a girlfriend then. . . .

SECRETARIES: Oooooh!

AUTHOR: That's enough. Got it?

SECRETARIES: We got it!

[AUTHOR *and* SECRETARIES *exit.* OLD SAM *looks after retreating* SECRETARIES, *winks at audience.*]

OLD SAM: Rowff! I was quite the sheik in my youth. First in town to have a luminous hat band. . . . Had just started travelling for Apex Novelties. . . .

[YOUNG SAM appears in the distance. He's sharp; nervous, full of energy, carrying a suitcase. OLD SAM gestures toward him, then toward himself. YOUNG SAM is gone.]

I had a girlfriend then. Did I say that? We were engaged. Her name was Lila. . . . She worked in a club here in town. She was a hostess.

[LILA appears. The Nightclub. The same two entertainers as at the opening singing a song, exaggerated romantic gestures. YOUNG and OLD SAM are gone.]

SINGERS: *[Lip synching.]* Cross over the bridge, cross over the bridge

Change your reckless way of living, cross over the bridge

Leave your fickle past behind you, and true romance will find you

Sister—Cross over the bridge.

[JAKE, a tough-looking man, drinks at a table alone. Other customers. The MC steps into the spotlight.]

2

MC: Good evening to all you wonderful people here in the Club dez Morts. That's French for parlez-vous and how are you. You don't have to nudge her, sir. I think she got that one. Either you're all sleeping and I'm awake—or vice-versa. Hey—you be in my dreams, I'll be in yours. Love it. You know, these moments before the show where I get to be in close personal touch with all you wonderful people—hey, it's my life. What can I say? You're beautiful, each and every one of you, and it's beautiful that you're here with us tonight. No lie. Heart to heart. This story about My Uncle Sam is really something special. It can give you a lift—if you get me. Cure your warts. Heal cancer of the blood, save your marriage and ease your mind. When you go home tonight, tell it to your children. Whisper it in their ears while they sleep, like a brand new dream. . . .

WOMAN AT TABLE: Get off!

MC: Before we begin, I want to say hello to a very special someone—met her only last night down at the Trailways Terminal, and tonight, she's with us in the audience.

WOMAN: Get off!

MC: Hey—I want you to take this performance as my gift—personally—you know who you are.

WOMAN: GET THE HELL OFF.

MC: *[Retreating offstage.]* Heart to heart to heart to heart. . . .

    [The singing DUO *takes the stage, continuing their song as before.* LILA *crosses to* JAKE.*]*

DUO: If you've built a boat to take you to the
    greener side
    And if you've built that boat of every lie
    you've ever lied
    You'll never reach the promised land of
    love I guarantee
    For lies can not hold water and you'll
    sink into the sea.
    Cross over the bridge. . . .

    [Over the song, the WOMAN *at the table narrates:]*

WOMAN: A nightclub in Pittsburgh. A man and a woman

[*She gestures toward* LILA *and* JAKE.] at a corner table. He wears a loud sport jacket. She wears a black taffeta evening dress. He drinks beer. She sips a pink lady.

LILA: The least you could do, since we're *engaged,* you come to my place of employment, you could look like something.

JAKE: Whattaya want me to look like?

LILA: Something. You could wear a tie, at least. Where do you think you are? The turkish bath? This is a nightclub.

JAKE: Drink your pink lady, Lila.

LILA: I've never been so humiliated.

JAKE: I'm warning you, baby.

LILA: I do nothing but brag about you around here, Jake. I tell everyone you're gonna find my brother for me, and then we're gonna get married—and you come in looking like something they dragged outta the Monongahela river. When are you leaving?

JAKE: First thing in the morning.

LILA: You remember everything I told you?

JAKE: Yeah.

LILA: All the people?

JAKE: Yeah.

LILA: You know how to get to the light?

JAKE: Yeah.

LILA: Find him, Jake. He owes me. Daddy left us both that dough from the tunnel job. Fifty-fifty. Only I was a kid, so he tells my brother where he stashes it. Then Daddy is sitting in the Teepee Tavern drinking an Iron City, when his partner in the job shows up and asks a question. Where's the money? Daddy was reticent. His partner put an ice pick through his chest. Three days later my brother disappeared.

JAKE: Who was the partner?

LILA: You ever hear of the Bottler?

> *[A cop,* PLAINCLOTHES, *enters.]*

JAKE: Shut up!

LILA: What. . . .

JAKE: Shut up and reach under the table. I'm handing you a gun. Grab it.

LILA: Whatsa matter?

JAKE: Grab the heater, willya. A cop I know just walked in.

LILA: What am I gonna do with it?

JAKE: I don't care what you do with it. Sit on it.

LILA: OK, Jake. OK.

JAKE: Make some conversation. He spotted me.

LILA: They make pink ladies with gin. Gin and something red. . . .

NARRATOR: Meanwhile, on his way to visit Lila at the club, Sam stops in at the Chinese laundry to see if his shirts are ready.

> *[In another area,* YOUNG SAM *appears fumbling in his pocket in front of a wire cage, Chinese letters above.]*

Uh-oh! He lost his ticket.

CHINESE LAUNDRYMAN: No tickee, no washee.

> *[This scene fades as we return to the nightclub—]*

PLAINCLOTHES MAN: Hello Jake. Out for a good time?

JAKE: It just got ruined.

LILA: Well, if you gentlemen'll excuse me . . . *[*LILA *walks off, concealing the gun. . . .]*

PLAINCLOTHES MAN: Cute kid.

JAKE: Yeah. Class.

PLAINCLOTHES MAN: Stand up Jake. I said, stand up. Let's see what you got on you. *[He frisks him.]*

JAKE: I'm clean.

PLAINCLOTHES MAN: Jake, I come in here now and then, and I don't want my digestion getting upset by seeing your face.

JAKE: I'm leaving town in the morning.

PLAINCLOTHES MAN: Not soon enough. Get outta here— *now.* Move.

    [As JAKE exits he passes LILA.]

LILA: *[To JAKE.]* See ya, big boy. Get your man, get his money, and get out.

JAKE: So long, Lila. Keep it warm for me, hah. *[To COP, pointing at LILA.]* Like I said, class.

PLAINCLOTHES MAN: Yeah. One in a million. Move.

    [JAKE takes a step toward exit, freezes.]

NARRATOR 1: Jake's going off to find Lila's brother. *[JAKE exits.]* If he finds him, and gets the money, Lila says she'll marry Jake. I think Lila tells the same story to all the boys. . . . *[YOUNG SAM enters.]*

YOUNG SAM: Lila!

    [They embrace, move to the same table LILA sat at with JAKE.]

NARRATOR 1: In a few moments, Lila and Sam are deep in conversation. . . .

LILA: In Port Desire, a gentleman with a bright light—

YOUNG SAM: A bright light.

NARRATOR 2: *[To audience.]* In Port Desire, a gentleman with a bright light—

LILA: A gentleman who is a teacher—

YOUNG SAM: A teacher—

NARRATOR 2: A gentleman who is a teacher.

NARRATOR 1: Now Lila's telling Sam she'll marry *him* if he finds her brother.

LILA: I'll marry you if you find my brother.

NARRATOR 1: She's listing some people who might have some information about his whereabouts. . . .

LILA: A gentleman with a big book—

YOUNG SAM: A big book—

NARRATOR 2: A gentleman with a big book.

LILA: A lady in a golden vest—

YOUNG SAM: A golden vest—

NARRATOR 2: A lady in a golden vest.

LILA: A man with eight flags—

YOUNG SAM: Eight flags—

NARRATOR 2: A man with eight flags.

LILA: A lady in a violet gown—

YOUNG SAM: Violet gown—

NARRATOR 2: A lady in a violet gown.

LILA: A gentleman who is a gardener—

YOUNG SAM: A gardener—

NARRATOR 2: A gentleman who is a gardener.

> [*An* OLDER WOMAN *who has been seated with a young* GIGOLO *rises and slaps her companion.*]

OLDER WOMAN: Why do I do this to myself? [*To* LILA *and* YOUNG SAM.] Love is for fools.

NARRATOR: Love is for. . . .

OLDER WOMAN: On the other hand. . . .

> [*The* OLDER WOMAN *spots the* PLAINCLOTHES *cop. He beckons. They exit together. The* GIGOLO *pouts.*]

YOUNG SAM: I need a photo of your brother, so I'll know him.

LILA: No photos. If there were they'd be out of date. He's been missing for ten years.

YOUNG SAM: How do I recognize him?

LILA: By his habits. Smokes Luckies.

NARRATOR: Smokes Luckies.

LILA: Chews Doublemint gum.

NARRATOR: Doublemint gum.

LILA: He has very light eyes.

NARRATOR: Light eyes.

LILA: He needs his medicine.

NARRATOR: Needs his medicine.

GIGOLO: Needs his medicine.

CLUB SINGER: Needs his medicine.

LILA: Got it?

YOUNG SAM: Got it.

LILA: Find him, Sam. My brother robbed me of the family inheritance. I could have opened a beauty salon in Market Square, instead of working in this dump.

YOUNG SAM: When I find him, how do I get the money?

LILA: Ask him for it.

YOUNG SAM: What if he won't give it to me?

LILA: Take it.

YOUNG SAM: Right. Take it.

LILA: Right.

YOUNG SAM: Lila, I love you.

LILA: I know.

YOUNG SAM: When I come back, we'll . . .

LILA: Two more people. And the most important. My brother's wife, Darlene. When he disappeared, she went with him. Darlene was a dancer at the Go-Go-Rama Lounge here in Pittsburgh.

> [DARLENE *appears. Loud Go-Go music for 10 seconds, as she dances. It cuts off suddenly. She freezes.*]

> She was also a sensitive and intelligent person.

She read the poetry of Emily Dickinson between sets.

DARLENE: "I'm nobody. Who are you?"

LILA: Twenty minutes on, twenty minutes off. My brother owned the place. Darlene thought he was a quote.

DARLENE: Nice guy.

LILA: Unquote. One night Darlene arrived for work to find that the Go-Go-Rama had burnt to the ground.

LILA'S BROTHER: *[On mike, unseen.]* Must have been a dissatisfied customer.

LILA: Said my brother. Darlene was not amused. She was out of a job, and the sunglasses she'd left in her dressing room had melted in the blaze.

DARLENE: "Hope is the thing with feathers."

LILA: Said Darlene.

BROTHER: *[On mike, unseen.]* Yeah.

LILA: Said my brother.

BROTHER: *[On mike, unseen.]* But I owe people.

DARLENE: We'll think of something.

LILA: Said Darlene.

BROTHER: *[On mike, unseen.]* Yeah.

LILA: Said my brother, and called a cab to take her home. At 6:30 A.M., as Darlene was dreaming of an Aztec City, the phone rang. My brother had been arrested for setting fire to his own club, for the insurance money.

BROTHER: *[On mike, unseen.]* They're holding me on Easter Island.

NARRATOR: Said my brother.

BROTHER: *[On mike, unseen.]* Visiting hours are two to four.

LILA: Darlene thought she'd cheer him up. He was expecting her. There was a circle in the glass. . . .

[*As* LILA *says the following,* DARLENE *alone mimes this prison visitor room conversation.*]

His mouth, her ear. Her mouth, his ear. His mouth, her ear. Her mouth, his ear. . . . He made bail. Darlene married my brother. Then they disappeared. [DARLENE *is gone. Handing* YOUNG SAM JAKE'S *gun.*] Take this. You might need it.

YOUNG SAM: What? I don't even know how to. . . .

LILA: Watch out for the *Bottler!*

ALL: THE BOTTLER!

YOUNG SAM: Who's the Bottler?

LILA: Remember. Get your man, get his money, and get out. When you come back, I'll be waiting for you. . . .

3

YOUNG SAM: To prepare myself for finding Lila's missing brother, I wrote for an instruction cassette from the Universal Detective Agency and College. Lesson One.

[*A group of actors—the "lesson cassette," surrounds* YOUNG SAM. *Various voices and effects are "on the cassette:" i.e., sounds of footsteps, machine guns, and the lesson itself. The lesson is performed by various voices, on mike.*]

CASSETTE: THE MISSING PERSON KNOWS WHERE HE HIMSELF IS. THE ONLY TROUBLE IS THAT YOUR CLIENT DOES NOT KNOW.

YOUNG SAM: Playback.

CASSETTE: *[Different voice.]* . . . DOES NOT KNOW. The missing person often seems as if he has had a chunk of his mind removed, like a slice out of a watermelon. *[A slice of watermelon appears. Women's voices, alternating:]* I.D. POINTS: scars, tattoos, hair, moustache.

YOUNG SAM: Stop. Start.

CASSETTE: Beard, limp, dragging walk. Brand of gum. Brand of smokes. Et cetera.

YOUNG SAM: Playback.

CASSETTE: Et cetera. D.O.R.—Discharged on own recognizance, D.O.B.—Date of birth. *[Man's voice:]* D.O.A.—Dead on arrival.

YOUNG SAM: Playback.

CASSETTE: Dead on arrival. *[Woman's voice:]* Don't drink on the job. Unless you've been specifically invited to join your client for meals, bring your own sandwiches and coffee. Keep your coat and tie on, unless someone invites you to remove them. Allow no one to examine your gun. Don't take it out of its holster unless you intend to shoot someone with it. Don't shoot someone unless you intend to kill him.

   [ALL:] No one vanishes without a trace.

   [MAN'S VOICE:] This trace may be small, hard to find, but it's there. The only people you may never be able to find are the very criminal, the very rich, or the very dead.

YOUNG SAM: Stop.

CASSETTE: *[WOMEN:]* That's all.

   [The "cassette" is gone. OLD SAM *appears in another area, his hotel room.]*

OLD SAM IN HOTEL: That stuff about her brother was the most interesting thing Lila ever said to me. Something deep in me was interested. He sounds like a guy who might be worth my time. . . .

YOUNG SAM: He's missing from the world—so he must be nutso, or he's got amnesia, or he's scared. So I figure he won't be too much trouble over Lila's dough. The trouble is finding him. But, I can work on the way . . . ain't my usual route, but what the hell. So, I pack a nice selection of novelties outta the Apex catalog . . . so it shouldn't be a total loss. . . .

[YOUNG SAM packs novelties as OLD SAM speaks. We see goozelum goggles (the kind of glasses where the eyeballs dangle on springs), X-ray specs, joy buzzer, etc.]

OLD SAM: So it shouldn't be a total loss. . . . I sell those things to amuse. People need something. I mean, if you work for a living, you are probably not thanking God every morning for giving you the gift of life. I mean the kids are spilling the Wheaties all over the table, and the old lady don't look so good. . . . I mean we don't live in magazines. I live here. Alone. I get up in the morning and drink God's coffee and here I am. Sherman Arms . . . and there you are with everything you got, and everything you don't got hanging around your neck, and then a Chinese fingertrap comes into your life . . . vampire teeth . . . a joy buzzer. Stupid little things. They work—cause of people's ideas. These gags break the rules in people's heads. If there weren't any rules, I'd be outta business.

[YOUNG SAM finishes packing, closes his case.]

YOUNG SAM: I guess I'm going. I must love her like crazy.

NARRATOR: At the travel agency, scene 12.

> *[The* TRAVEL AGENT *and his female* ASSISTANT. *She is holding a map of the world.]*

AGENT: Port Desire, you say?

YOUNG SAM: Yeah.

AGENT: *[Looking on world map.]* We can't send you there if we can't find the place. Be sensible. How about Australia?

ASSISTANT: HA HA HA.

YOUNG SAM: Look again, will ya. That's the *world.* It's gotta be there somewhere.

AGENT: Ah! There's the little bugger. Port Desire. Sorry. You can't get there from here.

ASSISTANT: HA HA HA.

AGENT: However, I can send you to Port Satisfaction, which is right in the Port Desire neighborhood, sailing today on the S.S. *Guernsey.*

ALL: Mooo! Moo!

YOUNG SAM: Sounds like a cattle boat.

AGENT: Certainly. Extra fare.

YOUNG SAM: Extra fare?

AGENT: Worth it, believe me. You travel with prize- winning cattle, and they put a bed in your stall.

ASSISTANT: HA HA HA.

YOUNG SAM: All right, dammit. How do I find the boat?

AGENT: Go down to Pier 52, and follow the flies.

ASSISTANT: HA HA HA.

AGENT: By the way, *[takes out large hypodermic.]* do you have your inoculations? Ten bucks. You're travelling with pure-blood cattle and the owners don't wanna take no chances. . . .

> *[*YOUNG SAM *leaves the agency, avoiding the* AGENT, *who*

pursues him with his hypo. The AGENT *is gone. Music, as* YOUNG SAM *moves down a line of dancing farewell well-wishers, with* LILA *at the end of the line. They give advice as they dance past him.]*

MUSIC: *[Song.]*

> The wheel of fortune, keeps spinning around.
> Will the arrow point my way?
> Will this be my day?
> The wheel of fortune, etc.

MAN: People want blood for ten cents.

DARLENE: I'm nobody. Who are you?

LAUNDRYMAN: No tickee, no washee.

> *[*LILA *kisses him.]*

LILA: Sam—be careful.

YOUNG SAM: Lila. . . . I. . . .

LILA: Get your man, get his money, and get out.

> *[Music, "The Wheel of Fortune," continuing. All wave.* YOUNG SAM *exits.]*

4

The LIGHTHOUSE KEEPER *and his* DOG, *inside their light-house, the* DOG *to be played by an actress. The light above them sweeps 360 degrees.*

NARRATOR: At the lighthouse, scene 27.

KEEPER: This is the Port Desire Lighthouse. I'm all alone here.

DOG: Bow wow.

KEEPER: With my faithful dog. We haven't seen a soul for five months and thirty days. Only a boat or two in the distance . . . cruise liners. *[A boat appears.]* I can spot them through this telescope, playing shuffle-board on deck. . . . Red in ten! Six month shift. Captain said he'd bring out something to cheer me up when he came to relieve me. Don't need it. My nerves are steady. *[Holds out hand.]* That'll show Captain. "Ignore the visions," he told me. I told him he had nothing to worry about. I've never felt better in my life. *[The boat is gone.]*

I've learned to love it here. . . . Out here we breathe the sea mist. *[He takes deep breaths, as does the "dog."]*

The sea mist is half air, half saltwater. It rises up off the waves. It's been breathed by pelicans, by tuna, by krakens. It purifies us of all evil thoughts, puts us in touch with something deeper, stronger. And we're safe here. Safe. These cylindrical walls are thirty feet thick. No storm ever born could shake these walls. Safer than in church.

DOG: Bow wow.

    [Storm begins. Thunder, rain.]

KEEPER: Uh oh. Wind is up. *[Peers through telescope.]* Must be thirty miles an hour. Black clouds on the horizon. The waves look higher than I've ever seen them before.

    [A voice from below. . . .]

YOUNG SAM: *[Shouting through storm.]* Hello! Hello!

KEEPER: What?

YOUNG SAM: Hello! There's a storm out here! Let me in! My life is in danger out here.

KEEPER: Who are you?

YOUNG SAM: My Uncle Sam. I got some things here you

might like! Novelties! Knick knacks! Funmakers! Open the damn door!

>[KEEPER *lets* YOUNG SAM *in.*]

DOG: Bow wow.

YOUNG SAM: Yeah. . . . Uh, thank you. You the lighthouse keeper?

KEEPER: Now about those things. . . .

YOUNG SAM: I got party favors? Tricks? Puzzles? Household helpers? No, hah. You say you want more for your money? You say that what you've heard so far just ain't enough. Tell you what I'm gonna do. This—*[he shows it.]*—is the luminous crucifix. A recent advance in chemical technology has transformed the home crucifix—from a piece of bric-a-brac—to this living symbol of Christ's agony.

> The time for prayer is the nighttime, when the cares of the day are ended. The difficulty *has* been that it's impossible, at night, to *see* the *ordinary* crucifix. In the darkest room, this cross of perpetual light gives a wonderful warming glow, representing the luminous body of Jesus. What a comfort to the children on a stormy night. And this luminosity is not only lasting. It is permanent.

DOG: Bow wow.

YOUNG SAM: Next time you see me, you're gonna thank me. How many can I put you down for?

KEEPER: One.

YOUNG SAM: Just the one?

KEEPER: *[With a look at his* DOG.*]* Two.

>[*Thunder. The storm builds.*]

YOUNG SAM: By the way, I'm looking for a friend of mine . . . he used to work here, I think. Lila's brother.

KEEPER: Lila's brother? I remember him. Someone named Jake was here asking questions about him. He said he'd hurt me if I didn't tell. He didn't have to do that, did he?

YOUNG SAM: Did you tell him?

KEEPER: Breathe! Breathe the sea mist! Ah . . . that's better. You know, Lila's brother was the best man who ever ran the light.

YOUNG SAM: Where did he go from here?

KEEPER: He wasn't afraid of the tower, the rocks, the evil music of the gulls.

YOUNG SAM: Where is he now?

KEEPER: Got any gum?

YOUNG SAM: Gum?

KEEPER: Doublemint. It's my favorite.

NARRATOR: The missing man has a chunk of his mind removed, like a slice out of a watermelon.

　　　[The watermelon appears.]

KEEPER: Got any gum?

YOUNG SAM: Gum?

KEEPER: Doublemint. It's my favorite.

YOUNG SAM: I've only got exploding gum. By the way, do you have a sister?

KEEPER: I'm an only child. Can't you tell?

　　　[The watermelon is gone.]

YOUNG SAM: Then just tell me, where did Lila's brother go?

KEEPER: I like you. You should stay here. I'll teach you everything. . . . how to work the light, how to breathe in the salty mist. You'll be safe, like we are. I'll teach you the language of the gulls, caught between heaven and earth.

DOG: Bow wow.

> *[In the distance, a boat appears.]*

PASSENGERS: FUN! FUN! FUN! FUN!. . . .

YOUNG SAM: *[Aside.]* This guy's a jerk.

BOAT CAPTAIN: Meanwhile, on the approaching boat, bringing the lighthouse relief crew, a fabulous party is in progress.

PASSENGERS: FUN! FUN! FUN! FUN! FUN! FUN! FUN! FUN!

> *[The PASSENGERS, including the CAPTAIN, pile into the lighthouse, begin to crawl lasciviously around and over the DOG, LIGHTHOUSE KEEPER, and YOUNG SAM. YOUNG SAM backs away. Thunder.]*

KEEPER: The sea mist! The walls!

YOUNG SAM:. *[Shouting.]* Where did he go? Lila's brother?

ALL: FUN! FUN! FUN!

KEEPER: To the University! Professor Finley!

YOUNG SAM: The University. Professor Finley. Thanks a lot. Sea mist, my ass.

DOG: Bow wow.

> *[YOUNG SAM backs away from the orgy in progress as all lights fade but the lighthouse light, cries of passion mix with thunder as the storm builds. A last glimpse of the lighthouse, as it begins to topple, party and all, into the sea.]*

5

> *A LITTLE PERSON by the side of the road, wearing a dirty yellow vest. Nearby, a device for showing magic lantern slides, essentially a box with a peephole, with a*

Ray Xifo and Kristine Nielsen in *My Uncle Sam*
Martha Swope Associates/Susan Cook

place to insert a large glass slide. From below the box
hangs a sign: See the World. 10 cents.

LITTLE PERSON: *[Singing.]* The wheel of fortune, keeps
    spinning around. . . . *[Holds up, points to a slide.]*
    Peasants on the Yangtzee. *[The PERSON inserts it, sits.*
    JAKE *enters.]*

JAKE: This the road to the university?

LITTLE PERSON: May be. See the world?

JAKE: I'm seeing enough of it already.

LITTLE PERSON: Got a butt? Got any food? Got any
    money?

JAKE: Get out of my way, pops.

LITTLE PERSON: Why you going to college? Ain't you edu-
    cated yet?

JAKE: None of your damn business. *[JAKE shoves the LITTLE*
    PERSON *aside, exits.]*

NARRATOR: A GARDEN INTERLUDE! With Mr. Capa-
    bility Brown. *[CAPABILITY BROWN enters. 18th century*
    costume.]

CAPABILITY BROWN: I perceive that these grounds have
    never been touched by the finger of taste. Allow me
    to wave over them the wand of enchantment. These
    rocks shall be blown up, these trees cut down, and
    the wilderness with all its goats and monkeys will
    vanish like mist. A garden shall rise upon its ruins.

NARRATOR: Mr. Capability Brown was a master of space.

CAPABILITY BROWN: I am a master of space.

NARRATOR: What's missing for most gardeners to make
    them feel like artists, is a sufficiently hare-brained
    plan.

CAPABILITY BROWN: A true garden provides settings for

sensation, reflection, and repose. It must contain summer hermitages, winter hermitages, terminaries, bowling greens, Chinese pavilions, natural grottos, cascades, mosques, huts, pagodas, rustic seats and Druidical temples, many of which may be executed with flints, irregular stones, rude branches, or the roots of trees. An Eden to live in.

I intend to create this Elysium in this very countryside, and to. . . .

NARRATOR: END OF GARDEN INTERLUDE.

[CAPABILITY BROWN *is gone. The* LITTLE PERSON *is still on stage. In the distance,* OLD SAM *appears. He is looking into a Viewmaster.* YOUNG SAM *enters.*]

LITTLE PERSON: [*Singing to self.*] The wheel of fortune, is spinning around. . . .

YOUNG SAM: Excuse me, is this the way to the university?

LITTLE PERSON: Maybe. See the world?

YOUNG SAM: Thanks, but I'm doing O.K. on my own. . . .

LITTLE PERSON: Think so? You got a butt?

YOUNG SAM: Yeah . . . but it's my last one.

LITTLE PERSON: Can I have it?

YOUNG SAM: [*Hesitating.*] Sure. Here. Have a nice day. [*Handing a cigarette.*]

LITTLE PERSON: What happened to your face?

YOUNG SAM: Wha. . . . Nothing. I mean. . . .

LITTLE PERSON: Watch out for room 33.

YOUNG SAM: What?

LITTLE PERSON: You're a nice boy. Going to school?

YOUNG SAM: To the university.

LITTLE PERSON: When you're there, go dancing.

YOUNG SAM: Dancing?

LITTLE PERSON: Keep moving, give all of yourself away.

You're a nice boy. These days, people want blood for ten cents. Get it, too.

YOUNG SAM: Do they? What else you got to say?

LITTLE PERSON: Be careful. Watch out for the Bottler.

YOUNG SAM: Who?

LITTLE PERSON: THE BOTTLER.

YOUNG SAM: *[Aside.]* I've heard that before. *[To* LITTLE PERSON.*]* Any other words of wisdom?

LITTLE PERSON: Yeah. Don't let your mouth write no check that your tail can't cash.

> *[The* LITTLE PERSON *returns the cigarette* YOUNG SAM *gave. He takes it.]*

YOUNG SAM: Thanks, I guess.

> *[Blackout.]*

6

The BOTTLER, MISS SIMMONS, *dressed in violet,* MR. FLEA-GLE, *and the body of* JAKE.

NARRATOR 1: There were four people in a room at the Ramada Inn. Room 33. One of them had been shot several times in the chest. The people who shot him were not exactly green peas at their business. He lay across an orange bedspread and blood bubbled in his throat. He was about to die.

MR. FLEAGLE: Fucker's taking his time about it.

NARRATOR 1: The dying man, except for the blood that soaked his shirt front, was just another tough guy with a bald spot—although he had more stamina than most guys with bald spots. He was dying hard.

JAKE: Uggghhhh. Uggghhhh.

MISS SIMMONS: He's going. Maybe, Fleagle, you went too
  far.

BOTTLER: Ask him again.

  *[*MISS SIMMONS *slaps the dying man hard across the
  face.]*

MISS SIMMONS: *[To* JAKE.*]* Talk to me, darling. I love you.
  Any man in pain is so attractive. . . . It's hopeless.

NARRATOR 2 *[*THE AUTHOR*]*: The group in this room
  would stand out in a crowd of ordinary humans like
  whores in church. Miss Simmons had gone out to
  the far east in her youth, as a governess, but once in
  Hong Kong, she soon found other occupations. She
  was even a singer once, at a place outside of
  Pittsburgh called the Neptune Inn.

MISS SIMMONS: *[Singing.]* Whose honey are youuuuu. . . .

NARRATOR 3: A lady in a violet gown. . . .

NARRATOR 2 *[*THE AUTHOR*]*: Mr. Fleagle had been a clerk
  in a banking firm in Allentown, Pennsylvania. His
  very ingenious system of embezzlement obtained
  his discharge. The bank president was found some
  days later, the victim of a hideous freak accident
  involving a toaster and a high voltage line.

  *[*FLEAGLE *hisses at the* NARRATOR.*]* This is the
  Bottler. No one knows anything for certain about
  the Bottler. Perhaps he used to be a business partner
  of Lila's father. The Bottler does seem to feel that
  something belonging to him has gone astray, and
  that Lila's brother has it, and could be persuaded to
  return it—if he could only find him.

  *[*AUTHOR *exits.]*

FLEAGLE: Finish him. He won't remember anything else.

MISS SIMMONS: Yeah. Let's get out of here. This room gives me the creeps. . . .

FLEAGLE: Let's get on the other guy she sent out. I'm itching for it. I want that do-re-mi in my pocket as I percolate down the boulevard, with my entire residue behind me.

MISS SIMMONS: Fleagle, you are nowhere, you will be nowhere, and you can't be anywhere, as you are nowhere in front.

FLEAGLE: Shut up, you stupid bitch.

BOTTLER: Quiet. *[Looking at* JAKE.*]* Jake, memory is like an old music box. It lies silent for years, and then a mere nothing, a tremor will start the dusty spring, and the melody plays once more. Remember, Jake. What else did she tell you? Some memories are stirred by the sight of a faded flower, a hotel bill—a sudden stab of pain . . . the sound of a voice, a bar of music, a flavor on the tongue. . . . It seems he's dead.

FLEAGLE: I didn't know the gun was loaded.

BOTTLER: He had nothing more to tell us. Just another one of Lila's fiancés . . . though this one got further than most. . . . "The University." . . . That's all he remembered from the bitch's instructions. . . . Hmmm.

MISS SIMMONS: I'm nervous. Let's get out of here.

> *[Lights out, and up on* YOUNG SAM *approaching a hotel desk.]*

YOUNG SAM: I'm beat. Better check in and get some sleep.

CLERK: Yes.

YOUNG SAM: I'd like a. . . .

CLERK: *[Handing key.]* Room 33. Pleasant dreams.

> *[*CLERK *is gone.* YOUNG SAM *enters room 33. It's empty.]*

YOUNG SAM: Room 33. Uh oh. Looks normal enough. *[Takes out* JAKE'S *gun.]* Better be on the safe side. Hey, maybe the man I'm looking for lay here. . . . Lila's brother—the missing man. Was he awake all night . . . frightened? Or sleeping? Dreaming? Is he dreaming me following him? I'm a spectre in his sleep. . . . Is he angry? Is he laughing? Or crying? Has he lost his way?

*[*JAKE'S *body falls out of the closet with a crash. . . .]*
I've seen him somewhere before.

[The phone rings.] Hello. My Uncle Sam here, novelties, notions. . . . Lila!

[Lights up on LILA *in another area, with phone.]*
It's you! . . . O.K. . . . Right. . . . Right. . . . Uh, this guy Jake is here. Yeah, I've seen him in the club. He's dead. What do you think he's doing here? . . . Me neither. . . . O.K. Lila—I love you.

*[*LILA *hangs up phone. Lights dim on* YOUNG SAM *in room.]*

LILA: I know. Cry and you'll get a red nose, Lila my darling. Jake's dead. And Sam. . . . *[*LILA *energetically dresses to go out at a mirror.]* Not bad, Lila my darling. Only one left now, and he needs all the help he can find. Just get yourself together, go out into the world and make yourself as welcome as a snowflake in hell.

TRAVEL AGENT: *[With map of world.]* Where to, Miss?
Blackout. Lights up on. . . .

7.

COLLEGE CHEERLEADERS: *[Cheer.]* Be aggressive, Be Aggressive! B, E, A, G, G! R, E, S, S, I, V, E!

NARRATOR: AT THE UNIVERSITY, scene 14.

YOUNG SAM: Before I get there. . . .

ANOTHER NARRATOR: Stella! *[As* STELLA *enters.]* Her furnished room wasn't very far from the university. Now she stands gazing out over the college town, smiling a triumphant smile.

STELLA: Fundamentals of Botany. That's one course I won't have to worry about anymore.

NARRATOR: Stella opens the closet, unhooks a slinky black cocktail dress from the rack. . . .

STELLA: It's time to roll out the big guns.

MITZI: *[Coming in.]* Stella! Say, where are *you* going?

NARRATOR: It was Mitzi, Stella's roommate.

STELLA: Got a heavy date tonight, Mitzi.

MITZI: It isn't a blind date, I hope. I wouldn't fool around with any blind dates these days.

STELLA: Oh cut it out, Mitzi. So three girls disappear from campus. Is that any reason to start ugly rumors about murderers and maniacs?

MITZI: I didn't *start* the rumors, Stella. Who's the guy?

STELLA: Professor Finley.

MITZI: Finley? The botany teacher? Are you out of your mind? He's an old creep.

STELLA: He may be an old creep, Mitz, but if I don't pass Botany, I don't graduate, and what I know about botany wouldn't fill a thimble.

MITZI: I get it. . . .

STELLA: Not a word. I promised him I wouldn't tell a soul.

MITZI: Don't worry, honey, your secret romance is safe with me.

>   [MITZI *exits.*]

STELLA: Poor Professor Finley. If only he knew what he's letting himself in for. . . .

>   [PROFESSOR FINLEY *enters, moving slowly toward* STELLA. *He caresses a plant.*]

NARRATOR: Stella had planned it all carefully, ever since that first week when they'd covered roots and stems, and she knew, with pistils and stamens still to come, she'd never be able to pass. She'd worn her sexiest outfits to class, sat in the front row, and finally he'd bitten. . . .

STELLA: You wanted to see me, Professor?

FINLEY: I read your paper on chlorophyll, Miss Sharp. Frankly, I'm worried about how much you've grasped from my lectures.

STELLA: I'm a little worried myself, Professor. Perhaps if you reviewed it for me, say some evening. . . .

FINLEY: That would be highly irregular, Miss Sharp. The faculty frowns on fraternization.

STELLA: Well, I wouldn't want to get you into any trouble.

FINLEY: Perhaps if no one knew . . . if it was our little secret. I mean I'd like to help you Miss Sharp. You're a very nice . . . girl.

NARRATOR: He'd taken the bait. Hook, line, and sinker.

FINLEY: Shall we say, tonight. At eight. At my house.

STELLA: Oh Professor! This is so sweet of you. I could kiss you. . . .

[FINLEY *exits.*]

NARRATOR: Professor Finley's house was one of those old piles that had been fashionable a century ago. Stella walks through the dark garden, up the steps, lifts the huge door knocker, and the hollow sound echoes down long corridors, dies away in dark corners within. The door creaks open.

FINLEY: Why, Miss Sharp. You're all dressed up.

STELLA: Just a little something I picked up for cocktails. Like it?

FINLEY: It's a very nice gown, Miss Sharp. Come in.

STELLA: Call me Stella, Professor.

FINLEY: Would you care for a drink—Stella?

STELLA: Why, thanks.

NARRATOR: The wine was sweet, syrupy, with a heavy aroma. The corridor was dark, as Stella followed Professor Finley down . . . down . . . toward a wooden door covered with odd carvings. The nagging thought that she was alone with this strange old man. . . . Those three girls who disappeared so recently? . . . Had they been students in Finley's Botany class? She couldn't remember. . . . That wine he'd given her must have gone to her head. Finley opened the door, and as they stepped inside, Stella could hear the click of the lock behind her. At one end of the room the floor was covered with earth. Growing in the earth—twisted green things with bulbous crimson tops pulsating open and shut like lecherous mouths. . . .

STELLA: Oooooooooh!

FINLEY: Yes, Stella! Flesh-eating plants are my forte. These are native to the Amazon. These plants Stella,

they need life! They need blood and flesh, Stella. . . .
[As he picks her up to throw her into plants.] Their
digestion is a fascinating process, I assure you. . . .

STELLA: NO!!! AHHHHHHH!

YOUNG SAM: *[Entering.]* Excuse me? Professor Finley?

FINLEY: Yes?

YOUNG SAM: I'm My Uncle Sam.

FINLEY: This is Stella. *[Putting her down to shake SAM'S hand.]* May I ask what you're doing here?

YOUNG SAM: Uh . . . I've got a few novelty items here—
[Opening suitcase.] I thought you and the little lady
might find interesting to have around the home.
Start your own Ant Farm. Watch them work, wor-
ship and play! Goozelum Goggles!

FINLEY: Do you think a university professor would be
interested in Goozelum Goggles?

> *[Behind FINLEY'S back, STELLA exits.]*

YOUNG SAM: You're a big reader, I bet.

FINLEY: Of course I am.

YOUNG SAM: Tell you want I'm gonna do. Special price
for you and the missus on any of the selection of
exciting books I have to offer. Here's one called
Confessions of a Nun . . . this one's written in the kind
of plain language anyone can understand. I can see
you're a man of the world. Here's a copy of *From
Ballroom to Hell* by an ex-dance teacher . . . awful
dangers to young girls in the dancing academy.
How about *HIRAM BIRDSEED AT THE WORLD'S
FAIR* ?

> *[Aside to audience.]* This *Hiram Birdseed at the
World's Fair* is my biggest seller. These books are all
published by the same company in Philadelphia.

For men only. You know the kind—*Sam Savage in
the South Seas* . . . "the naked maidens surrounded
him . . ." and so on. It's like the same guy wrote
them all, though they got different names on 'em.
But Hiram Birdseed is different. It's like this writer
of all of them was hit by fantasy exhaustion one day
and he hadda stay in bed, so for one time he hired
another guy . . . a little guy with a dirty green cardi-
gan sweater and glasses, and he was given this title,
Hiram Birdseed at the World's Fair, and the idea: farm
boy gets involved in international sex in New York
City, and this little guy goes back to his furnished
room, and he writes. He stays up all night, his mind
at white heat, and as the dawn filters through the
venetian blinds he finishes the first half. He falls
into a fitful doze. The pages on the desk flutter in an
early morning breeze. . . .

In the first half of this book, Hiram Birdseed
does not even get to the World's Fair. He does not
even get to New York. In chapter one, he's on the
farm. He looks at a cow sleeping. In the second
chapter he eats breakfast. A page and a half details
how the gravy looks dripping over the biscuits. The
third chapter is called "Hiram Birdseed's Dream."
There's a glowing garden of unearthly trees in
which Chinamen in violet robes are tormenting this
porcupine with long golden sticks. By the time you
get to about page ninety eight, Hiram is at last on a
train to New York, and he's looking at the blonde
hairs on the back of the neck of a girl seated in front
of him. Then suddenly the style changes, like the
old hack rose up out of his sickbed in horror, and

took over. All at once, Little Egypt is shakin' it, and Hiram, the same Hiram who watched the cow sleep in chapter one, is watching the bouncing breasts. *[To* FINLEY.*]* My best seller.

FINLEY: You're a bright boy, but you don't actually *know* anything—do you? Why don't you enroll. Here at the university there's knowledge, sex, and the companionship of intelligent minds.

YOUNG SAM: I'll think it over. Got a cigarette?

FINLEY: Of course, Luckies are my brand. You don't mind?

NARRATOR: Smokes Luckies.

YOUNG SAM: Not at all. By the way, does the name Lila mean anything to you?

FINLEY: No.

YOUNG SAM: How about "Lila's brother"?

FINLEY: Brilliant boy. An ex-student of mine. "A" in my graduate botany seminar. Quite the inventive geneticist. Then he dropped out. Pity.

YOUNG SAM: Yeah. What a shame. Look. I'm trying to find him, and I need to know where. . . .

FINLEY: *[Looks at watch.]* You'll have to excuse me. It's time for my dance class.

DANCE TEACHER: Ready! Everybody in plac*e!*

   [All company, but YOUNG SAM, *prepare to dance. The* BOTTLER, MISS SIMMONS, *and* MR. FLEAGLE *together on an end of the dance class away from* SAM *and* PROFESSOR FINLEY. OLD SAM *and* LILA *on opposite sides, toward the rear.]*

YOUNG SAM: I'm not here for the class. I just. . . .

TEACHER: IN PLACE! CHIN UP! SHOULDERS BACK! GUT IN! Thank you—*[He gets in line with the whole*

class, next to PROFESSOR FINLEY. *Music: Cha cha cha.]*
ONE TWO CHA CHA CHA. THREE FOUR CHA
CHA CHA, TURN AND CHA CHA CHA. . . .

MAN IN CLASS: A gentleman with eight flags.

YOUNG SAM: *[Still dancing.]* What?

ANOTHER MAN IN CLASS: A gentleman with a big book.

YOUNG SAM: *[To* FINLEY.*]* What? Professor, where did he
go?

FINLEY: Who?

YOUNG SAM: Lila's brother!

FINLEY: Try Chinatown.

YOUNG SAM: Chinatown?

FINLEY: Yes. Needs his medicine—Follow my laundry
man.

TEACHER: ONE TWO CHA CHA CHA. . . .

> *[The* CHINESE LAUNDRYMAN *appears, a large bag of
> laundry on his shoulder. He exits.* YOUNG SAM *separates
> himself from the dancers, exits, following the laundry-
> man. He in turn is followed off by the* BOTTLER'S *trio. All
> other dancers leave except* LILA *and* OLD SAM. *He watches
> her. She exits.* OLD SAM *alone, cha-chas hesitantly, then
> more strongly as the music builds. Black out. Lights up
> as* YOUNG SAM *follows the laundryman. He punches a
> button on his cassette player.]*

CASSETTE: Universal Detective Agency. Missing Persons,
lesson 2. . . .

> *[During the following "play" of the cassette, per-
> formed by the Company on mike, as* YOUNG SAM *follows
> the laundryman to Chinatown, the* BOTTLER, MISS SIM-
> MONS, *and* MR. FLEAGLE *appear and follow him.]*

To locate the missing man, it is often necessary
to employ the basic techniques of *shadowing,* or, *tail-*

ing. There are two kinds of tail: the close tail, where your main concern is not to lose the subject, and the loose tail, where your main concern is not to be spotted. If your subject spots you, you've blown it. Avoid this. Look ordinary. Leave those flashy clothes at home. Disguises should be simple: a hat, or a pair of glasses. A subject who is suspicious, may use windows or mirrors to try to spot you. The investigator may even find *himself* followed by someone trying to find out why he's following someone else. Avoid this. If you think you're being followed, go into a theatre or restaurant and out another door. Above all—identify with the missing man. *[All followers freeze.]* What would you do if you were him? Where would *you* go? It's easy. After all, we're all missing. The only difference is for how long . . . a minute of daydreaming in an unfamiliar park or garden . . . a half hour in a strange bar and grill when no one knows where you are. You're gone. Before you know it, you're on a bus . . . a new city . . . a new name. Missing. Don't get confused by the meaning of it all. Do your job.

[All followers again begin to follow each other.] Do what you were sent for. That's all.

[The laundryman exits. YOUNG SAM follows. The BOTTLER, MISS SIMMONS, and MR. FLEAGLE follow him.]

8

An opium den, its denizens scattered about on low bunks, smoking set-ups next to them. One of them stares into a

Viewmaster. They smoke. An elderly Chinese center, the
owner, with a parrot on her shoulder.

DENIZEN 1: Do not think ill of me for frequenting this
place. Remember times when you too wanted to
disappear, to find a place where the world could
never reach you. That place is only in your mind,
when the smoky walls swing shut and you live
within. . . . I have been a visitor here for years. After
all, my dreams are harmless enough. . . .

NARRATOR: A bad poet.

DENIZEN 1: This room is a place of passage between the
worlds. . . .

DENIZEN 2: *[A woman singing.]* The wheel of fortune,
keeps spinning 'round. . . .

DENIZEN 3: . . . she was eaten by raccoons, or beavers or
something. . . .

　　　[The LAUNDRYMAN *enters, takes a pipe from the*
OWNER, *lies down.]*

NARRATOR: The owner of the place is a cultivated chink.
An opium peddler, yes, but also a philosopher.

OWNER: Ugliness and beauty are opposites. But when the
black smoke fills your head, one is as good as the
other. *[*YOUNG SAM *enters.]*

YOUNG SAM: This is an opium den!

DENIZEN 4: As Brother Brigham said when he crossed the
border into Utah. . . . Children, this is the place!

YOUNG SAM: Maybe some of the gang would be interested in purchasing a few entertaining. . . .

DENIZEN 4: They're only interested in their medicine.

YOUNG SAM: O.K., O.K. Then I'll get right to the point.
I'm looking for Lila's brother. . . .

DENIZEN 4: Quiet. Quiet, before someone slits your throat. He was here. He's gone, long ago. He ascended from this house devoted to ruin—up to the third heaven. . . .

YOUNG SAM: Where?

DENIZEN 3: Shh. . . . Eveyone here has already heard your stupid braying . . . in their dreams. Have a pipe . . . and wait.

OWNER: You seek the black smoke? . . .

> [She hands YOUNG SAM the pipe. YOUNG SAM lies on a bunk, waits. MISS SIMMONS enters. Approaches YOUNG SAM.]

NARRATOR: [OLD SAM from a bunk.] Then she appeared. . . . She flowed across the room like hot molasses. She sat down, crossed her legs slow, gentle, taking care not to bruise any of that smooth tender flesh. She had lips that would burn holes in asbestos. She smiled, but she didn't say anything Maybe she couldn't talk. Maybe she was an idiot. I didn't care.

YOUNG SAM: [To MISS SIMMONS.] Lady, whatever it is, it's eight to five I'll do it.

MISS SIMMONS: You're right, but I'd say even money.

YOUNG SAM: I'm My Uncle Sam. . . . You come here often?

OLD SAM: Miss Simmons was able to project a fatal combination . . . a capacity for unending self absorbed sensual pleasure, and a cute little fear of this capacity in herself that could let a man be a man. Deadly. For a moment, she drove Lila completely out of my head.

MISS SIMMONS: Shhh. Let's smoke a pipe. I love to suck the black smoke into my brain.

YOUNG SAM: I never tried this stuff . . . though I always suspected that the chinks in Yip Man's Chinese Laundry in Pittsburgh were using the stuff in the back room. . . .

CHINESE LAUNDRYMAN: *[In another area.]* Hey, Wong! Take the iron for awhile and let me have the pipe. . . .

OLD SAM: Other devotees of the black smoke optically fondled Miss Simmons as we puffed away. They mumbled in their stupor.

DENIZEN: . . . gentleman with eight flags. . . .

OTHER DENIZEN: . . . gentleman with a big book. . . .

OLD SAM: My head was getting heavy. . . .

    [YOUNG SAM slips down onto MISS SIMMONS'S lap. She slips his gun out of his pocket, signals. The BOTTLER and MR. FLEAGLE enter.]

ALL: THE BOTTLER!

BOTTLER: Thank you. *[He looks down at YOUNG SAM in his opium dream. MISS SIMMONS hands him YOUNG SAM's gun.]*

    So this is My Uncle Sam. Lila's last chance. He's having a delightful dream. If we wish to interview him, we must wake him up. I doubt all of us will disappear. Fleagle!

    [FLEAGLE slaps YOUNG SAM around until he wakes.]

FLEAGLE: Filthy hophead.

BOTTLER: Why do I do this, you ask me. Why?

YOUNG SAM: Who the hell are you? *[Silence.]* Are you Lila's brother?

    [Hysterical laughter.]

BOTTLER: Sorry. I'm the Bottler.

YOUNG SAM: The Bottler?

FLEAGLE: He's a bright boy.

MISS SIMMONS: Very.

BOTTLER: To continue. Why do I do this? Faster horses? Younger women? For love? For wisdom? No. I need that few million in green Lila's brother's got because—I have a dream. The Bottler's dream. To put it shit simple, I intend to create paradise on earth. I was left a little spit of land in Florida in my father's will. From this prenatal strip of sand will rise, like Venus out of the sea, CHEZ BOTTLER, the finest resort hotel and casino operation in the hemisphere. Think of it!

YOUNG SAM: I'm thinking of it.

BOTTLER: Every room will have a heart-shaped bathtub with jacuzzi, steam, carpeting three inches thick, wall and ceiling mirrors, a king-sized bed equipped with magic fingers, and a projection video unit wired in direct to my library of erotic classics, including *Quick Henry the Flit, Dr. Kremser, Vivisectionist,* and *Pom Pom Girls Go Crazy.* Each room will also be equipped with electronic brain stimulation devices produced simply out of ladies' hairdryers, by my own patented process. Chez Bottler will have ten restaurants, including the Undersea Lounge with a wall size fishtank with dugongs, manatees, and electric eels. Siamese service personnel, an eclectic stable of whores, steaks flown in from Kansas City. Amusements! High stakes baccarat tables, miniature golf, water polo, lindy-hopping, a zoo, with a petting area . . . black swans fly across a red sky, and the moon, a thin glorious crescent, rises over Chez Bottler! A warm wind caresses the very stones. In the penthouse suite sit I, the Bottler, a magnum of champagne in one hand, a woman's breast in the other, looking out the window toward the horizon, where the sea touches the sky. This is the world the Bottler built, God save him. He came from nothing, and before he goes back to nothing, he made everything. So three cheers for the Bottler, my pom pom girls!

Miss Simmons, of course, will be in charge of Chez Bottler's social agenda. Fleagle will discipline the staff.

FLEAGLE: I want to push laundry hampers down this carpeted hallway in a red outfit. I want to vacuum. . . .

MISS SIMMONS: I want to walk in the garden, and torment the porcupines with a long golden stick. . . .

BOTTLER: Shut up. Now, Uncle, tell us—where is Lila's brother?

YOUNG SAM: I don't know. I've been looking for him myself.

BOTTLER: What instructions did Lila give you? What clues? *[YOUNG SAM is silent.]* Mr. Fleagle, hit him. *[FLEAGLE does so, more than once.]*

Fleagle, restrain yourself. He needs to talk to me. The man has already dropped his hole card.

YOUNG SAM: Lila didn't tell me anything.

BOTTLER: You're lying. Lila tells all her fiances the clues.

YOUNG SAM: What?

BOTTLER: I know her. Take a look.

[BOTTLER shows YOUNG SAM a photo.]

YOUNG SAM: It's Lila! And she's naked! Where'd you get this?

BOTTLER: I have nude photos of everyone. Talk!

YOUNG SAM: Never!

BOTTLER: I'll find him. I've got a line on his soul, and that line is like a trail of blood in snow. He's dripping blood on the snow for me to follow. He's stolen my dream! When I find him, I will dig his greedy eyes out, and fill the hollow cells with two dim burning bulbs—then place his body by the graveyard gate, to light the coffins in. Fleagle—kill this fool, and catch up to us.

    [The BOTTLER *and* MISS SIMMONS *exit. Silence.* FLEAGLE *puts a gun to* YOUNG SAM'S *head.]*

FLEAGLE: We'll play American roulette. Put one bullet in, spin the chamber, hold it to the head, and pull the trigger six times. I'll take five seconds between trigger pulls, so you can contemplate the nature of time.

    *[*OLD SAM *rises, steps forward to watch. "Click." The* AUTHOR *appears, steps forward to watch. "Click." "Click." The* LITTLE PERSON *in the yellow vest rises up suddenly from bunk, and rushes toward* MR. FLEAGLE *from behind, a heavy opium pipe raised overhead to strike. All freeze.]*

DENIZEN 1: It is time for another dream, is it not?

    [He raises a pipe to his lips. Blackout.]

INTERMISSION

ACT II

9

Darkness. In the dark, voices.

YOUNG SAM: Hey, I'm sorry your opium den got wrecked, O.K. I didn't bring those people here. Look, they beat me up bad. I think my nose is bro—

CHINESE VOICE: How much money you have, my flend?

YOUNG SAM: Money? What about them? The Bottler. The rest of them?

CHINESE VOICE: They are gone. How much?

YOUNG SAM: Thirty bucks.

CHINESE VOICE: That will cover the parrot. How do you intend to pay for the rest of it?

YOUNG SAM: I'm gettin' out of. . . .

    [Sounds of blows, grunts, a beating going on. Sounds fade. . . . The AUTHOR *appears. He is holding an old-fashioned egg-candler. This is a tin can painted black and rigged up over a lightbulb. A hole to fit the end of an egg into is cut in the side of the can.]*

AUTHOR: My Uncle Sam taught me how to candle eggs. He had never said more than two or three words to me before that Saturday afternoon. He took my hand, and led me down the street to his brother's, my grandfather's, grocery store. Locked. Closed on Saturday. My Uncle Sam had a key. We went into the back room, full of old newspapers, and the smell of cheese. Cool in there. And stacks of eggs in cartons, ready to be sorted for the bins. Candling eggs.

You stick an egg in the hole, *[Demonstrating.]* turn
on the light, and you can see inside the shell. . . .
You look for cracks, or tiny blood spots on the yolk
inside. Those are grade B. The perfect ones are
grade A. So there we were, My Uncle Sam and me,
lighting up eggs in the dark. Once I got the hang of
it, Sam sat there on a pile of newspapers in his cashmere coat and watched me. He lit a cigar.

  [A cigar lights in the dark on stage.] I couldn't see
him in the dark, but I felt him watching me, careful,
like I shouldn't make a mistake, and at the same
time I had the feeling he was a million miles away.
. . . Now he's still telling his story to himself, and
I'm still telling it to myself, and we're both still
telling it to you. Someone's telling you a story. . . .

  [Lights up on OLD SAM. He's in his hotel room.]

OLD SAM: Out my window, there's Market Square below,
  and beyond it to the west, there's Shady Hill and the
  docks by the river, and then the low outline of the
  military barracks at Fort Pitt—National Guard. On
  some days I can hear the band in the distance, playing those same bad marches, all the young boys
  march forward and back, forward and back. Out
  past the barracks, open fields, and on to Florence,
  Slovan, west to Steubenville. Over to the east, there's
  that green dome of the observatory at the University
  of Pittsburgh, where those professors try to spy out
  the secrets in the stars, and on past the interstate,
  further east to New Alexandria, Wilkinsburg, and
  Turtle Creek. To the north, behind my back, the
  Monongahela, traffic on the Ninth Street bridge
  crossing over by the stadium, out beyond the Jones

and Laughlin stacks to Avalon, then up Route 57 to New Castle, through to Lake Erie, and across the border into Canada, where the reindeer roam. Market Square below, and to the south, the suburbs, breaking up into scattered patches of tract homes, blurring away to green and brown, further south past Uniontown and Wind Ridge, following the river, where it rushes into the Ohio, and on into the Mississippi, Mississippi to New Orleans, spreading out through the delta marshes into the blue Gulf of Mexico, with its shrimps and sharks, and sailing on over the Caribees, a gull, lost between heaven and earth, high over the Southern continent, over Cape Horn, and in the great distance it all goes white, cold white, and the great sea birds fly before me into that whiteness and are swallowed, white on white. . . .

I'm not feeling any better. The pain is everywhere, especially in my chest. It comes and goes. I can't sleep. The doctors tell me I can't drink. I don't like TV. So I talk.

[YOUNG SAM *appears, bleeding, dizzy, exhausted.*] They left me, behind some billboard. I could barely stand there and watch myself bleed. Missing Man, my ass. What about me? I look in my wallet to remember who I am. Driver's license.

OLD SAM & YOUNG SAM: "My Uncle Sam."

YOUNG SAM: Sounds right. Hey. . . . there's a photo of somebody's kid in here. It's my nephew's son. He's three, and he's got a sailor suit on—The moon's spinning around in little circles—

[YOUNG SAM *holds his arm. He's in pain.*] I'm hurt. I got to find a doctor.

OLD SAM *comes strolling, looking at the moon. A young boy appears, looking into a Viewmaster.*

OLD SAM: Nice moon.

YOUNG SAM: Yeah. Uh, Mister,where can I find a doctor?

OLD SAM: Don't you remember?

YOUNG SAM: Remember? I never been. . . .

OLD SAM: Head that way, little house right over the Mexican border. Say, long as I've got your attention here, I happen to have with me a small packet of itching powder. Only ten cents. Sprinkle a little down the ladies' backs at parties.

YOUNG SAM: I'm not going to any parties. Besides, I'm. . . .

OLD SAM: Breaks the ice. Starts the ball rolling. Mix and mingle.

YOUNG SAM: I'm mingling, all right.

OLD SAM: *[Whipping on gozzlelum goggles.]* How about a pair of goozelum goggles?

YOUNG SAM: *[Opening his case, shows own goggles.]* Look, I'm in the business. How would *you* like some rubber pretzels? Rubber doughnuts? Try a few on your unsuspecting guests and watch the fun! How many can I put you down for? Now get out of my way. I'm hurt . . . I need to cross the border, find that doc. . . .

*[*YOUNG SAM *exits. The* YOUNG BOY *is gone.]*

OLD SAM:Not feeling well, eh. You don't know the half of it. . . . *[To audience.]* Punchboard party games? Kissy-kissy? Funny fortune? Nickel a try! *[He coughs.]* Feels like weeds wrapped around my chest here. . . . I better lie down . . . my younger mind is stifling . . . like being in a cage full of monkeys, all chattering at once. *[He pulls out a rubber banana.]* These rubber bananas defy detection. EVEN WHEN YOU KNOW, THEY FOOL YOU.

> [OLD SAM *exits. The* MEXICAN DOCTOR *appears, along with some equipment.*]

NARRATOR 1: THE MEXICAN DOCTOR. Scene 57.

NARRATOR 2: Common sense suggests that excellent medical care is unlikely to be found in Mexican border towns. However, one never knows, do one?

> [YOUNG SAM *enters.*]

YOUNG SAM: The trouble here is that this is actually my life. I mean there is no difference between who I am and who I think I am and who I can make people think I am. This is just it, you know . . . bleeding into my boots. . . . Doctor!!

DOCTOR: [*Looking him over.*] You're not running from the law are you? Federales? I'm strictly legitimate.

YOUNG SAM: No. Just patch up this bleeding. . . .

DOCTOR: You can't be too careful with the law. Especially in Sonora. I had an associate who was arrested for pleasuring a pig. In this very state.

YOUNG SAM: What was the charge?

DOCTOR: Rape, of course. But he claimed he had the pig's consent. Complicated case. Still in the courts, I believe.

> [*The* DOCTOR *examines* YOUNG SAM.] Nasty, nasty. We can take care of you just fine.

> [*Lights fade on* YOUNG SAM *and the* DOCTOR, *as in another area, the* BOTTLER'S *trio enters, followed by a* NARRATOR.]

NARRATOR: Meanwhile, the Bottler is on the move, with Miss Simmons and Mr. Fleagle, and they stop by the roadside, and Miss Simmons says—

MISS SIMMONS: Uh oh. The Bottler's thinking.

NARRATOR: And the Bottler says—

BOTTLER: Why "Uh oh?"

MISS SIMMONS: Thinking's O.K.

NARRATOR: —says Miss Simmons.

MISS SIMMONS: But I'd rather do sex, play the piano, or kill someone than stand here and watch you think.

FLEAGLE: Yeah.

MISS SIMMONS: Watching you think is boring. . . .

 [A fortune teller appears, who is the same LITTLE PERSON *we've met before. This time, the* LITTLE PERSON *has a long speaking trumpet to talk to the fortunee, so that no one else can hear the inquirer's fate. The teller stands on a box, and a lantern hangs off a tree branch nearby.]*

LITTLE PERSON: The future revealed! Ten cents.

MISS SIMMONS: I want my fortune told. Fleagle, you got a dime?

FLEAGLE: Ask the Bottler.

MISS SIMMONS: You got a dime?

BOTTLER: *[To* FORTUNE TELLER.*]* We'll pay *after* the fortune.

LITTLE PERSON: *[To* BOTTLER.*]* What happened to your face?

BOTTLER: Skip the insults. Fortune first, or Mr. Fleagle will turn out your light.

LITTLE PERSON: O.K., already.

 [The PERSON *speaks into* MISS SIMMONS'S *ear with the trumpet.* FLEAGLE *and the* BOTTLER *attempt to overhear.* MISS SIMMONS *is shaken by whatever she's hearing. She wants to cry. The* BOTTLER *grabs the speaking trumpet and pulls it away from her ear.]*

BOTTLER: We got business. Let's get out of here.

LITTLE PERSON: Ten cents.

BOTTLER: Fish for it.

> [*They begin to exit, but the* FORTUNE TELLER *calls after the* BOTTLER.]

LITTLER PERSON: I'll tell your future for free. Your dream will come to nothing. Crows will tear your eyes out, and you'll go blind and silent into old age, alone and without the strength to kill yourself.

BOTTLER: You don't frighten me. Let's go.

> [*This scene fades, as we return to the* DOCTOR'S *office. As the* DOC *works on* YOUNG SAM, OLD SAM *appears behind them.*]

OLD SAM: Doctors are liars and thieves. The body screams for help, and they give it a shot and say goodnight. Last time the nurse is sitting at my bed, blonde, and she holds my hand and talks to me . . . and then someone says "Give him his shot. . . . Lots of others on the ward, honey. Give him a shot and say goodnight. . . ."

> [OLD SAM *is gone.*]

NARRATOR: [AUTHOR.] The doc has a pharmacist's degree from a correspondence school in Pittsburgh, Pennsylvania. But after his third conviction, no one would let him stand behind the counter. He could not find a wheel to turn. One night he sucked up a little juice and thought it over at a place called Ernesto's near Three Rivers stadium. The answer came to him. He moved to Mexico, right below the border.

DOCTOR: [*Finishing with* YOUNG SAM.] Good as new. You're healed. [*He reaches into a box, takes out an amulet on a chain.*] Want one?

NARRATOR: [AUTHOR.] The doctor is holding a little amulet, actually a rose-colored cameo of the doctor himself in profile, with the words "Believe in me" inscribed on the back in a florid hand.

   [The AUTHOR is gone.]

DOCTOR: It's free. Helps keep up the faith.

YOUNG SAM: No, thanks. But perhaps you'd be interested in a few choice. . . . Ah, the hell with it. You did a good job. How come you're down here?

DOCTOR: [Sings.] "South of the border, down Mexico way—that's where I fell in love, the stars above . . ." I prefer it.

YOUNG SAM: You hiding from someone? [The Doctor laughs.]

DOCTOR: That's what all my patients say . . . except one. Years ago. You remind me of him.

YOUNG SAM: Yeah. Who?

DOCTOR: Lila's brother. He was here for awhile, after I patched him up. Brilliant man. Quite the chemist. We distilled a few powerful psychic energizers from some interesting local flora. By prescription only, of course.

YOUNG SAM: When he left, did he say where he was going?

DOCTOR: No, but he did leave this *map.*

   [The DOCTOR *takes a map out of his pocket, hands it to* YOUNG SAM. *Lights fade, and up on* LILA, *in her travelling clothes.*]

LILA: Can't trust men to do damn all. Ten. Ten fiancés in the last three years. I sent all of them to find what's mine. None of them ever came back. I had a feeling about Sam, though. He was the dumbest—or maybe he just loved me the most, and I thought maybe he'd stumble through to the end, where all those other guys just. . . . I don't know what happened to them. Maybe they got lost. Maybe they met the Bottler. Maybe they failed, and were too ashamed to come back. Maybe once they got there, they forgot all about Lila. . . . Now *I'm* going wherever it is I sent everyone else.

Sometimes when I look in the mirror, my face frightens me. There's some need I don't understand right below the skin, that wants to tear through. Sometimes it feels like as long as I'm flesh and bone, I'll never rest.

That's not true. I'll end it, and then I'll rest—one way or another. [LILA *exits.*]

10

A NARRATOR *appears, holding a putter.*

NARRATOR: At the miniature golf course, scene 10.
[*The* NARRATOR *goes off as* YOUNG SAM *enters.*]
YOUNG SAM: Lila's brother marked out a route—and I'm following his faded pencil line. So this map is a tool to figure where I am in relation to something a helluva lot bigger than me. Kind of religious, don't you think?
[*In a wooden booth, the* MANAGER *of the golf course appears, reading a large book. He has a row of golf clubs and balls. Over the booth, a sign with a painting of the solar system and the words: Solar System Miniature Golf—Eight Holes Only.* YOUNG SAM *approaches.*]

MANAGER: Get outta my light.

YOUNG SAM: Uh, I'm quite the reader myself. Looks like an old book you got there.

MANAGER: Old? It's new as tomorrow. This is—"Secret Councils of a Certain Exile." Among other tidbits, it includes the architect's complete plans for the tower of Babel.

YOUNG SAM: That's very interesting. You know, I happen to have with me a number of books, including one you may have heard of—*Hiram Birdseed at the World's Fair. [Aside to audience.]* This *Hiram Birdseed at the World's Fair* is my biggest seller. These books are all published by the same company in Philadelphia. For men only, you know the kind. . . .

MANAGER: Not interested. I already have this excellent book.

YOUNG SAM: How do you know? You barely started it.

MANAGER: I wrote it. Are you playing? Or looking for Lila's brother?

YOUNG SAM: I. . . .

MANAGER: Why didn't you say so? He helped me build this place. Every hole a different planet. In fact, it was his idea to have only eight holes. "Leave out the earth," he says. "Too dull."

NARRATOR: A gentleman with eight flags.

MANAGER: I used to have another miniature golf course. Earth only. Had a first hole called Constantinople. The ball needed to go through the door of the palace of the Imam, then between the Bosphorous and the Hellespont. Second hole was a bridge at Florence, the ball rolled among carriages and men on horseback crossing over in both directions. Underneath, an aquatic expedition set out on the Arno. Third hole had a . . .

YOUNG SAM: About Lila's. . . .

MANAGER: I know exactly where he is. *[The* MANAGER *hands* YOUNG SAM *a club.]* Play a round.

YOUNG SAM: I don't play golf.

>   *[The* MANAGER *picks up another club, leaps out of his booth, and fences with* YOUNG SAM, *until* YOUNG SAM *is backed into a corner, the club poised over his head.]*

MANAGER: Golf? What has all this to do with golf? You want to *know*, don't you? Get on the course.

YOUNG SAM: O.K., O.K.

>   *[*YOUNG SAM *takes his club, heads for the course.]*

MANAGER: Start with Hole One, Mercury. The one that looks like a cracked landscape of ice.

YOUNG SAM: I thought Mercury was hot.

MANAGER: Not in my brain, it isn't. When you finish, I'll have a surprise for you.

>   *[The company, as other miniature golf customers, enter.]*

Ah, more truth seekers.

>   *[*YOUNG SAM *exits to begin play. The company golfs.* CAPABILITY BROWN *enters with a vine covered putter. As he speaks,* OLD SAM, *the* BOTTLER, MISS SIMMONS, *and* FLEAGLE, *(caddying),* LILA, *and the company members play different holes, each separately, not seeing each other.]*

NARRATOR: A GARDEN INTERLUDE, with Mr. Capability Brown.

CAPABILITY BROWN: THE RULES FOR THE CREATION OF ELYSIUM IN THE ENGLISH COUNTRYSIDE. A Paradise for all seasons.

NARRATOR: WINTER.

CAPABILITY BROWN: The evergreens: holly, ivy and the well attired woodbine. Juniper for gin.

NARRATOR: SPRING.

CAPABILITY BROWN: Violets, daffadillies, sweet briar, peonies and honeysuckle.

NARRATOR: SUMMER.

CAPABILITY BROWN: Columbine, apricocks, wild vine and laurel.

NARRATOR: FALL.

CAPABILITY BROWN: The apple, poppies, pumpkins, and all melons come to fruit. HAVE THE FOLLOWING: IN THE EARTH: Mounds, grottos, crypts. ON THE EARTH: groves, labyrinths, fountains. IN THE AIR: aviaries containing the ostrich, peacocks, swans, and cranes. Buzzy bees. A slew of automata among the rocks. Include my patented mechanism for the production of artificial echoes.

NARRATOR: Echoes.

CAPABILITY BROWN: Statuary as follows: Voluptia, goddess of pleasure; Sylvanus, god of the woods; and Agerona, goddess of silence. Areas should be set aside for a medical garden, a spiritual garden, and for garden burial. This garden should be so linked to nature that a man could stumble in without realizing he is in a garden at all. In fact. . . .

NARRATOR: End of Garden Interlude.

   [OLD SAM *enters with putter, playing as* CAPABILITY BROWN *moves on.*]

OLD SAM: [*Calling after* CAPABILITY BROWN.] Dollar a hole? [*To audience.*] I'm too old to waste time being clever. All this really happened, and nothing is changed to amuse you. This is not some story I've told myself so often that I believe it. It's true as death. Come the end, it's over and it don't play back. Unlike life, death doesn't happen in your mind. It's a cool clear note from outside, high and sharp enough to break the shell.

[*A* WOMAN *approaches* OLD SAM. *She's holding a '46 Pontiac carburetor, and a putter.*]

WOMAN: Last night, I was playing through, 3 a.m., they landed right there on the seventh. Neptune. Took me right inside the ship. This big one says "I, the advance scout of the invasion force, have proven we are invincible. Is it not better to live as our slaves, rather than be exterminated?" What could I say? Let them know back in Pittsburgh. They said we were living wrong here on earth. "Stop all that stupid shit," they said. They gave me this signalling device, if I ever want to contact THEM!

OLD SAM: That's a '46 Pontiac carburetor.

WOMAN: Is it now? [*As* OLD SAM *leaves, the* WOMAN *turns to audience.*] Let 'em know back in Pittsburgh!

[*She exits, and the* BOTTLER, MISS SIMMONS *and* MR. FLEAGLE *enter.* FLEAGLE *carries the* BOTTLER'S *putter. As they play. . . .*]

BOTTLER: It's 3 A.M. at Chez Bottler. Down a hallway carpeted in Astroturf. . . .

MISS SIMMONS: Shade?

BOTTLER: Crimson—a clown with an enormous pair of shears skips toward room 33. On the roof of Chez Bottler the anti-aircraft guns swivel slowly on their turrets, fingers of light probe the sky. . . .

[FLEAGLE *hands the* BOTTLER *the putter. The* BOTTLER
putts. All look.]

FLEAGLE: Nice shot!

BOTTLER: Wasn't it? We're close. I can feel it. Next stop . . .
next stop and we'll have him.

[*The* BOTTLER *and his crew exit.* YOUNG SAM *plays
the last hole, and the* MANAGER *comes out to greet him.*]

MANAGER: You played through.

YOUNG SAM: Yeah.

MANAGER: Did you . . . get it?

YOUNG SAM: Get what?

MANAGER: Never mind. Note my eyes.

YOUNG SAM: Very light colored. Almost white.

NARRATOR: Very light eyes.

MANAGER: They were always light, but now—exception-
ally. The powerful use of the brain makes the eyes
lighter. What color are yours?

YOUNG SAM: Brown.

MANAGER: Of cours*e. [He embraces* YOUNG SAM.] You
found me at last! I am Lila's brother! Got any gum?

YOUNG SAM: What kind do you want?

MANAGER: Doublemint.

YOUNG SAM: I've only got exploding gum. . . .

MANAGER: Well, tell me all about Lila. How'd you know
where to find me? What'd she tell you about the
money?

YOUNG SAM: Bullshit. You're not her brother. You're not
the missing man. You try to find someone, you get
to know him. . . .

MANAGER: If I'm not Lila's brother, how would I know
all these details? You saw the man with the light?
Didn't you? I smoke Luckies, don't I?

YOUNG SAM: Somebody told you that stuff. I'm leaving. Here's your golf club.

MANAGER: Damn right somebody told me. All Lila's other "fiancés" who've been coming this way for ten years.

YOUNG SAM: You're lying. You gotta be.

MANAGER: Deadheads and suckers. Nobody finds him, or that money. Leave, why don't you. I'm gonna play a round. *[Picks up putter.]* Don't think that if you find him, he'll have more to show you than this! Fore!

> *[The* MANAGER *is gone. The* LITTLE PERSON *in the dirty yellow vest appears. The* PERSON *is carrying a box with holes in the top.]*

LITTLE PERSON: Got a butt?

YOUNG SAM: It's you again. Who are you?

LITTLE PERSON: I'm nobody. Who are you?

YOUNG SAM: My Uncle Sam. Hey . . .

LITTLE PERSON: Just kidding . . . I'm in show business. Show's in here. *[Holds up box.]*

> Rats. I run a rat theatre. But the show's not in A-1 shape. Yesterday, we were doing a matinee of *Romeo and Juliet* when a dog broke into the show tent and ate the cast. These are only the understudies.

YOUNG SAM: You been following me.

LITTLE PERSON: Or vice-versa. I'll put my cards on the table. In fact, I'll put my cards on the floor. You got troubles ahead. Go to the church of St. Christopher. Watch out for Lila.

YOUNG SAM: Lila?

LITTLE PERSON: Then go to the Blowhole Theatre. Gotta run. There's the travel agent.

YOUNG SAM: Hey—wait. . . .

> [*The* TRAVEL AGENT *appears with his female* ASSISTANT *as the* LITTLE PERSON *runs off.*]

TRAVEL AGENT: Hey! How you been? Where to this time? You know, from the looks of you, you got quite a streak of bad luck going.

WOMAN: HA HA HA.

TRAVEL AGENT: Mister, you must have done something real bad in this life to get paid off that way. Or in some other life. You ever consider. . . .

YOUNG SAM: I wanna make some travel arrangements.

TRAVEL AGENT: So it's like that, is it? Passport?

YOUNG SAM: Uh . . . I didn't think I needed. . . .

TRAVEL AGENT: The little book, sir. The one that tells you who you are.

YOUNG SAM: I know who I am.

TRAVEL AGENT: Do you now?

WOMAN: HA HA HA.

TRAVEL AGENT: Purpose of travel? Business? Or pleasure? *[*YOUNG SAM *takes out some money, holds it up. The* AGENT *takes it.]* Where did you say, sir?

YOUNG SAM: The Church of St. Christopher.

TRAVEL AGENT: Wonderful choice, sir. My most popular destination this year.

YOUNG SAM: Where *is* this church exactly?

TRAVEL AGENT: In the city of Pittsburgh, state of Pennsylvania, land of enchantment.

YOUNG SAM: You're kidding.

TRAVEL AGENT: Sir, you'll love it. Pittsburgh is noted for its wonderful humidity. On the average night, you can take an easy chair out on the tarantula, and relax in the cool breeze.

WOMAN: HA HA HA.

TRAVEL AGENT: Majestic mountains, sparkling rivers, breathtaking buildings, gorgeous gardens. The scenery's nice too.

WOMAN: HA HA HA.

YOUNG SAM: I can't believe this.

TRAVEL AGENT: Your tickets.

YOUNG SAM: Thanks.

TRAVEL AGENT: You'll love the boat ride. Ocean all the way.

WOMAN: HA HA HA.

YOUNG SAM: There's no water between. . . .

TRAVEL AGENT: And remember our motto: Everywhere you go, there you are!

    [The TRAVEL AGENT *is gone.]*

NARRATOR: While in transit, My Uncle Sam studies his final lessons from the Universal Detective Agency.

YOUNG SAM: Here goes.

    [The following "cassette," as usual, is performed by the company on mike around YOUNG SAM.*]*

CASSETTE: GETTING YOUR MAN: Be sure you've got the right party. Remember: people *can* change, and not just their height, weight, sex, and facial structure . . . even the nature of the twinkle in their eye. The cub detective can easily drop into the chief pitfall in the search for Missing Persons. Philosophy. If you find yourself beginning to search for its own sake, or thinking of your search as a quest of some sacred kind, or feeling that the search itself is the goal and whether you find the missing man or not is simply a question of plot: THESE ARE DANGER SIGNS. STOP! Remember the client! And most vital of all—if you find yourself not calling in to the office, not seeing your friends, getting a divorce, telling your girlfriend you won't be seeing her for awhile. . . if you have a strange attraction for anonymous hotels on side streets, faceless coffee shops. If you lose the ability to tell one city from another. If you see a sign that says "transients only" and you say "home sweet home" . . . *you yourself are becoming missing* . . . and the Universal Detective Agency will have to send a student out to find you. That's a joke—but being missing is not funny.

[Raucous laughter.]

11

The Church of St. Christopher. Appropriate music and prayers. In semidarkness, penitents who could be the BOTTLER, MISS SIMMONS, *and* FLEAGLE.

NARRATOR: At last My Uncle Sam arrives to pay a pious visit to the Church of St. Christopher—and to ask a few questions. He arrives at the sanctuary—late.

PENITENTS: Mea culpa, mea culpa, mea culpa. In nomine Patri, Filii, et Spiritu Sanctu. . . . *[repeats]*

[A SACRISTAN *approaches* YOUNG SAM.*]*

SACRISTAN: I'm sorry to tell you that the Holy Crows have already gone piously to roost. These are not the original Holy Crows, of course, but their descendents . . . the grandchildren of the very Holy Crows that tore out the eyes of the murderers of Saint

Christopher. However, I could officially arouse them for a small fee. Ten cents.

NARRATOR: Sam was broke, and besides. . . .

YOUNG SAM: I'm not interested in any crows. I'm looking for a guy called Lila's brother. Do you know anything about. . . .

SACRISTAN: I believe you will find what the Holy Crows have to say on the subject to be not devoid of interest.

YOUNG SAM: The crows?

SACRISTAN: Ten cents.

NARRATOR: Sam was broke. He hadda unload something on this holy father.

YOUNG SAM: Uh . . . father, I got here a French ring, with a view. The ring is genuine imitation platinum, and set in the top here is your choice of picture. Bathing Beauties! . . . Uh . . . Views of the Panama Canal? How about a luminous crucifix?

[He shows it. The SACRISTAN *stares at it.]*

SACRISTAN: You are out of your mind. The insane are God's special children. For you, I'll wake the crows for nothing. Follow me.

NARRATOR: The sacristan led My Uncle Sam toward the far end of the cloister, where there sat two curious birds.

[The HOLY CROWS *are revealed on their perch. They are two gigantic black crows, with bright yellow beaks.]*

SACRISTAN: These birds, by the holy mathematics of the silver wires and instruments winded among their entrails, and on into their small throats, freely whistle their natural field notes.

[The birds are silent. The SACRISTAN *pokes them with a stick.]*

CROWS: Caw! Caw! Caw!

SACRISTAN: They are able to move with natural grace in all their parts. But so closely beneath the feathers are all these instruments obscured, that the pious renounce conjectures of art, and say it is done by God's grace. The cause of many conversions. Pressure on this stone in the floor sets them in motion.

YOUNG SAM: They're fakes.

SACRISTAN: Of course. I built them myself, with God's guidance.

YOUNG SAM: But they couldn't fool anyone. Too big. Everyone knows. . . .

SACRISTAN: All the holy secrets are what everyone knows. Obvious. God is love, yes? All flesh is grass. The wages of sin is death.

NARRATOR: In the back pew, three worshippers. Their expressions were pure and holy—almost tragic. In fact, the trio were overdoing it a bit even for the Church of St. Christopher. They looked like they were discussing the medical expenses of a dying patient.

*[*YOUNG SAM *spots the* BOTTLER, MISS SIMMONS, *and* FLEAGLE. *They spot him, rush toward him.]*

YOUNG SAM: I think I'm in some trouble here, father.

SACRISTAN: What trouble, my son? Does God not exist? Are we not men?

FLEAGLE: *[Screaming.]* You were warned!

[The SACRISTAN, *behind* YOUNG SAM'S *back, slips away.]*

BOTTLER: What, may I ask, are you doing here?

Rocco Sisto, Olek Krupa, Margaret Whitton, and
R. Hamilton Wright in *My Uncle Sam*
Martha Swope Associates/Susan Cook

YOUNG SAM: I'm uh . . . security man for the church . . . guarding the crows. Ask the Sacristan.

MISS SIMMONS: What Sacristan? There's no one here but us.

FLEAGLE: We warned you to change your act, or go back to the woods.

BOTTLER: That money's mine. I'm meeting the missing man first, and only. But you'll go further than anyone who's just disappeared. Much further. I'm going to have Mr. Fleagle and Miss Simmons— [FLEAGLE *grabs* YOUNG SAM, *takes him down to his knees, holds him helpless.*] —administer to you a tremendous overdose of a certain drug that will cause you to forget who you are.

[He *hands a hypodermic to* MISS SIMMONS.] Permanently. Then we'll leave you to wander off about the world. Simpler than killing. A corpse is dirty. You'll be listed as missing. A missing person is as transparent as glass. Nothing left to clean up or throw away. . . . I have a dream. Gently, Fleagle . . . soon. No one can be allowed to interfere with the creation of Chez Bottler! As you are still disturbed by these impossible fantasies of finding someone, when you can't even find yourself, the sooner you lose your mind entirely the better. Perhaps some charitable institution will provide you with a dark room and clean straw, where you can dream forever of Lila, and her brother, and the Bottler. Now, Miss Simmons. Now!

[As the BOTTLER *says this, he steps beneath the* HOLY CROWS, *stepping on the stone that activates them. They writhe forward off their perch, attacking the* BOTTLER.]

CROWS: Caw! Caw! Caw!

[They peck out his eyes. Blood streams from between the BOTTLER'S *fingers as he holds his face. He's in agony. The crows return to their perch.* FLEAGLE *and* MISS SIMMONS *stare, letting* YOUNG SAM *go. The* SACRISTAN *enters,* LILA *behind him.]*

SACRISTAN: The principal virtue of these marvelous crows, beyond their efficacy in conversion, is that they have no practical use. Like music, they are solely for the recreation of the mind.

[The BOTTLER *staggers off, blind and in pain.* FLEAGLE *and* MISS SIMMONS *follow. Before she exits,* MISS SIMMONS *turns back.]*

MISS SIMMONS: You never understood him, any of you!

[She exits.]

YOUNG SAM: Lila! You're here!

SACRISTAN: Lila's brother is close. Nearby. Go through the Blowhole Theatre. *[*YOUNG SAM *heads toward* LILA *and the church entrance.]* Those doors are locked for the night. You can't go back the way you came.

[The LITTLE PERSON *in the dirty yellow vest emerges from behind the* HOLY CROWS.*]*

LITTLE PERSON: Follow me.

12

The LITTLE PERSON *leads* YOUNG SAM *and* LILA *away. The cloister is gone, and the Blowhole Theatre appears.* YOUNG SAM, LILA, *and the* LITTLE PERSON *reappear at one side of this "theatre." At the rear of the Blowhole Theatre set is a multicolored house exterior, with a lunatic's grin-*

*ning face painted on the door. A tree stands in this
house's very green front yard. Hot dogs grow on its
branches. There's a large pink doghouse. A seascape is in
the distance, with moving waves. In front of it all, a low
white picket fence, with flowers. On the side of the set
furthest from* YOUNG SAM *and* LILA *there is a large sign
reading EXIT—with an arrow, pointing to the only way
out. This exit sign is at the base of a large papier-mâché
elephant, with crimson tusks with yellow tips. A man is
in a howdah up above on the elephant's back with his
hands on control levers. A* FARMER *[overalls, corncob
pipe] peering through a telescope and holding a cattle
prod, is onstage along with a rather sinister-looking*
CLOWN, *other Blowhole Theatre personnel.*

*[NOTE: The set specified here for the Blowhole
Theatre is meant to be suggestive. In any case, a garish
American sideshow.]*

NARRATOR: The Blowhole Theatre—A passageway!
Scene 42.

[A PITCHMAN *enters. Music, loud, as the Blowhole
personnel and set come alive. The* PITCHMAN *holds a
Viewmaster.]*

PITCHMAN: YOWZAA! YOWZAA! YOWZAA! The world
famous BLOWHOLE THEATRE has got it all! This
show is all meat and no potatoes. Remember, ladies
and gentlemen, that the cool of the evening is the
perfect time to see the BLOWHOLE THEATRE, and
to mark its many pee-cool-i-arities! Pay at the door.
No tickee. No washee. *[To self.]* People want blood
for ten cents.

[Another PITCHMAN *enters, with a large scale.]*

ANOTHER PITCHMAN: Not a show you go *to!* A show you go *through!* Guess your weight, occupation or age! Winna prize! Just one thin dime, the tenth part of a dollar. Guess your age! *[To the* LITTLE PERSON.*]* Hell, I'll even guess your sex!

*[*LILA *grabs* YOUNG SAM'S *hand, pulling him toward the Blowhole stage.]*

LILA: Sam, let's go. We're so close.

[He stops her.]

YOUNG SAM: You sent a lot of other men on this crazy search, didn't you, Lila? Did you promise to marry them too?

LILA: I'm sorry, Sam. I lied to you, I wanted what was mine, and it was the only way I had . . . I was hoping you'd be the one. *[Beat.]* I was. That's the truth.

LITTLE PERSON: Leave him alone. She knew you could be killed.

YOUNG SAM: Did you think the Bottler would kill me, Lila? Did you care about that when you sent me for your money? Or maybe I'd kill him? Or we'd find it and kill each other, and both be out of your way.

LILA: Sam, I knew something bad might happen—but I didn't *want* it to—

LITTLE PERSON: Lila, go home.

[The LITTLE PERSON *takes off her hat, and the rest of her disguise. She is a young woman, now in a dress, with long hair.]*

LILA: Darlene . . . ?

YOUNG SAM: You're Darlene? Lila's brother's wife?

DARLENE: There's no money anymore, Lila. He spent it all long ago, and he doesn't want to see you.

LILA: Bastard. Both of you—bastards. Is that true? What
    did he do with all that money?

DARLENE: He made a garden. *[The exit sign of the Blowhole
    Theatre revolves, revealing the words TO THE GAR-
    DEN.]*

NARRATOR: Last Garden Interlude.

    [CAPABILITY BROWN appears.]

CAPABILITY BROWN: Gardens are maps of paradise, but
    tricky ones. Certain gardens are dependent for their
    effect on being viewed in a certain order, like words
    on a page. Some gardens are puzzles, and demand
    solutions. . . . Others have made their most beautiful
    areas impossible to reach . . . like a goal in a dream.
    And there are gardens that lead us to believe we've
    been all through them, and then we realize we've
    only been in a small corner, a simple temple or
    grove. Outside, the entire garden awaits us still.

        Our true life, the spirit in everything—is invisi-
    ble. Yet it moves men, and beasts, rivers and trees,
    and in their movements, we can learn to see it, even
    in a single leaf, in the blink of an eye.

        On these nearby grounds lives a hermit. He
    built all this: the Opium Den, this Blowhole Theatre,
    the lighthouse, the nightclub in Pittsburgh, and the
    pleasant walks and groves between. Then he made
    himself a simple cottage, with an herb garden. He
    then built a place yet simpler, a kind of hut. Now he
    lives by a stick he has stuck into the ground, and
    he's hung from it a water gourd. I think he may
    soon move again. . . .

        Perhaps I'll write a garden book. I have no
    doubt I would produce, a volume of uncommon

use, that will be worthy to be placed, beneath the eye of men of taste. What man of taste my right will doubt to put things in—or leave them out.

Perhaps I'd do better to live in a tree—sleep my days away on a sofa of goosefoot vine.

[CAPABILITY BROWN *is gone.*]

LILA: [*To* YOUNG SAM *and* DARLENE.] It looks like I'm not wanted here.

YOUNG SAM: Did you ever love me, Lila?

LILA: I don't know. Maybe I did—and I didn't know it. Sam, I'm leaving. There's nothing for me here. Come back with me. . . . please. This time, no promises. You wouldn't believe them anyway.

DARLENE: You're a liar, Lila. You're scared and lonely now, so you'll beg him to hold your hand. He's much too good for you.

LILA: You coming, Sam? [*A long beat.*]

YOUNG SAM: No, Lila. I'll stay.

[LILA *exits.* YOUNG SAM *looks after her. To* DAR-LENE.]

That was wrong. You shouldn't have done that. [*Long beat. To himself.*] I shouldn't have done that.

[YOUNG SAM *hesitantly starts off after* LILA, *but* DAR-LENE *stops him.*]

DARLENE: You want to meet him, don't you? You want to see the garden, don't you? This is the only way to go!

[*She pulls* YOUNG SAM *down with her onto the stage of the Blowhole Theatre. Music. The* FARMER *and the* CLOWN *leap into action. The* CLOWN *blocks their way. The* FARMER *pulls down a window shade from a tree limb. On it is a painting of the sun and moon. The elephant's eyes light up red. Other Blowhole Theatre performers dance.]*

CLOWN: Do you do the cakewalk? Sarabande?

FARMER: Black Bottom? Gavotte?

[FARMER uses his cattle prod to make YOUNG SAM and DARLENE dance.]

CLOWN: *[Dancing.]* Have you trod the quaint mazes in the wanton green? Done the hokey pokey?

[The music ends abruptly. The FARMER grabs YOUNG SAM'S face and appeals to the man in the howdah, who is suddenly wearing a white wig. A trial.]

FARMER/ATTORNEY: Look at the face of my client! Is this the face of a guilty man? An undeserving man? A man who shouldn't receive his perfect birthright!

[The HOWDAH MAN/JUDGE growls and snarls.] These allegations are false! I demand to cross examine the alligator! *[The FARMER/ATTORNEY turns to DARLENE.]* You his accomplice?

DARLENE: I just helped him to. . . .

CLOWN & FARMER & PITCHMAN: We thought so!

[HOWDAH MAN/JUDGE growls again.]

FARMER/ATTORNEY: *[Stage whisper.]* Sam, it's hopeless. Your case won't hold water.

[The FARMER/ATTORNEY rubs his fingers together— a gesture for money. He winks.]

YOUNG SAM: I'm broke. *[DARLENE hands YOUNG SAM a dime.]* I've got ten cents. *[He hands it to FARMER.]* Will this plug the leak?

FARMER/ATTORNEY: This'll not only plug it, it'll water-proof it at the same time.

[FARMER hands the dime to the CLOWN, who hands it up to the HOWDAH MAN.]

HOWDAH MAN/JUDGE: Let me rebalance the scales of justice. . . .

CLOWN: If he can't rebalance it, I knows a man, who knows a man, who can rebalance it. . . .

FARMER & CLOWN: Shhh!

HOWDAH MAN/JUDGE: Innocent!

CLOWN: Innocent!

FARMER/ATTORNEY: Innocent!

PITCHMAN: Innocent?

HOWDAH MAN/JUDGE: Head for the exit!

DARLENE: Let's go.

> *[Music. The floor wiggles, tossing them to the ground. The* CLOWN *leaps about hysterically. A blast of air blows* DARLENE'S *dress up above her waist. Other Blowhole personnel dance. Faces of other characters appear grinning in the house's windows.* DARLENE *grabs* YOUNG SAM'S *hand.]*

FARMER/ATTORNEY: *[Shouting.]* Keep moving! Give all of yourself away!

> *[They bolt through the exit. They're gone, and so is the Blowhole Theatre set. The Blowhole Theatre actors place themselves in a straggly line, except one, who gawks at the others.]*

NARRATOR: In its infancy, the Blowhole Theatre Company once performed an adaptation of *Hiram Birdseed at the World's Fair.* It consisted of mindless gawking by one member of the company, while the others paraded by dressed as all the people of the earth.

> *[They do so, and exit.]*

13

The garden. The stage is almost bare. Green. DARLENE *and* YOUNG SAM. OLD SAM, *alone, toward the rear.*

NARRATOR: IN THE GARDEN.

OLD SAM: He's not doing so badly. I even like him. He's doing his very very best. You know, you get on, and you cross over somehow. I can feel in my mind my entire life there for me—all at once. Confusing after so many years of being stuck in time. Floating between gears—I'm here and I'm in the garden. It's no choice. It's all together. I don't need to make those choices anymore.

DARLENE: *[To* YOUNG SAM.*]* You've come a long way. My husband disappeared to lose himself, to hide from everything he was. The money helped. He built a place to forget himself in, to make someone new. *[Laughing.]* He doesn't even remember his name.

YOUNG SAM: Does he know you?

DARLENE: *[Laughs.]* There are things he hasn't forgotten.

YOUNG SAM: Why did you help me get here?

DARLENE: We wanted company. Someone to help us. The garden needs care. Wait here. I'll bring him. The truth is that this world is paradise. If you don't believe me, look around.

        *[*DARLENE *exits.* YOUNG *and* OLD SAM *onstage,* OLD SAM *at some distance behind* YOUNG SAM. *The* AUTHOR *enters.]*

AUTHOR: And he did. And it seemed to My Uncle Sam that everything was there for his sake, and that everything spoke to him. The flowers nodded in greeting, the clouds above foretold great wonders, and the statues smiled their enigmatic smiles. He was sure beyond any doubt that an urgent meaning was there—but he couldn't read it—not so he could tell it back to you. That it was there was enough.

[The AUTHOR is gone.]

YOUNG SAM: I saw the river flowing through the garden, and on either side of the river, trees bearing all manner of fruit, and the fruit of the trees were for the healing of nations. . . .

[Young Sam takes a few steps toward the audience.]

At this moment, it doesn't seem, after all the way I've come, that there's any stopping place. Seems to me I go from one place to another in the blink of an eye . . . Even this garden's only one step . . . seeing it all from over my head somewhere. . . .

OLD SAM & YOUNG SAM: . . . like a gull, wandering between heaven and earth and looking down, all so easy. I'm floating out everywhere and turning like the rolling earth itself in this travelling of mine. . . . I can be everywhere, and the world—the world just can't help itself in some beautiful way. . . .

YOUNG SAM: *[Alone.]* . . . and I saw all this in the garden, and my own life jumped up at me like a puppy inside.

[Long beat.]

OLD SAM: *[Alone.]* I didn't stay.

[YOUNG SAM exits. OLD SAM'S hotel room returns, and he goes to it, sits in his chair. In the distance, the singing duo. This time they actually sing, no lip sync, and no music.]

DUO: This is my story, I have no song
　　Just a lone and broken heart,
　　Just because I fell in love, in love with you
　　I pray, that you'll come back to me
　　Just to hear you say you love me
　　And we'll never, never part. . . .
　　　　[They fade, and are gone.]

14

OLD SAM: Sioux City Sue . . . soo city soo . . . her hair is blonde her eye is blue . . . swap my horse and dog for you. . . . Lila was gone when I got back. I asked everybody, searched everywhere. Nothing. She was gone, that's all. Disappeared. . . . Soo city soo. . . . I used to want my own place to live, where I could just die without inconveniencing anyone. Now I don't mind that the maid'll scream when she finds my body.

White frost covers the garden. The flowers freeze in the night, wake up before dawn as white ghosts of themselves, shapes alone, with no life left. All one whiteness in the pre-dawn dark, and then the morning sun rises and melts the frost, and it flows down into the roots, and gives us life. Ice and water. Same stuff. A pine cone drops in the winter garden. Frost on the chrysanthemums.

Lila's dead now. I see her, and she's laughing, and her memory draws me toward the grave. Who says that the dead don't think of us? Lila thinks of me all the time. . . .

This morning I woke suddenly, and wasn't sure where I was . . . like a gull, lost between heaven and earth. . . . Downstairs, there's a woman, got two kids and a black eye, moved in three weeks ago, running away from some man. I believe the Child Services pays her bills. He hasn't found her yet, and she's looking better. Not so scared. This morning she says "Hello, My Uncle Sam" in the coffee shop. Tonight those two kids of hers can't sleep. They feel I'm gonna die. So they sit up in bed, eyes wide open, waiting. Their momma comes in and says, "You got school tomorrow, go to sleep," and they say "We can't sleep momma, something's gonna happen. . . . *[He holds his chest in pain.]* No doctor. Don't call a doctor. I don't need no doctor. It's all right. If you don't know it, it's a two lane road, and I'm coming back the other way. I got a return ticket. See you all again sometime. . . .

[Lights dim on OLD SAM, *as* YOUNG SAM *appears.]*

YOUNG SAM: I am My Uncle Sam. What can't be said, can't be said, and it can't be whistled either. . . .

*[*YOUNG SAM *strolls off, whistling, past* OLD SAM, *who is very still. The* AUTHOR *appears.]*

AUTHOR: There's My Uncle Sam . . . sitting alone in his hotel room in Pittsburgh . . . Sherman Arms. There's his cashmere coat, and his cigar in the ashtray. He's got the sweetest expression on his face. . . .

I got a nephew, name's Jesse. He sees me every now and then, and I say "How you doin', Jess," and we go down to the video arcade, and I lay five bucks worth of quarters on him. He sees me all right, with my cashmere coat and my cigar. Corona

Corona, get 'em five for a dollar, cigar stand, Sherman Arms. Come dusk, last sun through the lace curtains, and I sit in a leather armchair in the lobby. I am My Uncle Sam. . . .

Statues of My Uncle Sam across America! Winter, and there's snow on his shoulders, and a little perfect mound of snow sits in the crown of his hat where no one can see it but the birds. In the summer, someone wreathes the brow of the statue with flowers.

FIN

American Notes

Tho' obscur'd, this is the form
of the Angelic land.

—WILLIAM BLAKE: *America*

American Notes was first presented by the New York Shakespeare Festival Public Theater on February 18, 1988. The cast, in order of appearance, was as follows:

MAYOR	Rodney Scott Hudson
CHUCKLES	Olek Krupa
PAULINE	Lauren Tom
FABER	Stephen McHattie
PITCHMAN	Thomas Ikeda
KAREN	Mercedes Ruehl
REPORTER	Andrew Davis
TIM	Jesse Borrego
LINDA	Laura Innes
PROFESSOR	George Bartenieff

Director: Joanne Akalaitis
Set: John Arnone
Costumes: David C. Woolard
Lighting: Frances Aronson

PRODUCTION NOTE

The set for *American Notes* is basically six places: motel reception area; Karen's motel room; Pitchman's banner and showfront; Professor's house; Tim and Linda's bar; and the Mayor's area. Where these are in relation to each other, and whether all the areas are onstage all the time are questions that I hope will be answered by each individual production according to its needs and interests. The settings in a particular production can be very full and movie-like—realistic places, or sparse theatrical arrangements that indicate the nature of place through significant objects. In either case, we should have the feeling that a great dark sky is overhead, that the distances surrounding our places below are vast. The music is all American music, and can range from rock and roll to muzak to country and western. It can come from radios and televisions, and/or just be there—as soft background for the voices, punctuation, or moments of violent energy and pulse.

Please leave space in the language, and between the people, for silence.

It is night, we are in America, and the time is now.

ACT 1

An open field, outskirts of town. An older man sits in the dirt, some food and a bottle alongside him. This is the MAYOR. *A traveller enters, dusty, ragged, having walked a long way. He holds a battered suitcase. This is the man who will be called* CHUCKLES. *He stops, as if unsure which way to go. He hesitantly approaches the* MAYOR.

MAYOR: Bound for somewhere, buddy?
    *[*CHUCKLES *nods. He points in one direction, then hesitates, points in another direction. He looks around confusedly.]*
    Well, little buddy—stay or walk.
    *[*CHUCKLES *moves about uncertainly, stops.]*
    You want advice, or directions?
    *[*CHUCKLES *stands silent, ill at ease.]*
    You want advice.
    [The MAYOR *looks* CHUCKLES *over carefully.]*
    You been travelling, little buddy. Probably looking for it, but you ain't found it yet. Hmmmm . . . your eyes been sucking up so much world they got swelled up like beachballs, poppin' outta your face. Ooo weee! You know, you keep moving and peeping in everywhichplace, you can raise up a big wind in your head, special if you don't know exactly what you looking at. Why just yesterday I was out taking my constitutional—past the flag go flap flap on the village green, past the newstand, past a man slicing another man's face with a breadknife, past old Mr. and Mrs. Whoever's house and she's pray-

ing with her thumb up her Bible and he's rubbing his moneymaker, and I stop to take a leak behind the barn and who do I see hailing a cab in the dark but little Miss Muffet, and her hair's all tangled and she ain't wallking right. Hey, I seen a guy follow somebody's daughter into the all night launderama and he's got his dick hid inna boxa Tide. I see 'em go in there and she's folding up her underwear, and I'm looking through the keyhole and all that wash is spinning round and round and round.

I seen a man, 'bout this time yesterday, slit his own throat in the bathroom mirror. Home sweet home, you betcha. Run around to nowhere till they drop, ain't even looking. Am I right?

[CHUCKLES *nods in agreement. He shyly eyes the* MAYOR's *food. The* MAYOR *eyes* CHUCKLES.]

Hey . . . uh, [*Naming him.*] Chuckles! Chuckles, you want something to eat?

[CHUCKLES *grabs the food, begins to chomp away.*]

Hey . . . my lunch. You are supposed to leave me something.

[CHUCKLES, *frightened, drops the food quickly, pushes it back over to the* MAYOR. *The* MAYOR, *in turn, places the food carefully back between the two of them.* CHUCKLES *hesitantly takes something to eat. The* MAYOR *nods.*]

Now I been on that road myself. Got tired one day, and settled down. Right here. Got a wife and three kids. Why just last week I got elected mayor. Ain't much in it but I like the honor you know, from my fellow citizens. Nasty and slow as they may be, they got glimmers, glimmers way down in their

Olek Krupa and Rodney Scott Hudson in *American Notes*
Martha Swope Associates/Carol Rosegg

underpants. Know what I mean little buddy? Down there—and in the very center of the eye, in the black dot.

I got a good idea where you're headed. Why you know there's nine rivers between here and there, and you moving like you gonna get there Tuesday. There's the Muskinggum, an' the Chatahoochie, the Raritanic, the Monongahoola, the Gahoolamonga, the Belly-up, the Snake, and the Skunk. Whooooooo! You counting? There's one so fearsome it either doesn't have a name or I'm scared to tell it. You think this some tiddlywink country like Alboonia you step outta your shack to take a piss and if the wind's right you are watering foreign soil? This is the land of Rootie Kazootie and the Appaloosa, sea to shining sea. Go somewhere and die! Whooboy! You moving on to somewhere cause you think this ain't it, but you don't know this country or these people around here, little bitty buddy, so there's nothing but wind in your head. It's whistling between your ears, bitty buddy. Just wind.

You got your lips loose yet? No talkee, eh? Wanna wrestle? Wanna swap socks?

[MAYOR conceals his socks with his hands.]

No peeking. Look in my pocket. Waddaya see?

[The MAYOR holds open his pants pocket. CHUCKLES peers into it.]

Pocket fulla darkness—hooboy! Hey, Chuckles, wiggle down in the dirt here.

[They both sit on the ground.]

Hey, eat some more stuff here.

[CHUCKLES eats.]

Ease your weary mind. This is some place, all right. You lucky you here. You oughta get work, stay awhile. . . . I might be able to place a man of your talents. . . .

[*Lights up in another area on* PAULINE, *a young woman standing motionless in the center of a motel office.*]

Look around. Hey, see there's Pauline. She works late. . . .

Hey, Chuckles. Suck up some of this juice I got here. . . . Made it special for ya. . . . [MAYOR *hands* CHUCKLES *his bottle, and* CHUCKLES *drinks.*] . . . and open your eyes. . . .

[*Lights fade on the* MAYOR *and* CHUCKLES, *come up more strongly on* PAULINE. *In the motel office, a counter closes a small area off from the rest of the space. Behind the counter, a chair. On the counter, a bell, a register, some books, a small TV, a phone. A radio plays. Out in the space, a few chairs. Through a screen door, extending away from the office, the "outside": perhaps a sign reading "OFFICE" with an arrow, parking stripes on cracked asphalt.* PAULINE *the nite-clerk suddenly rushes over to the screen door, opens it, and leans out.*]

PAULINE: GET OUT OF HERE! Leave me alone, please! You're drunk, you know that? GO AWAY AND STOP BOTHERING ME! I'm gonna call the police if you don't get outta here, NOW!

[PAULINE *goes back behind the desk, reaches for the phone, then changes her mind. She's nervous, listening for any noise. Suddenly the screen door opens. A man enters in a rumpled suit and tie. He goes up to* PAULINE, *and looks at her expectantly.*]

FABER: I'm in 4. I left my key.

PAULINE: Oh . . . yeah. *[She hands his key to him.]*

FABER: Thanks. Good night.

> *[He heads for the door, but her voice stops him.]*

PAULINE: Uh, excuse me. Mr. Faber?

FABER: How'd you know my name?

PAULINE: It's in the register. Room 4.

FABER: Right. I've never seen you here before.

PAULINE: I'm the nite clerk. I don't come in till twelve, so if you don't stay out late, or get up early, you don't see me.

FABER: Uh, right. Good night, miss. . . .

PAULINE: Pauline. Mr. Faber, did you see anyone hanging around on your way in?

FABER: Not a soul, Pauline.

PAULINE: Would you mind doing me a favor? Could you go outside and take a look around the parking lot?

FABER: I'll play. What am I looking for?

PAULINE: There's this drunk guy who's been hanging around here bothering me, and I think he's gone now, but I'm not sure. . . .

> *[*FABER *hesitates, then shrugs his shoulders.]*

FABER: O.K. I'll take a look.

> *[*FABER *exits.* PAULINE *waits nervously. Lights up in another area on an older man, the* PITCHMAN, *in front of an enclosure with a curtained entrance. Some carnival lights. A huge painted banner depicts the lush landscape of Egypt, the pyramids, and the river Nile. The* PITCHMAN *is seated on a stool. He has a microphone. Near him stands* CHUCKLES, *who has a container half full of water in his hands.]*

PITCHMAN *[on mike]:* Come in and see the crocodile, Papa

Crocodile, the biggest, oldest, mightiest of them all. Man killer. Swamp monster. Alive on the inside. Listen to him kick and splash. Sounds like he's coming out of there . . . *[looks at* CHUCKLES*]* . . . sounds like he's coming OUTTA THERE! *[*CHUCKLES *shakes his container, making a splashing sound near the mike.]* From the land of the pharoahs, the sphinx and the pyramids comes the crocodile, the colossus of reptiles, twelve hundred pounds of tail lashing, jaw gnashing danger. Bonecrusher! See him now. Listen to him thrash about in there. Sounds like he's about to come outta there, doesn't it? *[*CHUCKLES *splashes.]* No danger at all. You'll be separated from him by two sets of steel bars. Go right in. The show is always open. Go right in. . . .

[From a distance, a MAN'S VOICE, *screaming]*

MAN'S VOICE: *[offstage]* Pauline!

[The PITCHMAN *pauses a moment, then continues.]*

PITCHMAN: See BONECRUSHER, the summum bonum of nature's awesome power and cruelty, etcetera, etcetera and so forth. That's the pitch, which is one thing. The attraction's another. Some shows, what's on the inside ain't worth spitting at. Crusher's the real thing. You got the real thing, people come. Even in Boobopolis, or Chump Junction, or Hayseed Center, or wherever the fuck we are this week. People go on in and tell me, Mister, you didn't say enough, and come back with the family.

See Bonecrusher, the monster of the Nile, alive on the inside. No sir, this is not a movie. . . . Alive!

[The PITCHMAN *and* CHUCKLES *are still, as lights on them fade out. In the motel office area,* FABER *returns.]*

FABER: There was this guy leaning over the one car in the parking lot . . . mine. He's vomiting on the hood. So I say, "uh, buddy, get off my car," and he heaves again and then he turns around to me with puke all over his football jersey and he says "You're the one." I do believe he thought I was your boyfriend. I was flattered. I figured I wouldn't disillusion him. I say "I am the one. Go—and be sick somewhere else."

PAULINE: Did he?

FABER: First he took a swing at me. He missed, and he falls down and sort of crawls away. Then he stands up and he howls.

MAN'S VOICE : *[Howling O.S.]* PAULINE!

FABER: You probably heard that part. Then he just wanders off into the dark. I see him again when he hits the highway light near the junction, and he bobs and weaves a bit under the light, and he's gone. He the town wino? Or a lover you won't see no more?

PAULINE: Just some guy.

    *[*FABER *takes a seat.]*

FABER: Hey . . . you want a favor, and I don't even know you, and I go to shoo this guy away. He's mean drunk, bigger than me, and could have been carrying the kitchen cleaver. I take my life in my hands out there, and you won't answer a little question to help me pass the time.

PAULINE: It's true, what I said. He's *just some guy.*

FABER: No. That's me. I'm just some guy. I'm staying here, you never saw me before, you say hello cause that's your job, and I'm gone. He's somebody. He's got a name. He may even have a mother. Right in town . . . that's where he's going now. Home, and his mom is sitting in the kitchen in a flower print nightdress, waiting up. Radio's on, some kinda endless traffic report. She's reading the back of a box of Fab, and when he hits the screen door, she looks up. "Where you been, Bobby? Your hair's all tangled and you ain't talking right. Oooh wee, you got puke and blood all over you. . . ."

PAULINE: Blood? He's got blood all over him?

FABER: Thought I'd leave out that part. I kicked him.

PAULINE: You kicked him? I asked you to look around, not to kick him or something. Why'd you do that? Oh, Jesus, why. . . .

FABER: I kicked him cause he was lying on the asphalt and he says "goddamn cunt I'm going back there and fuck her up." He said something along those lines. So I kicked him in the face. He bled a little. Discouraging him seemed like a good idea at the time. You got someone who can stay with you for a few nights till he cools off? Hell, he'll probably be back with a shotgun. . . .

PAULINE: You're kidding, aren't you? I hope. . . .

FABER: Yeah. He's gone. Who is he?

PAULINE: Nobody. I teach exercise twice a week, in town. The studio has a window on the street, so it's kind of advertising, but anyone can just look in and see us jumping around in leotards. One day, there's this guy I never saw before, and he watches the whole fifty-five minutes, like he's hypnotized. Next day he comes inside and says he wants to sign up. I tell him the class is full. That was a lie, and I didn't like saying it, but there's something funny about him, like

he's not seeing what's there, but something else *he*
likes better—but you're not too sure *you'd* like it better—and he's seeing it *all the time.* Then he asks me
out. I had to get Elaine to make him leave. Then he
showed up here tonight. He was drunk. I was
scared. Thanks for helping me out.

FABER: He got caught by something is all. Your hair,
some angle of your body, something in your face
locked in to a dream of his and he grabbed at it only
way he had. He'll forget it—till some other time and
place, somebody else in a window tilts her head a
certain way, and the rusted old gears mesh, and he
once more presses his nose against the glass. It's a
great life. What time is it?

PAULINE: After two.

FABER: I'm wide awake.

PAULINE: Me, too. You want some coffee? I've got a hot
plate in the back, and some instant. . . .

FABER: Yeah . . . that's good. That's fine. I like that.

PAULINE: O.K.

> [PAULINE *exits through a rear door behind the desk.*
> FABER *alone.* CHUCKLES *enters. He carries a vacuum
> cleaner. He stares suspiciously at* FABER. *He exits.*]

FABER: [*calling offstage*] Hey, am I the only one staying
here? Tonight, I mean.

PAULINE: [*from off*] Well, we really have only one other
guest. Another single. God, she's real beautiful.
Hasn't been out of her room for three days. She's
been calling over, though, for messages.

FABER: Yeah?

> [PAULINE *returns with two coffee cups and a jar of
> powdered cream. She sets them down on the counter.*]

PAULINE: I got Cremora, the powder?

FABER: That's fine. Uh. . . .

> [He gets up and goes over to PAULINE, *who is behind her desk.*] I got a bottle of whiskey here in one pocket, unopened. Maybe we just adulterate the coffee a little. What do you think, Pauline?

PAULINE: [hesitantly] O.K., but just a little for me. I've gotta work till eight.

FABER: I know. You're on the job, Pauline. [FABER *adds whiskey to the coffee.*] If I ring the bell, you'll ask what you can do for me. [He rings the bell. Silence for a moment.]

PAULINE: Mr. Faber, where've you been tonight? I know you didn't take your car cause it's been sitting there since I came on, so I thought hey, Mr. Faber in 4 must have friends in town. After all, he's been here a week, and what else is there to stay around here that long for?

FABER: Pauline, I bet you figure out a lot of things, don't you?

PAULINE: I bet it's a girlfriend. She's got a car, and picked you up, and you. . . .

FABER: You got this one wrong. I don't know anyone anywhere near here. I was out walking. In town.

PAULINE: Everything's closed.

FABER: I wasn't shopping. I was walking. So, Pauline. What do you do here all night long?

PAULINE: Homework, mostly. I got an English lit assignment for tomorrow. I just started, part time. At the community college, out on 119. It's going O.K. so far.

FABER: Sounds like something, I guess. . . .

PAULINE: All my friends went to college a year ago. But my mom wouldn't have the county nurse before.

FABER: Mind if I ask just what you're talking about?

PAULINE: Oh . . . sorry. My mom's not real well, and someone's gotta be around her almost all the time. Now, the nurse is there, and I can work this job, *and* start school.

FABER: Uh, Pauline, long as we're having this coffee and all, I'd feel better if you just came out from behind the desk, and we'd just sit around here like people do, you know.

PAULINE: I'm not supposed to be out there where the guests sit.

FABER: We're not gonna be having any more company tonight.

   [PAULINE *comes hesitantly out from behind the desk, sits in a chair by* FABER. *They drink coffee.*] Now, uh, Pauline, are you single?

PAULINE: Sure. I told you. I live with my Mom.

FABER: Well, for all I knew your husband was living there too, and the two of you had a little room up in the attic where you baked brownies or something, ran the volunteer fire department, a little palmistry scam . . . and then the two of you being real quiet till your Mom goes off to sleep, then once you hear the sick old lady snoring you leap at each other, tearing. . . .

PAULINE: No. Just me and my mom.

FABER: Let me make a comment here, Pauline. I was downtown there in the downtown tonight, and it seemed as if someone had pressed the pause button on the whole neighborhood around 1942. Quiet.

Sort of permanently still. Awful slow for actual people. And out here, right now, even stranger. No
wind, no traffic. . . . I can hear the breath going in
and out of you.

PAULINE: I think that's your own breath you're hearing,
Mr. Faber.

FABER: Yeah, You're right. That's what it is.

PAULINE: I'm gonna get to my book for awhile, O.K.?

FABER: You don't mind if I sit up here a bit?

PAULINE: Make yourself at home. There's nobody here
but us . . . [phone rings] . . . and the girl in 7.

   [PAULINE picks up the desk phone. Lights up in a
   room of the same motel. A stocking hangs out of a suitcase on a stand. Empty liquor bottles. A girl in a slip,
   KAREN, is sitting on an unmade bed, the phone in her
   hand.]

   Office. Can I help you?

KAREN: Yeah, uh Jenny. . . .

PAULINE: Pauline.

KAREN: Oh. Yeah. Pauline, the nite clerk. Listen, Pauline,
what time you got?

PAULINE: Exactly . . . [looks at watch] . . . 2:45.

KAREN: Zat daylight savings or what? Just kidding. . . .
Uh, anything for me?

PAULINE: Uh, I'm sorry. No messages.

KAREN: Thanks.

PAULINE: It's no trouble. Good night. [PAULINE hangs up
the phone, as does KAREN; to FABER.]

   The girl who's waiting. . . .

   [PAULINE reads. FABER sits quietly. In her room, we
   hear KAREN in VOICE-OVER or LIVE, as indicated. She
   looks down at a cigarette burnhole in the bedspread.]

KAREN: *[V.O.]* Oh Jesus, Karen darling. Look at that. You coulda set your bed on fire. *[She looks around the room.]* *[V.O.]* Musta been a helluva party. I hope I had a good time. Hell, nobody else showed up. . . .

[She opens a liquor bottle, pours a drink, shakes out two aspirin.]

[LIVE] Well, onward Christian soldiers. *[She takes the aspirin with a chaser.]* Ugh. What's the worst? He got hit by a truck or something and he's laid up in a hospital, and his face is all bandaged so he can't call. Or, he's dead, so he can't call.

[V.O.] You'd almost like that Karen darling, cause what's likely is that bastard's out on the road somewhere and he forgot you. You just went right out of his head. "Karen? Who the fuck is that? I don't remember."

[LIVE] No. That's not fucking possible. I can tell.

[KAREN'S MEMORY evokes the REPORTER, and he appears in another space. He holds a letter from the PROFESSOR.]

REPORTER: Hey, I've been in heaven for two days, and I am not about to walk away from it and not come back. It's a three hour drive, I'm only gonna be with the guy an hour maybe, tops. Just to take some pictures and notes for the story.

KAREN: *[LIVE]* You know it's *four miles* to town, Chump Junction or whatever, only shoes I got are these heels, I got about seventy-five cents in my purse, half a pack of Pall Malls, some groceries, and a bottle of vodka.

What am I gonna *do* here?

REPORTER: How should I know? Read a magazine. Watch the TV. They got TV in the rooms.

KAREN: *[LIVE]* This professor you're gonna see . . . he got a phone number?

REPORTER: *[checking the letter]* Baby, he lives in the middle of god-forsaken nowhere. He doesn't have a phone. I think he doesn't believe in 'em.

> *[Lights come up on the* PROFESSOR *in his farmhouse. A door with many locks, boards nailed over windows, piles of disorganized books, odd electronic equipment, complex charts and diagrams. Strange atonal music plays, softly. The* PROFESSOR *addresses the audience. In his own space, the* REPORTER *looks over the letter his magazine's received.]*

PROFESSOR: There exist particular spiritual beings who hold certain information invaluable to humanity. In this place, I have entered into unrestrained dialogue with these beings on a variety of congenial topics. To accomplish this, of course, I've had to probe some rather isolated spiritual neighborhoods, previously accessible only by psychic helicopter. . . .

> I wrote to the newspapers, magazines, learnéd societies. Only one response—from a publication mired in lurid speculation and unsubstantiated horseshit. *Flying Saucer News.*

REPORTER: *[to* KAREN*]* Hey . . . see ya' in a l'il bit, hah . . . late tonight or tomorrow. Or tomorrow. Or tomorrow.

> *[Lights strong on the* PROFESSOR, *the* REPORTER, *and* KAREN. *A knock on the* PROFESSOR'S *door. He opens it warily.* CHUCKLES *enters, bringing the* PROFESSOR *some take-out food. He eats ravenously, as* CHUCKLES *listens.]*

PROFESSOR: These beings, these shadow people, they're around us, all the time. They can't fly, or raise the dead, or control the weather. They're very light, you know. The wind can blow them away, if they're not careful. Very light. Very beautiful.

[CHUCKLES *exits. The* PROFESSOR *locks the door quickly and thoroughly, continues.*]

Some say they've always existed, and will exist forever. I wouldn't say that. Some say they are the dead. I wouldn't say that. They're just there, alongside us, like feelings in the air.

[*Lights down on the* PROFESSOR]

KAREN: [*LIVE*] Three days in this hole. What day is it anyway?

[*V.O.*] Maybe it's Sunday, and I should go to church or something. [*She picks up the phone, dials. In the motel office, it rings.*]

PAULINE: Office.

KAREN: Hey, Pauline, what day you got?

PAULINE: It's Monday now.

KAREN: Any messages?

PAULINE: Nothing yet. Sorry.

KAREN: Thanks. [*They hang up the phones.*] [*V.O.*]On the way over to the motel he says let's get you some groceries to take up to the room. I say O.K. and we pull up at the 7-11 and on the way in I trip over a fucking tricycle some kid leaves there in front of the door. I ripped my stocking on the pedal. I guess I'm nervous or something cause I start kicking the bike. The kid comes rushing out, screaming at me. He's got a big container of purple snow in his hand.

[*LIVE*] The place's microwave is busted. He

buys me a frozen burrito and tells me it'll thaw, and an orange soda and a beer and some kinda dead french fries, all gonna taste like cardboard puke. He pays, and he hands the whole bag to me like it's fulla gold, with this shit-eating grin on his face. I smile back and say hey whyn't you just leave me fifty bucks and I'll get my own groceries. . . .

[V.O.] I could see I said the wrong thing. He'd been burned before. He just looked over my shoulder at a shelf full of motor oil. Forget it, I say, I don't need no money. You're gonna be back tomorrow, right? and I give him a kiss, a nice wet one with a little tongue in it. He smiles.

[LIVE] What a chump.

[V.O.] "Day after, the latest," he says . . . and he drops me here and he's gone. Frozen burrito and an orange soda. Purple snow.

REPORTER: See ya in a l'il bit, hah . . . late tonight. Or tomorrow.

[The REPORTER exits.]

KAREN: [LIVE] Hey, anything coulda happened. Car broke down. Couldn't find that professor. Maybe he forgot the name of this place so he couldn't call. Hey, Karen darling. Believe. He'll be here. . . .

[Lights up on the same PITCHMAN we've seen before, in front of the same crocodile exhibit: banner, entranceway in to see the crocodile. Near the enclosure is CHUCKLES. He holds the closed container of water, the splasher. CHUCKLES shakes his container. Sounds of splashing.]

PITCHMAN: [on mike] No, sir, it is not a movie. Alive on the inside. Bonecrusher, world's largest. . . . Hey, Chuckles. Wet Mr. B down, will ya?

CHUCKLES: Splushh splush?

PITCHMAN: Yeah.

CHUCKLES: Splush splush! Splish!

> [CHUCKLES *goes into the crocodile's enclosure. An attractive young girl and her boyfriend walk up to the exhibit. This is* TIM *and* LINDA.]

TIM: [*to* PITCHMAN] Hi! My name's Tim. This is Linda. Linda, say hello to the nice man.

LINDA: Hello.

TIM: We want to see, uh, Bonecrusher, you call him?

PITCHMAN: That's what I call him, and that's his name. His Momma gave it to him on the banks of the Nile, in Crocodilopolis. Enter and discover. Or you can go downtown to Penny's and watch the wax dummies in the window.

> [TIM *and* LINDA *disappear into Bonecrusher's enclosure. The* PITCHMAN'S *eyes follow* LINDA *as they exit. He turns to the audience.*]

You know what age is to me? It's a number. Sixty. Nineteen. Zero. That's all the fuck it is, a fucking number. Hey, couple of local girls come around wearing these shorts show half their ass when they lean over to look at Bonecrusher, and he ain't looking at them but I am and they say, Hey, how you doing, Pop? You want some of that, Pop? Hey, my name's Marty, cut that Pop crap, you know. Now I ain't saying it's exactly the same. If she tries to gimme a blowjob every ten minutes I'm gonna say, hey, what you doing you trying to kill me or something?

Been with Bonecrusher for thirty years. Got him when I got outta the army in '58. Hey, I'm different, he's the same, but that's on the outside. Inside, I'm just like him—no change at all.

That's Chuckles. Found him wandering around the lot when we hit town. I taught him how to hose out the cage, do some other little stuff around here. Boss wanted to throw him off the lot, I said, hey, no way, Chuckles stays with me. Cause I had an idea. I treat him good, feed him, let him sleep under the drop here. It's next to Crusher, and sometimes it don't smell all that good, but he don't mind. We got a deal, Chuckles and me. Chuckles is gonna feed me to Crusher when I die. I needed an idiot. Nobody else would do it. When I found Chuckles, I knew I found my boy.

I'm a religious man, in my way. If Bonecrusher eats me, I'll go on living, looking out of his eyes. You'll be able to see me in there, a little spark of red fire way back in those black slits of nothing. Hey, I'll be him, and he'll be me. Bullshit spook stuff, hah? I don't care what you think. Sense to me don't gotta be sense to you.

Listen and learn. What you think ain't all the thinking there is. Bonecrusher is a priest. It's all in *Job*, and I got it by heart.

Canst thou draw out Leviathan with a hook? Who can open the doors of his face? Or light the lamps of his mouth? Will he speak soft words unto thee? Will he make a covenant with thee? Will he take thee for a servant forever? Upon earth there is not his like, who is made without fear. He beholdeth all high things, and sorrow is turned into joy before him.

[TIM *and* LINDA *emerge from Bonecrusher's enclosure.*]

TIM: Hey, fella. I hate to tell you this, but your croc's dead.

PITCHMAN: You don't say. *[laughs]* You know anything about crocodiles, friend? They look deader'n hell most of the time.

TIM: Excuse me, but that animal in there is gone, finished.

PITCHMAN: That's Bonecrusher in there, and he'll outlive you or me.

TIM: He's dead. Probably been dead for a week.

PITCHMAN: Fuck you and your mother, friend. Chuckles!

[CHUCKLES *advances, as menacingly as he can manage, toward* TIM. TIM *grabs him suddenly, twists, and* CHUCKLES *is on his knees.*]

TIM: *[to* PITCHMAN*]* You're right about one thing. He is big. But he's not Egyptian, and he's not a crocodile. He's an American alligator. Do you want to sell the body?

[*The* PITCHMAN *doesn't answer.*]

LINDA: Bury him, or put him in the town dump where the birds'll strip him clean. Children can play with his bones.

[TIM *and* LINDA *exit, and from off, their laughter.*]

PITCHMAN: Chuckles, go in there and poke Mr. B.

[CHUCKLES *enters the croc's enclosure. A moment later, he slowly emerges. He looks down at the ground.*]

I been with him 30 years, Chuckles. I been on the road with him every season. I got repeat customers. These people bring their kids. Little goddamn kids.

"Know how he got so big, sonny? People think he grew fat on fear. That's not so. He's big with love. . . ."

[The PITCHMAN *slowly sits down again in his usual position, in front of the huge banner. He picks up his microphone.]*

[On mike.] See Bonecrusher, World's Largest Crocodile, Colosus of reptiles, monster of the Nile. Hear him splash around in there. I do believe he's coming out of there. . . .

*[*CHUCKLES *makes shaking motions, but his hands are empty. No splashing sound.]*

[Off mike.] No sir, this is not a movie. Alive on the inside. *[to* CHUCKLES*]* Bonecrusher ain't dead, Chuckles. He's sleeping, that's all. Needs his rest. After all the horrible things he's done his whole life long, he needs his rest. . . .

[The PITCHMAN *and* CHUCKLES *are still. In the motel office,* PAULINE *reads,* FABER *sits quietly.]*

FABER: Pauline?

PAULINE: Yes, Mr. Faber?

FABER: Pauline, now that we're sitting around here together and all—would you tell me a story?

PAULINE: I don't know any stories.

FABER: You already told me one, Pauline. About the exercise class.

PAULINE: That wasn't a story, Mr. Faber. It happened.

FABER: Story all the same, Pauline. Just like when some old lady comes down in her pajamas says Pauline honey I can't get a wink so give a listen to my life. It's the same as all the others so I guess the joke's on me. You could read it on line at the supermarket,

hear em shout it over the cornfields, but, hey—hear
it now, 'cause what you the nite clerk for anyway?
Tell me that one, Pauline, and when you're done I'll
comment, and we'll be having a conversation here.

PAULINE: I can't tell you a story, Mr. Faber. Not just like
that, anyway.

FABER: All right, then I'll tell you one, Pauline. All you
got to do is listen.

> *[Lights up on a bar somewhere. Over the bar, a TV
> plays: picture, no sound. There's also a video game, and a
> small stage at the rear. On that stage, TIM and LINDA, as
> a performing duo. They do a song, perhaps their version
> of Sonny and Cher's "I Got You, Babe." During the
> song, FABER enters, and sits at the bar. From the motel
> office, PAULINE watches. The song ends, and LINDA goes
> to the video game, plays. TIM comes over to FABER.]*

TIM: My name's Tim. I'm living at the hotel. Blaine Hotel
right up the street. Hey, after the accident, before I
had this job, I was working polishing airport floors
in the middle of the night. It's quiet, and I liked the
way the machine kept humming. If I stuck six
months they were gonna embroider my name on
my uniform. Tim. I left. Airport's for the planes
really, not the people, you know. Got this job, took a
room right up the street. Come over and see me. I
could put you so straight you wouldn't bend again
for days—years, maybe. *[Pointing.]* That's Linda.
Linda, say hello to the nice man.

LINDA: Hello.

TIM: You know why Linda stays with me?

FABER: I. . . .

TIM: 'Cause she's crazy, that's why. Besides, she's on the

four to twelve shift at Denny's out on Arctic, and
when she's done, she needs somebody to love. I flat-
ter myself. Listen, buddy. The truth is she sleeps on
the floor with her clothes on, in the bathroom next
to the tub, curled up in an old army blanket I got. I
lay there in bed and I whisper and I say Linda
Linda come on into bed here. It's warm and I took a
bath before I got in, and the sheets is clean, and I
ain't gonna do nothing—I'm just gonna hold you. I
say all that whispering loud so she'll hear me in the
bathroom, but she never answers. I never know if
she hears me, or if she's sleeping. When I say that
stuff to her I ain't lying, you know. I ain't lying, but
I'm hoping. . . .

Listen, Bob. You know Linda got two kids.
Would you believe it? Yeah, they live in Reno,
Nevada. She lost 'em on a bet.

Now she's here. You like her, Bob? She got very
nice tits. Not saggy at all, you know. She's like a girl
in a magazine—not a mark on her. Clean and
healthy. And she don't think about anything. Not
much anyway. Not anymore.

Listen to me, Bob. You got nothing, right? You
got a rented room, you got a Momma somewhere if
she ain't dead, you got what's inside your head,
which by peeking in through your eyes, those transparent windows of the soul, I can see ain't much.
You have fallen through an American crack, and
them is deep. Whole damn country is mined with
'em, it's like walking over quicksand, open up and
swallow a young man quick as say howdy want
some pancakes. You got trouble. Trouble is my

experteeze. I majored in trouble at a major university. We are talking English, *capish? Comprendo?* This isn't *sound.* This is the straight skinny, no tricks, no figure it out later, no get it in your dreams. This is get it now and take it home.

Me and Linda are here. That's fortuitous. Good graces is what you're in, friend. God loves you, and I could learn. So could Linda.

FABER: What makes you think you can come over here and say all this shit to me?

TIM: I gotta license. You wanna see it?

FABER: Do you think I'm stupid? That I'm gonna let the two of you just take my. . . .

TIM: No. You're not stupid. You had some bad luck is all. 'Scuse me, buddy. Look her over whiles I take a dump. I'll be back with ya shortly.

[TIM *exits into the bathroom.* LINDA *comes over and sits with* FABER.]

LINDA: Hello.

FABER: Hello. You, uh, come from around here?

LINDA: Sure. Sure I do. Right around here. I come from right here.

FABER: What do you do? I mean, what do you *do?* You work?

LINDA: I am *intending* to get work, so I can fuck who I like. I sing here for the hell of it. It doesn't pay. As they say, poverty sucks, but then, employment ain't much better. That's a bind, Mister.

FABER: Where do you live?

LINDA: With Timmy. But it's filthy. I have plans to get ahold of some amphetamines, and take 'em with a broom and a box of Brillo nearby.

Timmy's nuts, you know. He's here somewhere, 'less he left. He knows I can find my way back, so he doesn't have to stay, you know.

[CHUCKLES *enters, goes behind the bar, where he seems to be employed as bartender. He listens.*]

You know what love can do? Rip you to shit, then come upside your head with a two by four and knock what's left of you right into the street. Think so?

FABER: Yeah. I know so.

LINDA: Everything Tim told you about me is a bunch of lying shit. You know that?

FABER: I. . . .

LINDA: I mean, he thinks I exist only for him. When I go out into the hallway and slam the door behind me, he thinks I dissolve in the corridor before I get to the stairs. I reconstitute myself a moment before I come into his presence. Now you know that's not true, cause I'm here, and he's not . . . aren't I?

FABER: Yeah, you are.

LINDA: Touch me so you're sure.

FABER: I'm sure.

LINDA: Touch me, dammit.

[*FABER touches her.*]

FABER: Your hand is hot.

LINDA: No. Yours is cold. You're freezing. You're going below zero, with the negative numbers. You wanna buy me a drink?

FABER: Sure.

LINDA: [*to* CHUCKLES] I'll have a shot of wild turkey, black coffee, and a glass of water, please.

[CHUCKLES *looks around confusedly behind the bar to*

fill her order. To FABER.*]* Do I have lipstick on my teeth?

FABER: As a matter of fact, yeah. A little.

LINDA: Would you wipe it off? Use your finger.

[He does so. She catches his finger in her mouth, sucks on it gently, then suddenly bites hard. FABER *leaps away.]*

FABER: Owww!

*[*TIM *opens the men's room door, heads toward them.]*

TIM: She's cute. Don't pay attention to her now, Bob. She's not yours yet. No deal yet. Listen to me. You're here for a reason, right? You're a man in need. Am I right? I mean, you can tell me, us, you can tell us because we are nothing but need. We desire everything. You name it, we want it, and we want it bad. Hey, I'm talking to you, buddy. Hey, I'm asking you a question.

FABER: I wasn't listening.

TIM: Some people think their ears just hang there and work all by themselves. You know a smart guy can take his ears off and put 'em in his pocket in Guatemala or something. But that don't matter, Bob, cause you're full of shit on this one, and I say that with *conviction.* You were straining to hear me, like a kid can't take a shit. You been hearing every motherfucking word. Well?

FABER: I want her.

TIM: *[laughs]* You know, Bob, you and me we're gonna be friends. In fact, Bob, we're friends right now. What's your name? Shhhh. Don't tell me. What's a little name between friends. What's your offer? You keep sleeping alone, friend, you die inside. What you can buy by the hour ain't worth the chump

change you lay out for it. That is not heat to warm
you. You are a man who can smell true love when
it's coming down the street, you can smell it coming
to you cross the rivers and seas, its odor mixing
with the salt spray and the quick perfume of the flying fish. You know it—when it's sitting right here
alongside you. Gimme something. For Linda. All
you got. She's worth it. . . .

    [A long silence. FABER *doesn't move or speak.]* You
wanna play, but you don't wanna pay. This is true
of everyone. The piper will pipe till the gates of
dawn, drag your dancing body along, but you gotta
pay at the end of the road. *[sings]* "I ain't the devil
or the devil's son, but I can be the devil till the devil
come . . ." Well? After tonight, I won't be around to
fix you.

FABER: No deal.

TIM: Well, whaddaya know. Bright boy, maybe. Might
not have worked out too well for you, in the long
run. I coulda pressed you harder—but hell, why
hook you? Maybe you'll meet me again someday,
and I don't want no bad blood between us. I surely
don't. Come on, Linda. Let's go.

    *[*TIM *and* LINDA *exit.* FABER *sits alone, then crosses to*
PAULINE *in the motel office as lights fade in the bar.]*

FABER: *[to* PAULINE*]* Funny, hah? What do you think,
Pauline?

PAULINE: I don't know, Mr. Faber. What do you think?

FABER: I think they were extremely quick. Every time
they threw me one I fumbled, tripped, and fell over
in the grass. They had me looking like Mexican
money—with holes in it. They let me off easy.

Jesse Borrego, Stephen McHattie, and Laura Innes in
American Notes
Martha Swope Associates/Carol Rosegg

[A moment's silence.]

PAULINE: Mr. Faber, would you ever think about living here?

FABER: In the motel? Sure. Forever.

PAULINE: You know what I mean. It's not as slow here as it looks. Things happen, but kind of one at a time, like. . . . Are you interested in this?

FABER: It's not really coming through at the moment, Pauline. Maybe you should try something else.

PAULINE: O.K. . . . You know the high school a few miles down the road? Around this time of year we bring in a carnival, the VFW does it actually, and they move right onto the football field. It might be there right now.

FABER: So?

PAULINE: What do you mean, so?

FABER: So, what, uh, follows?

PAULINE: Nothing. Just a story.

FABER: Pauline, you gotta be more interesting. I mean to press this point here. Don't you wanna do things, or make things, or be what you read about in books, or see on your TV there? I mean, you could get where you feel O.K. cause you do this or that and other people think it's hot shit. Hey, keep humping back there behind the desk and you gonna turn into a zombie, Pauline. This place gonna be the Zombieland Motel. Tourists welcome.

PAULINE: What do you think I should do? I'm happy here, Mr. Faber, I think. I'm hardly ever bored. I got so many things I. . . .

FABER: That's cause you got a TV there, Pauline, for when you kind of hit a heavy patch of nothing.

PAULINE: I don't want to have an argument with you. Sure, sometimes I watch the late. . . .

FABER: TV's a little strange, isn't it? A tiny, lit–up, twisted replica of everything, that's trying to eliminate our world, and take its place.

PAULINE: Mr. Faber, you probably never worked nights. The TV helps pass the time.

    [Silence. CHUCKLES *enters, cleaning.]*

FABER: I been meaning to ask you. Who's that?

PAULINE: Him? He's just some guy. *[*PAULINE *laughs.]* That's Chuckles. He works around the place. He sleeps here somewhere, nobody really knows where.

FABER: Chuckles, hah?

PAULINE: Someone named him that. He doesn't talk. Except to say the motel motto. I think the owner taught him. Chuckles! The motto!

CHUCKLES: *[In a panic, articulating as best he can.]* We're easy to get to, but hard to leave.

    *[*CHUCKLES *exits.]*

PAULINE: We're easy to get to, but hard to leave. You like the coffee?

FABER: Yeah. Uh, you like the whiskey I put in it?

PAULINE: Yeah, warms you up.

FABER: Have some more, Pauline.

PAULINE: O.K. But just a bit. . . . *[He pours.]* Do you have someone, Mr. Faber? You know, like a wife. Or a girlfriend. You know . . . someone.

FABER: You ask a lot of questions, Pauline.

PAULINE: I'm just curious. It's the only way you can find things out.

FABER: I had someone. About a year ago she left me, her

and the kid and everything. I came in late one night, and I'd had a few, and I crawled into bed alongside her, and I'm out. Next thing I knew I hear a crash, open one eye, clock says 6 A.M. I get up and go into the front room, and there she is with her girlfriend Myra, and the kid is already in Myra's old Chevy, and so is all their clothes and stuff, but they can't get the kid's crib through the front door. It was their trying that woke me. I'm standing there naked, looking at her like a dying calf in a hailstorm, and she doesn't even blink. She bends over the crib again and tries to force it through. I wasn't mad. I felt funny and sad seeing her do that. It made me see how she saw me, you know, and that wasn't pretty, but it wasn't true.

I walked over to the door, and sat down next to the crib and started taking it apart. Only took ten minutes. Once I did it, she got it out of there and was gone. She didn't even say thank you. She wouldn't even let the kid kiss me goodbye. I saw her a few times after that, but it was like seeing someone else. So after a while, I just got up and left there. I had the car, and some money, so like I say, I just left. You think I did right, Pauline?

PAULINE: I don't know, Mr. Faber. I don't even know you.

FABER: Good as anyone, Pauline.

PAULINE: I couldn't tell if. . . .

FABER: I been here a week, Pauline, cause I don't know whether to go. Or where. I got some money. You want some money? How much would you like?

PAULINE: I can't take your money.

FABER: I'm serious here, Pauline. No difference to me if it's in my pocket or not. Either way, something's gonna happen. Take it all.

[FABER takes out all his money, including change, and dumps it on PAULINE'S desk.]

PAULINE: Mr. Faber! Stop! I wouldn't take any money from you, unless I earned it or something.

FABER: You already did that, Pauline.

PAULINE: Coffee's only forty cents, Mr. Faber, and this one was on the house.

FABER: I don't mean the coffee, Pauline.

PAULINE: I know what you mean. Take back your money. *[FABER takes up the money, puts it back in his pockets.]*

You're probably forgetting a lot of things, Mr. Faber.

FABER: I'm remembering a lot, Pauline.

PAULINE: I think you're forgetting.

FABER: You know more about me than me, Pauline? Are we having an argument here?

PAULINE: I wouldn't call it that.

FABER: What would you call it?

[A long silence between them.]

PAULINE: You know what? I don't know why I think this, but I do. I think, even after all you told me, that somehow you're a lucky person.

FABER: You do? Well, maybe I am. Then I don't have to worry, do I? Cause if my luck holds, pretty soon someone's bound to come up behind me and slit my throat.

PAULINE: There's not a lot to say to that, is there? Except that I hope it doesn't happen.

FABER: Do you?

PAULINE: Yes, Mr. Faber, I do.

> [*Silence.* PAULINE *picks up a book, reads. More silence. Then. . . .*]

> What are doges?

FABER: Doges? What are you doing, the crossword puzzle?

PAULINE: I got a poem to read for my lit class. It's a word in the poem.

FABER: I don't know.

PAULINE: They surrender.

FABER: Who?

PAULINE: The doges. Doges surrender.

FABER: Let's hear it, Pauline.

PAULINE: What?

FABER: The poem.

PAULINE: Safe in their alabaster chambers
> Untouched by morning and untouched by
>> Noon
> Lie the meek members of the resurrection
> Rafter of satin, and roof of stone.
> More?

FABER: Yeah. The doges didn't come in yet.

PAULINE: Grand go the years in the crescent above them
> Worlds scoop their arcs and firmaments row
> Diadems drop, and doges surrender
> Soundless as dots on a disc of snow.

FABER: Yeah.

PAULINE: You like it?

FABER: Yeah. I like it. I like you reading it.

PAULINE: What about the doges?

FABER: Not a clue, Pauline. It's a mystery.

[Long silence. The phone rings. PAULINE *picks it up.]*
PAULINE: Office.

[Lights up on KAREN *in her room. She's on the phone.]*

KAREN: Hey, Pauline, what time you got?
PAULINE: About . . . 3 A.M.
KAREN: Three A.M.? Are these nights getting longer or what?
PAULINE: I don't know.
KAREN: Me neither. . . . Long as I got you here, why don't you give me my messages. Reel 'em off.
PAULINE: I'm afraid there. . . .
KAREN: Please don't sound so damn sorry.

*[*KAREN *hangs up her phone, and* PAULINE *follows suit. Lights fade on* KAREN, PAULINE *and* FABER *as they come up on* CHUCKLES *and the* MAYOR *at the* MAYOR's *place in the field near town.* CHUCKLES *is sitting in the dirt, listening.]*

MAYOR: A Mayor's got a lot of responsibilities here, bitty buddy. You think I can put in time on cartography and transportation for every travelling boy comes through looking for where else and wherever? I got duties, bitty buddy. Duties. I got to shave every three days. I got to think about everybody all at once, including dead people, plus perambulations and looking around in present time so everybody round here can step sweetly into the future foot by foot, which they do every day thank you to God, good fortune, and the help of a few little doings I do here and there. The point is, Chuckles, my boy, we walk a fine line—between yesterday and tomorrow, between nothing and nothing. You can step right off the log. We don't wanna go down in flames here, do we bitty buddy?

This is amazing country. Sea to shining. . . . I'll tell you what it is. It's fertile. I was on my way out the door one day, little buddy of mine, about to take my mayoral constitutional, had a handful of pumpkin seeds to munch on the road. I turn around to wave goodbye to the wife and kids, and one seed fell outta my hand. Before I could turn back around that seed had taken root in the earth, sprouted up and spread so high and wide that I was dangerously surrounded by enormous serpentine vines, caught in their green clutches. The volunteer fire department had to break out the axes and cut me loose. *[The* MAYOR *pauses, remembers . . .]* Chuckles? You got a shovel, little buddy? I wanna go down to the dump, dig up that crocodile.

CHUCKLES: Splish splash?

MAYOR: Listen up now. You can have the head, the tail, and the part in the middle. *[*CHUCKLES *thinks, then looks questioningly at the* MAYOR.*]* All I wants is the heart. That roll of white fat around the heart of a dragon is good for the pecker. Puts lead in the pencil, woo boy!

CHUCKLES: Dragon?

MAYOR: Dragon, crocodile, allygrabber, same thing. You know, little brother, in the spring them dragons fly high and bring the rain. After harvest time they go down and coil in the depths of the sea. Friend of mine rose up to heaven on a red dragon, escorted by blue mice. Right here in town. By the way, you *still* want to get moving?

[CHUCKLES *nods, looks pleadingly at the* MAYOR.]

Well, you are stupid, but you're not dumb. Listen up. Where you're thinking you maybe wanna be is prob'ly west of here somewheres, you head out past the junction, up by the Shell station, hang a right by the tomb of the Holy Apostle Thomas, pass the railroad yards, left at the tower of Babel and straight on, feet on the white line and a smile on your face.

Dangerous journey to who knows where. You might be shipwrecked, more than once. Now, if *I* was *you*, I'd stick around here a while. You ain't seen nothing here yet. This is interesting country. Look around. Hey . . . you want a little of this stuff . . . I brewed some up special for ya.

[MAYOR *takes out flask, gives some to* CHUCKLES . . . *he drinks . . .]* Hey, you gotta get back to work. . . .

[CHUCKLES *remembers his job. He panics, rushes off. Lights up on* KAREN *in her motel room. The* MAYOR *calls after* CHUCKLES.]

Relax. There's the girl in 7. She's not going anywhere, is she?—not yet. She's waiting.

[KAREN'S *room. Liquor bottles, full of ashtrays, clothes everywhere. A sudden loud knock at the door.* KAREN *turns joyfully toward it. It opens, and* CHUCKLES *steps hesitantly inside, his arms full of toilet paper and towels.]*

KAREN: *[Screaming.]* GET OUT!

[CHUCKLES exits, *terrified.* KAREN *shakes out a cigarette, lights it.]*

[V.O.] These nights are definitely getting longer. Winter's coming. *[LIVE]* Fucking ice age. *[V.O.]*

Let's review the facts here, Karen darling. Raised in back of the Hi-Hat Tavern, down the street from Marty's Broiler and the Key Motel. That was a while ago, Karen darling, and now its getting a little late in the afternoon here. . . . *[LIVE]* I almost got married once. Right out of high school. He dumped me. I had to sit up for two nights picking his name outta my cheerleader jacket. Tick tock. Tick.

[KAREN turns on her radio. Music. She dances. The REPORTER appears in another space. He dances.]

REPORTER: You dance to this kinda music?

KAREN: *[Live]* Fluently—and we go from there. *[V.O.]* After a few hours, I notice he's actually listening to what I'm saying, and I say to myself, uh oh Karen girl, here's trouble and I like it. *[LIVE]* Asshole. God I shoulda just run something on him, taken his money, gone to the ladies, and disappeared. Next day, go shopping.

[V.O.] My grandma used to tell me, Karen sweetheart, keep away from cigarette smokers who show up under your window after midnight and play the banjo. Tick tock. Tick. Pay more attention you wouldn't end up waiting for someone you hardly know in some kinda lima bean hell here. . . . Even your own pain grows boring.

[LIVE] Fine. Where we at? Nighttime. And up above, the stars, little lit windows of the dead's town, where all the dead sit around being dead. Hey, you, Mr. Stupid! You don't know what you got here. You got a full size, moderately fucked up person here, and I have a lot of potential. What's the matter, hah? I'm not as good looking as those nine-

teen year olds. *[She goes over to the mirror, looks in.]* Bullshit. All right, some of it's missing, but most of it's there. Are you aware, Mister Not Here, that I am a model? *[V.O.]* Correction. Was a model. I was sixteen. I did catalogues. In my last year of high school I did Penney's for the whole state. *[LIVE]* I got the pictures. *[V.O.]* In a trunk somewheres. Maybe in my mother's house, if she didn't throw 'em away. . . .

[There's a knock at the door. She rushes over to answer it, pulls it open. CHUCKLES *is standing there again, his arms full of toilet paper, ready to change the roll. She stares at him.* CHUCKLES *doesn't move.]*

Come right on in. *[*CHUCKLES *goes through the room into the bathroom, strands of toilet paper trailing behind him.]* Care for a cocktail?

*[*CHUCKLES *peers out a moment, looks questioningly at her, goes back to work.* KAREN *waits for him to leave. He emerges, and while she's turned away, he leaves a badly crushed candy bar by her telephone. He walks toward the door, stops a moment and looks at her.]*

KAREN: Thanks, I guess.

CHUCKLES: *[mimes wiping his ass and nods vigorously]* We're easy to get to, but hard to leave.

[He waves goobye to her. He exits.]

KAREN: *[V.O.]* Where was I? *[LIVE]* Who the hell knows. *[*KAREN *notices the candy bar, picks it up. She looks back toward the door. V.O.]* Oh my God . . . am I that piti-ful? *[LIVE]* Snickers. Looks like it's been in his pocket in a heat wave. *[She tosses the crushed candy bar into a corner. V.O.]* Three days in this hole. Waiting's just like being dead, except you still have to pass the time. *[LIVE. Sings.]* "I will sing you a song of the New Jerusalem, that far away home of the soul. . . ." *[V.O.]* That's all I remember. *[LIVE]* Facts. He's late, *[V.O.]* he's very late, *[LIVE]* but he's on his way, knowing I'd wait forever, that I'd be here . . . *[V.O.]* . . . staring out the window for him till my eyes become two tiny swamps where moss floats, till my lips are food for crows, till deep in the grass grown up through this crumbling floor, my white bones rot.

    [LIVE] Fuck that. Hell, he'll probably show up any minute, with a hard-on and a mouth full of sorry. *[A moment's silence]* You know, after a while, you wait long enough, you say to yourself, well, actually, this is it. This is my life. Not what's gonna happen, but now. I'm here.

    *[*KAREN *is still. Lights come up on* PAULINE *and* FABER *as before, in the motel office.* PAULINE *is reading a book.* FABER *sits. In another area, lights up on the* REPORTER. *He's walking through a field: mud, trees. He carries a camera, notebook. He stops, turns to the audience.]*

REPORTER: I'm freelance. I take what I can get. My current employers, an association of screwballs known as *Flying Saucer News*, has been running me into the ground. I been over half the state in the last three days. Three days. Damn. I gotta remember the name of that motel I left her in so's I can call. I been trying, but it won't come to me. I can find it, I know the town. . . . Hell, she'll be there. She could tell I was . . . you know, sometimes you get another chance. You think you'll never get another chance, and God gives you another chance. I'm gonna need some loving after this ring of loons I been chasing.

The job? Photo stories on three reported sightings. First one was a group of housewives who claimed they witnessed the levitation of an entire shopping mall by alien beings. If that sounds like one valium too many—check. Number two was a Mex ranch hand who was shearing sheeps up country, and got taken aboard a big one. Got him up there stripped naked as a chicken and put him in a room with a space girl, looked like Marilyn Monroe in silver spandex, but bald and with gills like a fish. He claims they wanted him for breeding purposes. I expect he had a real vivid dream out on the prairie. Number three? This one's an ex-professor, lives in the farmhouse up ahead. Once I finish with him, it's pick up Karen, and hit the road. . . .

[The REPORTER *turns away, continues walking as lights dim on him, brighten on* PAULINE *and* FABER *in the motel office. The radio plays quietly.]*

FABER: Pauline, would you . . . could you sing me a song?

PAULINE: *[laughs]* I can't sing.

FABER: That's a lie, Pauline.

PAULINE: O.K. I *won't.* You wouldn't want to hear it, Mr. Faber, believe me.

FABER: You're wrong there, Pauline. I'd like it.

PAULINE: I don't know any songs.

FABER: You must know *one* song, Pauline, the one you learned in the third grade, where everybody stood in a row. Sing it, and I'll be sitting here much happier, I think.

PAULINE: I'm not responsible for your happiness, Mr.
   Faber.

FABER: Yes you are, Pauline, and I'm responsible for
   yours.

   [A silence]

PAULINE: We didn't stand in a row. We sat in a circle.

   *[FABER reaches over and turns off the radio. PAULINE
   sings, very quietly and simply.]*

      Down in the valley, valley so low
      Late in the evening, hear the train blow
      Roses love sunshine, violets love dew
      Angels in heaven, know I love you
      Down in the meadow, down on my knees
      Praying to heaven, give my heart ease
      Give my heart ease, love, give my heart ease
      Praying to heaven, give my heart ease. . . .

   That's all I know. *[FABER applauds solemnly.]* Are
   you making fun of me?

FABER: I am extremely serious here, Pauline.

PAULINE: Good, cause I'd like you to consider something,
   Mr. Faber. This conversation is not just your conversation with me. This is our conversation, Mr. Faber,
   and now it's your turn. Sing.

FABER: I can't sing, Pauline.

PAULINE: That's what I said, Mr. Faber.

   *[FABER, with much hesitancy, begins to sing some
   romantic ballad poorly. He stops.]*

FABER: *[Sings much louder, and bangs on the chair in
   rhythm.]*

      Let's twist again, like we did last summer
      Yeah, let's twist again, like we did last year

Do you remember when, we were really
    humming
C'mon, let's twist again, twisting time is
    here. . . .

PAULINE: Shhhh. . . . You'll wake everybody up.

FABER: All the customers are wide awake, Pauline. One
is upstairs walking the floor, and the other one is
me. [FABER *stands, and twists, along with very loud
singing.*]

Round and round and up and down we
    goooooo again
Baby let me know, you love me so, and then . . .
Let's twist again, like we. . . .

PAULINE: STOP!

[FABER *stops singing abruptly.*]

FABER: What kind of lipstick is that you got on, Pauline?
Flamingo pink? Tangerine blush?

PAULINE: I'm not wearing any lipstick.

FABER: What kind of perfume you wearing? Lily of the
Valley? Tiger Musk? Orange Blossom Special?

PAULINE: I'm not wearing any perfume.

FABER: I smell something, Pauline.

PAULINE: Maybe it's my shampoo.

FABER: Answer me something, Pauline. What kind of
shampoo?

PAULINE: Apple something . . . with keratin, whatever
that is. Why are you interested in. . . .

FABER: That's private stuff I'm asking about, Pauline.
You buy it in the supermarket, but you rub it right
on your body. Have a drink. [*Takes out bottle.*]

PAULINE: I think I've had enough.

FABER: The last one. . . .

[PAULINE *still refuses.* FABER *refills his own. The bottle is empty.*] We got a dead soldier here. [*He drops the bottle in the trash.*]

PAULINE: You know, Mr. Faber, I've been thinking about what you said, about me sort of . . . doing more. Maybe moving away to a bigger place or something. I mean, if my Mom is. . . .

FABER: Don't blame me, Pauline.

PAULINE: Blame you?

FABER: One day ten years from now you're lying face down on a cot in some furnished room, crying into your pillow—and you remember. It was me told you to leave the bosom of your home and family. You hurry down to Woolworth's and buy one of those fat black magic markers and you go out to the graveyard and write insulting remarks all over my lily-white headstone.

PAULINE: That's an ugly story. And it's a lie. You won't be dead in ten years, and I won't be in a room somewhere crying.

FABER: You know the future, Pauline? Should hang a sign on your desk, LIFE READING, TEN BUCKS. You got gypsy blood?

PAULINE: I don't know. May be.

FABER: Maybe you do. [*silence*] You know, Pauline, I am convinced that for miles around, at this moment, we are the only creatures with their eyes open. The little raccoons and squirrels and stuff in the woods, they're all sleeping, and the people too, all snug in their beds, whole sky over the town is thick with dreams. . . .

PAULINE: [*looks at her watch*] Mr. Mason opens the Snack

Shop by the Trailways stop by six, so he's probably up now. And Dexter. He drew the graveyard shift this month, so he's. . . .

FABER: Pauline? I'd like to mention something here. It doesn't matter who the fuck is actually awake, or asleep, or dead. I'm talking about a feeling.

PAULINE: I'm talking about the facts.

FABER: You getting a little sarcastic here, Pauline?

PAULINE: Yes. You've been confusing me, Mr. Faber. And scaring me . . . a little.

FABER: I don't want to do that. I didn't mean to do that. *[a silence]* We're a bunch of poor bastards here, Pauline. Roam the planet like starving dogs, and never get it right. Find any little scrap of something in this world and it's thank God and step careful, cause you're likely to lose that too.

You spend a lot of nights talking to the itinerant sleepers, Pauline. The sleepwalkers. Whatta they have to say on the subject?

PAULINE: You're the only one who ever. . . .

FABER: Maybe you don't hear them cause your pretty head falls over and you sleep at the desk, and all the storytellers can't bear to wake you, so they keep it to themselves and tiptoe by.

PAULINE: I don't think so, Mr. Faber. Sometimes I do get sleepy, but I always wake myself, cause what if a car pulls in, and I'm sleeping with my head on the desk, like this. *[Does so.]* How does that look, to someone coming in, I mean?

FABER: I don't know. Looks all right to me.

PAULINE: *[sitting up]* It does not. I do all kinds of things to keep awake. Homework, the radio . . . You know, sometimes I just think about what might happen to me . . . if I'll ever get married, or even finish college and find some kind of interesting job. I think about my Mom, and start feeling sad for her and all. Then sometimes I go outside and sit in one of those lawn chairs in front of the office and just wait for it to get light. It happens real slow, so you have to slow yourself down to it or you get bored, cause it takes a few hours. When the first edge of the sun is up, I go back inside and make coffee. It can get real cold out there. Once I did that in the snow. I just kept shaking it off me, and walking around to get warm. I couldn't really tell when the sun came up. The snow was dirty gray in the dark and became white. The sky just got lighter and lighter—till it was light. *[PAULINE glances over to a corner, then jumps suddenly.]* Oooooh! Did you see it?

FABER: What?

PAULINE: A mouse. I'm sure I saw a. . . . There it goes!

> *[CHUCKLES bursts into the room, a broom raised over his head. He's trying wildly to kill the mouse or drive it away.]*

CHUCKLES: Meece! No!

> *[Suddenly, CHUCKLES sprawls to the floor. He stares around him desperately. Silence. The mouse seems to be gone. FABER silently points into a corner. The mouse! CHUCKLES is up, and rushing after it, swinging the broom wildly.]*

PAULINE: Chuckles! Stop! Don't hurt it!

> *[CHUCKLES doesn't hear her in his passion. He corners the mouse, and energetically smashes it.]*

CHUCKLES: Meece! Little meece! No!

[CHUCKLES *holds up the dead mouse by the tail. He speaks to it.*]

We're easy to get to, but hard to leave!

[CHUCKLES *pockets the dead mouse, and exits.* FABER *looks after him.*]

FABER: You know, this place looks ordinary from the outside. . . . [PAULINE *laughs.*] You ever feel there's strange things going on here. . . .

PAULINE: Strange things? Like a mouse? Or us talking?

FABER: I don't know. [*a long silence*] Last few weeks, I've seen a lot of dreams with my eyes open, just riding down the road. I drive through these towns, one after the other, and they all got a main street, and on it is a place to buy groceries, Food Town—a place to eat, Marv's Broiler—and a place to get fucked-up, Hi-Hat Tavern. And when you go through these places in America, the question is always "Anybody home?" The answer is obvious. No. Basically, there is nobody home in America, Pauline. Except you.

[*Again, a long silence between them.*]

There are people out there, after all. They go way back, and they came outta the sky and the dirt, just like us. And they got secrets, just like us. Right now, *at this moment,* in this town, everybody's waking up in their beds, eyes pop open, night still outside the window, and they rise up, and dress. There they go. There's the mailman scampering along Main Street, and the delivery boy, and the girl who works the checkout counter, and old Mr. Mason, slipping outta that ranch house. There's another, behind the Shell Station, and there's another in the river, in an ivory boat being hauled by a pair of

huge catfish, past green lily pads awash with
flames, and there's your Mom in a red dress dancing across the village green, all of them crawling
and prancing and snorting towards the woods outside of town, to a little clearing in a ring of trees.
They're out there, under the moon. Rumble and
bumble in the dark! Hop down! Jump up! Spin
around, and old Mr. Mason and a teenage girl from
the high school whirl round and round in the center, naked as jaybirds, and his fat belly wheezes in
and out with the pipes. . . . Know that tune? *[sings]*
O beautiful, for spacious skies, for amber . . . waves
. . . Look! They're all calling to you, Pauline, calling
for you to join them. But you're here talking to
Faber, and you forgot. They all got their party hats
on, Pauline, and you're the only one whose head is
bare. Go on. I'll mind the store.

PAULINE: There's no one out there, Mr. Faber. They're
home in bed.

FABER: Maybe so, Pauline. Maybe so.

[PAULINE *and* FABER *are quiet. Lights up on the* PRO-
FESSOR'S *house in the woods, somewhere in America.
Piles of books and papers, some of which are in cartons.
Strange electronic equipment. Arcane maps and charts.
A telephone. The* PROFESSOR *is packing. The* REPORTER *is
approaching. He stops, turns to the audience.]*

REPORTER: Funny. The closer I get to this professor's
place, the stranger I feel, sort of gloomy and
nervous at once, like I'm coming down off something. . . . Hell, maybe it's the air, seems kinda damp
or. . . . Well! Here we are.

[A *dog howls, loudly and suddenly, unnerving the*

REPORTER *for a moment.]* Coming along? Let's see how
the old duck is doing. Yoo hoo! Anybody home?

[The PROFESSOR *unlocks the door, opens it a crack.
Strange atonal music begins, softly.]*

PROFESSOR: *[loud]* Did you bring the pizza? You from
Pizza Hut?

REPORTER: *[after hesitating]* You order a large pepperoni
with anchovies and a diet coke?

PROFESSOR: Exactly. Come in, come in.

[The REPORTER *enters, and the* PROFESSOR *quickly
shuts the door and locks it behind him.]*

REPORTER: Professor, why are we playing charades?

PROFESSOR: Act normally, please. All your questions will
be answered in time. *[The* PROFESSOR *nervously looks
out the window, then back to the room.]* You are from
Flying Saucer News?

REPORTER: Yeah. You know something? I just remembered the name of a motel I gotta call. Can I use
your phone?

PROFESSOR: I told you in my letter. To the magazine. I
don't have a phone.

REPORTER: *[pointing to the phone]* What's that? A ding-
dong school phone?

PROFESSOR: The wires are down. They haven't come to
repair them in months. They get too many flat tires.

REPORTER: What the hell are you talking about?

[Loud noises from outside. CHUCKLES *bursts into the
room, panicked and upset. The body of a dog, wrapped in
a bloody towel, is in his arms.]*

CHUCKLES: Dead dog.

[The PROFESSOR *puts an arm around* CHUCKLES'
shoulder to comfort him. . . .]

PROFESSOR: Bury him in the garden. Next to the other one. I'll write the pound. This time, we'll get a dog so big that. . . . *[to the* REPORTER*]* This is Chuckles. He helps around the place. Chuckles, this is the man from the magazine. *[They shake hands awkwardly. To* CHUCKLES.*]* Keep packing! *[*CHUCKLES *exits. To* REPORTER.*]* Shouldn't you be taking notes?

REPORTER: My memory's sharp as a tack, professor.

PROFESSOR: Where were we?

REPORTER: Let's see if I have this right. You said in your letter that some kind of invisible creatures are out there in the woods, and you been talking to them.

PROFESSOR: In a word, yes.

REPORTER: If we *could* see them, what would they look like?

PROFESSOR: Like men . . . and women.

REPORTER: And you think they're from earth? Or Mars? Or outer space?

PROFESSOR: They come originally from the place of broken shells, a great sea of psychic debris from previous worlds, worlds that failed . . . a sort of spiritual version of the asteroid belt.

REPORTER: O.K. Moving right along. You might as well hit me with the rest of it.

PROFESSOR: *[pause]* The rest of it is . . . less theoretical. I left the doors open, so they could go freely, in and out. I was friendly, genial. They liked Chuckles. I won them over. They came when I called, drifting out of the woods. They guided me, taught me. . . . A man should marry for love. Don't you think so, Mister Reporter?

REPORTER: I know so.

PROFESSOR: I did. I married one of them. A woman of the shadow people. I loved her as I'd never been able to love one of us. She was devoted, at first, but she became unruly. Sexually demanding. She behaved badly. I couldn't help it. I had to. . . .

REPORTER: Go on. . . .

PROFESSOR: I locked her in the closet. She's extremely clever. She escaped, and fled back to them. They were furious. They told me to leave at once. Their speech, by the way, is a kind of gurgling, like a brook over stones. These last few days, they grow more malicious. She has inflamed them against me. They wait around the house, in the trees.

    You know, she never really loved me. They don't. . . . I have to leave here. . . . I'm a pauper. I'm unemployable. Perhaps I'll be hospitalized. . . .

    But I must go. You see, they'll kill me. I know they will. I have to tell the truth before they stop me. *They* explain everything. Parapsychology, mental illness, war, religion. The whole banana. They don't want their secrets known. Would you? Are you frightened?

REPORTER: No.

PROFESSOR: You should be. You can't hurt them, you know. And they won't die.

REPORTER: Why don't you just apologize to your . . . wife? For locking her in the closet. Make it up to her. Let them know you. . . .

PROFESSOR: She was wicked. She deserved punishment. You don't believe any of this, do you? *[The* PROFESSOR *goes over to a tape recorder.]* Proof positive! Their voices. . . . *[He presses "Play." The sound of a loud harsh bubbling and gurgling fills the room. Then suddenly the tape recorder begins to smoke, then bursts into flames.]* Damn them. You want more proof? Wait here.

[CHUCKLES enters with a pile of papers in his hands.]

Talk to Chuckles. He may be insane, but he's not dumb.

[The PROFESSOR exits. CHUCKLES stares at the REPORTER.]

REPORTER: What the hell is going on here? *[CHUCKLES begins packing.]* You all nuts or something? Look, I can take a joke, but. . . .

CHUCKLES: Go away. Go!

REPORTER: What's going on?

[CHUCKLES picks up some scattered papers, rushes out of the room as the PROFESSOR returns, holding a large plaster cast, with some odd markings on it.]

PROFESSOR: Their marks. Proof positive.

REPORTER: That could be a plaster cast of anything. A child could have made those prints, or you, or a tree branch, or . . . anything could have done this.

PROFESSOR: Anything didn't. The shadow people did.

REPORTER: I can't take anymore of this. There's a very visible woman waiting for me in a motel room, and I got to get back to her before she disappears. Goodbye, Professor, and good luck.

PROFESSOR: *[barring his way]* NO! Listen to me. Please. Write the story. Besides, you can't go. Out there, in the mood they're in, they may hurt you . . . or worse. They don't like the light as well as the dark. Wait until morning.

REPORTER: You should get some kind of help, you know that?

PROFESSOR: I know that. You are the help I was hoping to
    get.
REPORTER: I'm leaving.
PROFESSOR: It's your life.
REPORTER: Yeah. It is.
PROFESSOR: Chuckles! Let him out.

> [CHUCKLES *appears, unlocks the door for the* RE-
> PORTER, *who exits.* CHUCKLES *watches him go. A scream
> from outside. The* PROFESSOR *rushes to the window. The
> curtains stir in a sudden wind. They both stare out in
> panic, then slowly turn away.*]

> They've killed him. His body is lying there. . . .

> [*In the distance, what could be the sound of a car, or
> the wind, or . . .* CHUCKLES *listens.*]

CHUCKLES: [*mimes driving*] Brmmmmmm. Brmmmmmm.
PROFESSOR: No. That sound—the shadow people crying
    to each other in the trees. . . .

> They'll rush the house, I know it. Quick,
> Chuckles, the evidence! [CHUCKLES *hands him the
> plaster cast.*] Distract them while I run for it. They
> won't hurt you. Noises! [*The* PROFESSOR *grabs the reel
> of tape off the recorder.*] Now! [CHUCKLES, *frightened,
> begins to bang his hands together, then two pots, stamp
> his feet, make whatever noise he can.*] Goodbye.

> [*The* PROFESSOR *rushes out the door, leaving it open
> behind him. He's gone.* CHUCKLES *remains, making noise,
> hopping up and down in fear and panic. An electric flash,
> and the lights go out.* CHUCKLES' *noise stops for a mo-
> ment. Then it resumes in the darkness, louder and fiercer
> than before. It continues, and fades, as lights come up on*
> KAREN'S *motel room. She is holding a pad and pencil.*]

KAREN: [*V.O., reading what she's written.*] "If you ever

read this, that means you came back, and I'd already left. You think I'd wait around to . . ." *[crosses out, writes]* "You can reach me at . . ." *[crosses out, writes]* "My mom's phone number is 857-6621. I'll call there every day to see if you. . . ." *[She stops writing.]*

[LIVE.] He'll never see this. *[She crumples up the note and throws it in a corner.]*

[V.O.] Now how'm I gonna make it outta this hole. Paying the tab and leaving like a lady is out of the question. *[She begins to pack her suitcase.]*

[LIVE.] Without all this shit I could smile at the girl at the desk, say I'm getting some very fresh air, and hit the highway—but I am taking my worldly possessions. I got a blouse in there I haven't even worn yet.

[V.O.] O.K. Downstairs, suitcase in hand, deal with the girl at the desk, and hope she doesn't reach for the phone.

[LIVE. CHUCKLES, *in another space, dim light, listening.* KAREN *rehearses her pitch to* PAULINE.]* "Listen, Pauline, honey, I got in a bind. This can happen to a girl sometimes and if you don't know it yet, you will. Now I didn't find a window and stiff the place, did I? I'm right here in front of you. And you know why I'm standing here?

The cops? I'd be long gone. . . .

I don't give a shit about whoever owns this joint. I'm here cause I was concerned about you. If I skipped, it might come outta your salary. I couldn't stand the idea of fucking over another working girl. So what I got to say is this, and I'm saying please.

I will send you the money. That's the God's own truth. Soon as I get work, I will send you the money for the entire bill. Gimme the bill. I want it. It's got the address on it? Good. Pauline, some day if you hit a rough patch, I hope someone treats you the way you're treating me. Now listen honey, I want you to look at something. . . .

[Lights dim out on CHUCKLES *in the other space.* KAREN *takes a piece of costume jewelry out of her suitcase.]*

[LIVE.] My mother gave it to me. It's worth a hundred dollars if it's worth a dime. Here. You loan me twenty bucks on it, and when I send in the money for the bill, I'll pay you back and you can. . . . *[V.O.]* Forget the jewelry bit. The rest might go. It'll work. *[LIVE.]* And if it don't, well, what can they do to me that hasn't already been done? All right. It's time to take my old Granny's advice. *[*KAREN *gets into bed, sitting up, wide awake.]* When in trouble, pull down the shades and pay a visit to some other town, where the new girl is a pleasing novelty. *[LIVE and V.O.]* Karen darling, soon as it's light, we go.

[Lights fade on KAREN. *Lights up on* PAULINE *and* FABER *in the motel office.]*

FABER: Pauline—you think you're worth fighting for? If I was with you, I mean, if we were saying all this naked and with my mouth right up against your ear, and a huge gorilla with a baseball bat came up alongside the bed and said Faber get outta there, you gotta fight me first in the parking lot, you think I should just leave—or have it out with him?

PAULINE: Mr. Faber, I think maybe you should just relax and stop talking for a little bit. O.K.?

FABER: Well?

PAULINE: You'd do what you'd do, that's all. Depending.

FABER: Depending on what, Pauline?

PAULINE: A lot of things.

FABER: What things?

PAULINE: Mr. Faber, you're thinking about something that wasn't. And isn't. And won't be.

FABER: I got a tendency, Pauline. To do just that. You know, there's a lot of people who think their life is what happens to them. Get a job, get married, eat an ice cream cone. It's a great life.

There's another kind of people who don't connect what happens to them with their lives at all. Their life is something else . . . hopefully.

Shit. I gotta get out of here. You gonna run out of patience, and I'm gonna run out of money. But— if I just hit the road I'll end up in another place like this one, and for places like this one, this one's fine. What do you think, Pauline?

PAULINE: It doesn't matter much, Mr. Faber. The question is, what do you think?

FABER: I don't know, Pauline. I truly don't. . . . But, hey, I'm trying. . . .

PAULINE: Trying is just trying, Mr. Faber. You've got to *do* something.

FABER: Was that advice, Pauline? Are you telling me how I. . . .

PAULINE: Just forget it, Mr. Faber, O.K. I'm just talking. You got me trying to answer you. You know that? I don't even know what *I* should do.

FABER: Pauline, do you think our life is supposed to be interesting?

PAULINE: *Every moment* doesn't have to be interesting . . . but it is.

FABER: For you.

PAULINE: I don't feel sorry for you, Mr. Faber. I sort of want to, but I don't. I feel like laughing. Not at you. Just laughing.

> *[PAULINE is almost having a fit of giggles, but finally manages to stop herself. FABER stares at her. They sit quietly, as lights come up on the bar, and the carnival lot. In the bar, the TV is on, picture and low sound. TIM and LINDA are hanging out, watching the tube. In the lot, same setting as when we saw Bonecrusher: an enclosure, some carnival lights, but the banner of Egypt is gone. The PITCHMAN, hat on, and a suitcase in his hand, is standing where his chair and microphone used to be. He walks away from the carnival slowly, crosses the stage, and is gone. In the bar, the PROFESSOR enters, carrying his plaster cast. The reel of audio tape is in his pocket, some hanging out. He looks ragged, his clothes torn in places. He sits at the bar.]*

TIM: Hi. My name's Tim. This is Linda. Linda, say hello to the nice man.

LINDA: Hello.

> *[Suddenly, the TV image changes to a close-up of the PROFESSOR. He's on a street somewhere, clearly an interviewee on some sort of local television.]*

PROFESSOR: Turn it up, please. That's me.

> *[TIM turns up the TV sound. TIM, LINDA, and the PROFESSOR watch the show.]*

PROFESSOR ON TV: The shadow people are among us.

They're around us, all the time. They explain everything. Parapsychology, war, mental illness, religion.
They can't control the weather. Or fly. Or raise the
dead. They're very light, you know. The wind can
blow them away. Very light. Very beautiful. Some
say they've always existed, and will exist forever. I
wouldn't say that. Some say they. . . .

TIM: *[TIM reaches up and slaps off the TV. Silence.]* Come on,
Linda. Let's go.

    *[TIM exits. LINDA follows, but before she leaves, she
turns back to the PROFESSOR and the audience.]*

LINDA: Goodbye.

    *[LINDA exits. After a long moment, the PROFESSOR
moves toward the door as the lights dim on the bar, and
on the carnival lot. We return to PAULINE and FABER as
before. A long silence.]*

FABER: So. What do you think, Pauline? You think the
world's gonna end tonight? Twenty ton hypernu-
clear bomb drops right through the roof of the
motel. We're safe in the eye, sitting here in a great
crown of fire, while in the sky, all the dead from all
over America, each one a thin paper of ash—and the
fire dies, and the wind dies, and they float down
from where they been spinning in heaven, drift
down slow and easy, doing their last dead dance in
the air. Then it's quiet, just you, and me. *[CHUCKLES
enters, sweeping quietly. Long pause.]* No comment.
O.K. So. What do you think, Pauline? You think
we're supposed to be happy here?

PAULINE: At the motel?

FABER: You know what I mean.

PAULINE: I think . . . we *are* happy here. That happiness is

another word for our life. That we were made for
joy in everything, even our death.

FABER: Pauline, you hear that in church or somewhere?

PAULINE: No, Mr. Faber. I know it. Cause I saw it.

FABER: It's not a thing you *see*, Pauline.

PAULINE: You're wrong, Mr. Faber . . . I saw it in my
father's eyes before he died. I was standing there,
and he had all these tubes in him, and he was trying
to speak and no one could make out the words.
[CHUCKLES approaches them. He listens.] He was looking right at me, and then my Mom went over close
to him, and he spoke again. "What'd he say, Ma?"
"He says you're an angel." He was *seeing* it, and
then I could feel it, like a light all around me, and
him, and my Mom. It sounds terrible to say, with
him so sick and all, but I felt very happy. He died
that night, by himself, while everyone else was
sleeping. A little of that happiness is in me, still. It's
a truer thing than the other ways I feel sometimes—
so I try to . . . remember.

FABER: It was years ago . . . couple of months after my
father died, I went to the beach. I was lying there on
the sand, and I saw him. He was rising up out of the
water, but not like some religious painting or something. He was just walking out of the ocean in his
bathing suit. He always loved swimming in the
ocean. He came in dripping from a calm sea, and
walked over to me. I knew he was dead, and that it
was a . . . something in my head or. . . . He looked
very happy to see me there. He smiled, and
waved—and that little moment made me feel he
loved me in a way nothing in his life had ever done

. . . and that was it. Then he was gone, and I was smiling, almost laughing, and the tears were running down my face.

[A silence. CHUCKLES *rings the desk bell once. He moves away from them slowly, and exits.]*

You ever think about dying, Pauline?

PAULINE: I've thought about it, but not all the time or anything. I've got enough. . . .

FABER: One world at a time, right, Pauline?

[The phone rings. PAULINE *picks it up.]*

PAULINE: *[on phone]* Office. . . . Yes, she is. I'll connect you. *[*PAULINE *puts the call through, hangs up. To* FABER.*]* The girl in seven. She got a call. Goes to show.

FABER: Goes to show what?

PAULINE: Goes to show that . . . if I say, you'll say "you learn that in church or something, Pauline?"

FABER: Well?

PAULINE: Well, what?

FABER: Well, you gonna marry me or not, Pauline?

PAULINE: You didn't ask me, Mr. Faber.

FABER: I'm asking you now.

PAULINE: No.

FABER: O.K. Unrequited love, that's O.K. Better than no love at all. And I'll know you're here, Pauline. Right in the middle of America, like a fountain of snow.

[A long silence.]

PAULINE: How much longer are you gonna be staying, Mr. Faber?

FABER: You know something, Pauline. I better leave in the morning . . . I better go home, wherever that is. Keep the porch light on, Momma. Let it shine out

Complete cast of *American Notes*
Martha Swope Associates/Carol Rosegg

onto the lawn, and don't turn it off till sunrise, cause that's when I'm coming. There, that's me, little plume of dust rising, that's me in the dust cloud, coming from the east, with the sun behind me in splendour . . . hey, who knows? So. What do you think, Pauline?

PAULINE: I don't know, Mr. Faber. What do *you* think?

[FABER *and* PAULINE *are still.* CHUCKLES *appears, and alongside him, the* MAYOR. *Lights come up as well on all the other places we've seen:* KAREN'S *room, the bar, the carnival lot, the* PROFESSOR'S *house, the open field.*]

MAYOR: Interesting country, little buddy. You lucky you here.

[*The* MAYOR *steps back into darkness, as lights fade on all places.* CHUCKLES *alone. Light fades on* CHUCKLES, *and out.*]

END OF PLAY

Poor Folk's Pleasure

Poor Folk's Pleasure was first presented by River Arts Repertory Company, Woodstock, New York, on July 15, 1989, with the following cast:

Steve Coats
Saun Ellis
Laura Innis
Will Patton
Rocco Sisto

Director: Len Jenkin
Stage Manager: Rose Bonczek

1. Rowing in to Shore, with "I Have a Dog, His Name is . . . Bill"
2. The Lantern and the Bell
3. Dragging Dance-devil and angel
4. Hi-Hat Tavern
5. PhoneTalk with Hitting 1
6. The Man With a City in a Box
7. On the Corner, with "Ants in my Pants"
8. How We Eat in the USA, with White Courtesy Telephone
9. Fascination
10. Leroy Smiles, the Crab Man
11. Clown Show 1
12. Frankie the Finn
13. "I Have a Boyfriend Fatty"
14. A Woman on the Phone [Medicine], with "Ants in My Pants" & Belly Bump
15. Blind Man and the Lead Girl
16. A Film Extra Talks to the Audience
17. The Man on Crutches, and his Girl
18. Fascination 2, with trouble
19. Clown Show 2
20. The Man With Shaking Hands, with Hitting 2
21. Do The Stroll
22. In the Tattoo Parlor
23. Dance Call
24. Montage: Frankie the Finn, Fascination Girl on phone, Dragging Dance, Belly Bumps, Clown Show, Man with Shaking Hands, Boatman/Mandolinist, with White Courtesy Telephone
25. Do the Hokey-Pokey
26. Box of Fab
27. Over the Hump
28. "Row Row Row Your Boat"/"Life is But a Dream"

NOTE

Poor Folk's Pleasure is a theatre piece for five to seven performers. These performers take on a variety of roles. The set should be extremely simple: the bare interior of the theatre, and only those few objects necessary to the understanding of the scenes.

Poor Folk's Pleasure should feel like a concert for the acting company as band: a series of interconnected numbers, all coming from the same author and the same ensemble.

Where speech is indicated and no set text is given, this language is to be created by the performers and director, along with the dances, staging, and soundtrack.

1.

A MAN *rows, a mandolin in his lap, and a beatific smile on his face. He spots the crowd on shore (audience), and stops rowing, letting himself drift to a stop. He stands, steps toward the audience, tunes his mandolin. He sings.*

BOATMAN

I have a dog
His name is . . . Bill . . .
He . . .

The BOATMAN *pauses uncertainly. He exits.*

2.

In the foreground, a lantern and a bell on a small table. Quiet. A MAN *enters, holding a newspaper. He seats himself behind the table, and reads. He chuckles to himself. Then he folds his newspaper as, one by one, various people approach him, drop a fee into a tin cup on his table, and move to the far end of the space, looking intently at something we cannot see. A hush.*

The MAN *at the table speaks to us, in a language we cannot understand, explaining what the visitors are looking at, his own feelings about it, and the nature of his position there. He falls silent.*

He looks at his watch. He reaches for the bell, and as he does so, we can see his hand shake, so that an effort of will is required for him to raise the bell off the table. He

rings the bell, and sets it down. The viewers, one by one,
exit, again passing by his table. Silence. In the distance
one woman, still looking, remains.

3.

The Dragging Dance. Rock and roll music: uptempo
and strong. A silent and dreaming angel, borne on the
back of a wildly gesticulating and prancing demon, comes
toward us. They pause a moment, and then the demon
begins to back away, dragging the still dreaming angel
with him. The music ends abruptly.

4.

A salesman, *seated in a chair.*

salesman: I believe I'm in a hotel. I'm sure of it. I've
been in them before. Not exactly like this one.
Similar.

I have no conception of why my employers
imagined I would be able to sell here. The planet's
dead. I think I'll watch some local television. Uh oh.
No television in my room. I'll go down to the TV
viewing lounge, in the hotel basement.

He moves to another area, where a man *watches tele-*
vision.

The TV is already on. Kirk Douglas in *Spartacus*.
A man is watching. . . . I think it's the same man
who welcomed me at the desk . . . hmmm . . .

A portion of Spartacus *is performed, live: noble Romans with British accents, Kirk, slaves etc. The* MAN *watching turns off the TV.*

Now he's not looking at the TV anymore, but at a picture that hangs on the wall nearby. It's of a young girl. *[To* MAN*]* Excuse me. I'd like to pester you with some salestalk, if I may.

MAN: Look at her. Carefully. Tell me what you see.

SALESMAN: She looks very pretty . . . and a little sad. Perhaps she lost her . . .

MAN: She was a murderess. Sally was removed—ten years ago—for the murder of my brother Arnold in this very room of this hotel. She murdered him with that fire-ax hanging over there on the wall. It was a summer day. The guests were in the TV lounge, viewing. It was just after lunch. My brother was sitting in *that* chair, counting his loose change. Sally came across the room, the fire-ax cradled in her arms, humming a hymn . . . *[sings]* Row . . . row . . . row your boat, gently down the . . . stream. . . .

SALESMAN: Perhaps I'd better . . .

MAN: She was my wife. She never knew that. . . . Why don't you take a walk in the reality? Go on. You'll feel better. Go down to the Hi-Hat Tavern. Watch the show.

The MAN *returns to* Spartacus, *which returns, live—and then he and his TV are gone.*

The SALESMAN *walks. Around him, street scenes of violence, horror. A strange-looking woman hisses at him from a corner.*

SALESMAN: I believe I'm on the kind of street where they cut your throat to get your hat. Interesting, but I better be careful. I believe I'm lost. Ah—There's the Hi-Hat Tavern down that way, with that glowing hat and that glass with bubbles . . .

WOMAN: You don't want the Hi-Hat Tavern. They all just lie there. Now I can get into almost anything.

SALESMAN: I'd like to pester you with some salestalk, if I may.

WOMAN: You know, you're dead meat, darling. But that's all any of us are anyway. Just meat.

SALESMAN: Is that true?

WOMAN: Just as true as anything else.

> *The Hi-Hat Tavern appears. The Woman notices . . .*

WOMAN: Excuse me.

> *The* WOMAN *is gone. In the Hi-Hat Tavern, the* SALESMAN, *an* MC, *and a* GIRL *with her head lying on a table.*

MC: *[solemnly]* SHOWTIME!

SALESMAN: Can you help me? I'm lost.

> *The* MC *raises up the girl's head, shows her the salesman, and steps aside. Though she becomes more alert as he goes on, and looks at the salesman curiously, the* GIRL *doesn't reply to his "conversation."*

SALESMAN: Can you show me the way back to my hotel?

> Is anything wrong? . . .
> Can I get you a drink? . . .
> I have traveller's checks . . .
> Are you free this evening?
> I know a good discothéque.
> Shall we go to the cinema?
> I'll pick you up at your hotel . . .
> Can I see you again tomorrow?
> Where do you come from? . . .

Ted Davey, Warren Press, Bruce DuBose, and Jeff
Amano in "Hi-Hat Tavern" Undermain Theatre Production
Katherine Owens

I'm here on a business trip. The planet's dead.
What business are you in?

GIRL: I'm a dancer at the Hi-Hat Tavern. That's where
we are now.

SALESMAN: Is this your favorite kind of work?

GIRL: I've done it all. Right here. Mud wrestling, execu-
tive secretary, bikini boxing, Empress of China. You
name it, I've done it.

SALESMAN: What kind of career plans do you have?

GIRL: Just dancing.

SALESMAN: Are you happy now?

GIRL: What are you talking about?

SALESMAN: I'm sorry. I don't understand. Could you say
all that again, more slowly. Repeat yourself.

GIRL: Forget it, Mister. Forget all about it. Go home.

The MC *grabs the* GIRL *from behind.*

MC: [softly] Showtime!

GIRL: Hey . . . I gotta go on.

The MC *lays her head back down on the table, as it
was before. She appears to sleep. He stands alongside her.
Silence. The* SALESMAN *looks at them, then steps toward
the audience.*

SALESMAN: Excuse me. I'd like to pester you with some
salestalk, if I may.

5.

A TEENAGE GIRL *talks on the telephone to a friend of
hers: boys, clothes, problems. At the same time, the rest of
the performers in a kind of Hitting Dance, striking each
other repeatedly across the face, hard and realistically, in*

a steady rhythm. One of them interrupts the GIRL *on the phone, drags her up to join them. The* GIRL *is hit, and hits back, repeatedly. At first she laughs, then breaks into sobs and tears. The hitting continues.*

6.

A MAN *holding a shoebox moves rapidly and suspiciously from place to place. The* OTHER MAN *notices him.*

OTHER MAN: What you got in there?

MAN: Gimme a dime.

OTHER MAN: What for?

MAN: You wanna look, don't you?

OTHER MAN: I just asked what you got in there.

MAN: Fuckin' freeloaders. You understand English? You gimme ten cents American, I let you look.

OTHER MAN: It don't bite or nothing?

MAN: It don't bite. Make up your mind. I ain't got all day. I got things to do. Things.

The OTHER MAN *hands the* MAN *a dime. The* MAN *carefully removes the lid of the box. The* OTHER MAN *peers inside.*

OTHER MAN: It's dark in there.

MAN: Yeah. It's night time.

OTHER MAN: What?

MAN: Just look a little closer.

OTHER MAN: It looks deep. You got some kind of trick box here?

MAN: Yeah, sure. It's a trick box.

OTHER MAN: There's some lights . . . hey, it's like looking

down on someplace from an airplane. Look at all those little lights. Hey, man, you make this?

MAN: I didn't make it. I found it.

OTHER MAN: *[reaching into box]* Hey, they're streetlights! It's like a toy . . .

MAN: Keep your hands outta there. You don't get to touch for no dime. Just look.

OTHER MAN: Hey . . . now I can see cars moving . . . an stores . . . Christ. There's little people walking around in there. This a movie or something?

MAN: Yeah. It's a movie or something.

OTHER MAN: Lookit that. A girl is standing on this little streetcorner, realer than hell. You ever see this?

MAN: What's she wearing?

OTHER MAN: A kind of short red dress . . .

MAN: She going into an apartment building . . . the Raleigh Towers? In a hurry, like she . . .

OTHER MAN: No. She's just standing there, staring at the back of her hand. Ah—she's got a tiny smudge of lipstick on a knuckle. She wipes it away. Now this man is coming over . . . an' he starts talking . . .

7.

MAN: Why didn't you come over where we're at? I was waiting. You scared or something?

GIRL: We had homework. 'Sides, I don't like Rat.

MAN: The Rat's in the hole. They picked him up last night.

GIRL: He'll be out by s'afternoon.

Lisa Lee Schmidt and Jeff Amano in "On the Corner"
Katherine Owens

MAN: Un uh. Rat's got a hundred dollar bail. For Rat, that's a life sentence.

GIRL: So?

MAN: What you mean, so?

GIRL: Just so.

MAN: So Rat ain't gonna be home. That's what I'm telling you.

GIRL: I don't like Petey either. He makes me nervous, 'cause he's always so fucked up an' all.

MAN: Petey's in the hole too. He was with Rat. So you can come over any time. Be nobody to bother you. Just me an' Toad. You bring any of your girlfriends you wanna bring. Toad got his check last week so we hit the supermarket. Got a frig fulla beer, and we bought all these chips an' shit cause you an' your friend was coming. You didn't show, but we didn't eat 'em. I saved all that shit for you, little sister.

GIRL: What'd they do?

MAN: Who?

GIRL: Rat. Petey an' Rat.

MAN: They busted a window.

GIRL: Bull shit.

MAN: They got high an' went downtown. That's all. I wasn't there. Two uniforms an' a cop in plainclothes come over to the house last night. Toad was stoked, an' playing that same Captain Beefheart album over and over again, the way he likes . . . *[sings]* "Dust blows forward, an' the dust blows back . . ."

GIRL: What'd they want?

MAN: Who can understand what the police want? Not me, little sister. They went through all of Rat an' Petey's shit. Petey got all his shit in this trunk, man, and it was locked, but them fuckers didn't blink. One of the uniforms just goes out an' gets a tire iron an' fuckin' cracks it. Petey's gonna be mad. Those bastards don't give a shit about anyone's rights. They found Petey's stash, but I'm not sure they'll ever figure out what it fuckin' *is*. He takes weird shit, an' he mixes it with all that stuff the doctors give him for his head.

GIRL: So what'd they do?

MAN: I told you what they did. I don't know what they did.

     You coming over tonight?

GIRL: Maybe.

MAN: What's that shit, *maybe*?

GIRL: That is you just wait there, an' eat potato chips, an' see what happens. *[sings]* "Dust blows forward, an' the dust blows back . . ." I gotta go. . . .

    A MAN *in a straw hat appears in the distance. He looks at the couple, then the audience. He sings, with great passion, a slow blues.*

MAN IN STRAW HAT:

    It makes no difference, anywhere you go
    Cause I got something, want you to know
    I got ants, in my pants, baby for you!

8.

    A MAN *with a camera. In the distance, a family: father, mother and child. The* FATHER *reads the paper, the* MOTHER *knits, and the* CHILD *watches TV, as if the* MAN *with the camera was on it.*

MAN: I work for *Thrills Magazine*. Hey, how low can you go? And for how long? I'd quit, and do something a little less slimy, but I gotta eat. Don't we all.

FATHER: I like chicken pot pie.

MOTHER: Not me, Charlie.

CHILD: Daddy . . . shhhh.

MAN: Hey, no time for reflection here. I'm working. The job? To photograph Miss Charlene Mason, in the nude, these photographs to go with the centerfold theme for December, "I'm in love with Santa."

CHILD: *[sings]* You better watch out, you better not cry, you . . .

MOTHER: Shhh . . .

MAN: "Make her jump off the page," they told me. Charlene is actually an ex-hooker named Alberta Vignones who I hired for fifty bucks. The part of Santa will be played by yours truly, facing away from the camera. Cheaper that way. Don't have to hire some scuzzball with tattoos. Renting the suit was bad enough . . . got it right here in the bag, beard and all.

Alberta lives out along 509 with a kid and a husband named Charlie or something who works at a sand and gravel pit moving dirt around. He don't like her doing the posing every now and then, but they need the money. Wouldn't you? Same old story.

So I'm heading out toward Alberta's and I'm thinking I could eat something so I pull into this shopping mall. There's a place in there called the Wagon Wheel and I'm thinking uh oh I don't got my bowling trophy and then I figure what the hell and go in past the Pac Man machine and slide into the tufted leather and a blonde cowgirl is moving toward me in a little short white skirt that's got the skull of a cow on it in rhinestones and I think "Keep calm and don't do anything crazy" and she says "Welcome to the Wagon Wheel. You know what you'd like?" and I say "O my God" and she says "Scuse me?" and I say "Tuna melt, order of fries and a coffee." She says "Right" and I'm watching her go, little skirt flipping this way and that, and at that very moment some fool plays the jukebox and they dim the lights for the evening dating trade and I say to myself "O.K. It's time to play all the cards you got."

I wait. She comes back with the food like I knew she would and I give her time to set it down before I say "Honey, what time do you get off?" And she says "Can't you boys leave a working girl alone?" "Not when they're as pretty as you, Miss" I say. She says "Just shut up and eat or I'll call the manager. I don't need to get hassled by every slob who walks in the door."

She goes off, leaving me in bitterness and pain, and I take a bite, and another, and its not bad. And that's how we eat in the U.S.A. Some of us, anyway.

FATHER: I like chicken pot pie.

MOTHER: I'm making meatloaf, Charlie.

CHILD: Tuna melt, order of fries, and a coffee.

The man with the camera is gone, but the family remains. Silence.

AMPLIFIED VOICE: Mr. *[last name of actor playing the* FATHER*], Mr. *[first and last names of actor playing*

FATHER]. Please pick up the white courtesy telephone.

FATHER: I'm not expecting any call. I know. Must be for
somebody else with my name. But I better check it
out. *[goes to phone, picks it up]* Hello . . . yes . . . This
is _____ _____ . . . . Who is this? . . .
IS THIS SOME KIND OF A JOKE?

9.

*A bell rings. We see a silent row of "Fascination" play-
ers. Behind them, on a raised platform, a* TEENAGE GIRL
*who runs the game. Fascination is an old-fashioned store-
front game, where the players pay to roll rubber balls
toward a set of holes, trying for a prize-winning pattern.
The* TEENAGE GIRL *rings the bell again. While she speaks,
between games, the players are distracted, their attention
wandering. . . .*

GIRL: We have a winner, we have a winner! Number 18.
Seven tickets, any prize, bottom row. Known from
the rock-bound coast of Maine to the sun-kissed
shores of California, it's Fascination. Time for another game of Fascination. Time for another game of
Fascination. *[rings bell]* Roll 'em up! Roll 'em up!
And the first ball is out.

*The game has begun, and the players, though
remaining still and not miming any playing, have
become attentive, focused in front of them, tense. Silence.*

GIRL: *[rings bell]* We have a winner! We have a winner.
Number . . . *[and continuing . . .]*

She repeats her spiel, word for word, except that the

Laurel Hoitsma in "Fascination" Undermain Theatre Production
Katherine Owens

number of the winner has changed. As she speaks, the players repeat their distraction, and then their focus when the game begins again. Four games of Fascination. During game 3 the GIRL makes a phone call to her boyfriend, and we hear her talking to him as the game is in progress. She needs to ask him to "Hold on" when a winner comes up, and then she repeats her speech as before, and resumes her conversation as the following game is played. In the middle of the fourth game, the players break focus, and exit. The GIRL, busy on the phone, at last notices they're all gone. A bit disturbed, she asks her boyfriend to "Hold on. I'll be right back." And she quickly exits herself.

10.

LEROY SMILES *appears. He is seated on a low stool. He is legless, and has only two large digits on each hand. A* NEWSMAN *appears.*

NEWSMAN: LEROY SMILES, THE CRAB MAN! YOU BE THE JUDGE! Smiles, legless and with only two digits on each hand, is accused of mudering Jack Layne, 35, and his own 15-year-old daughter. LEROY SMILES, THE CRAB MAN!

The NEWSMAN *is gone. The three still figures onstage go into action.*

SMILES: Ungrateful little bitch! I swore I wouldn't go up on the platform again, and I went up there. I went up there in Dayton, and Akron, and I did some-fuck suburb of Cincinnatti where they had us on the asphalt. In a shopping plaza, Miss.

DAUGHTER: We went for a ride is all. Jack's got a car. He bought it from working. It's a Chevrolet. Caprice.

SMILES: Why was I on the platform, 'stead of watching TV, and relaxing in my own personal home? You know why, son? Jack? You know why, Jack?

JACK: No.

SMILES: So's I could pay the investigations place one thousand dollars to send some sonofabitch to find you. He found you, Miss. You went for a ride all right. Cross three states.

DAUGHTER: You didn't need to do that. I was coming back anyway.

JACK: We're gonna get married.

A long beat while LEROY SMILES *takes in this information.*

SMILES: Miss, I ever keep you home from school to do for me? One day?

DAUGHTER: No, you always been. . . .

SMILES: Come here, Jack.

JACK: What for?

SMILES: I want to show you something.

JACK: Oh yeah? Like what?

SMILES: You ever seen my hands, Jack?

JACK: Yeah, sure I seen 'em.

LEROY SMILES *lowers himself off his chair, and begins to scuttle across the floor toward* JACK.

SMILES: You ever seen them up close?

SMILES *moves closer to* JACK, *dragging himself along the floor, and then raises his powerful claws . . .*

DAUGHTER: Daddy! Daddy! NO!

The NEWSMAN *reappears, and as he speaks,* JACK
LAYNE, SMILES, *and his* DAUGHTER *return to the positions
they were in at the beginning of the scene.*

NEWSMAN: LEROY SMILES, the CRAB MAN! You be the
judge!

The NEWSMAN *is gone, and the scene of "Leroy
Smiles, the Crab Man" begins again, recycling.*

SMILES: Ungrateful little bitch! I swore I . . .

. . . *and continuing, until it is interrupted by the
scene that follows . . .*

11.

One PERFORMER *stands alone, stage center. An* ANNOUN-
CER *appears.*

ANNOUNCER: *[pointing to* PERFORMER*]* The laws of this person's existence are hideously simple. He [She] is
permitted to suffer, and commanded to amuse.

The ANNOUNCER *is gone. Music. The "Clown
Show." This is simply a desperate attempt by the* PER-
FORMER *to please the audience, using the barest minimum of words and/or props. He [She] tries one thing
after another. At last the* PERFORMER, *anxious and confused, abandons the attempt, to the tune of whatever
applause there may or may not be, and walks off. The
stage is bare.*

12.

In the distance, three WATCHERS. *In the foreground,* FRANKIE THE FINN. *He holds his head in his hands.*

WATCHER 1: Look!

WATCHER 2: It's Frankie the Finn!

WATCHER 3: Frankie the Finn's in his eighties. In forty-seven they foreclosed on the twenty acre farm he'd bought when he and his wife came over from the old country. She was buried there, in an open field. They told Frankie the bank owned it now.

FRANKIE: Fuck the bank.

WATCHER 3: Said Frankie the Finn. After he heard he stood in the middle of the field by his wife's gravestone and held his big head in his hands for about an hour. Everyone in town was watching from the road. Then he walked into his house and set it on fire. He sat there at the kitchen table with the room burning around him till the volunteer fire department went in and hauled him out. He was screaming in Finnish.

   FRANKIE *begins to shout and moan in what sounds like a mixture of Finnish and unintelligible gibberish. He stops suddenly.*

   They shipped him off to the cackle factory. Ten years later, he gets out, and comes back to town. He's got disability or something, and he rents a room, and sits around all day in front of the bank. [FRANKIE *sits*] He speaks only in Finnish now, as if everyone can understand him, or at least that's what we thought till a Finnish guy went over to talk to him and said it wasn't Finnish at all he was speaking. It sounded a little like it, but it was just nonsense he was saying, and smiling all the time.

So I guess that's how it is on this bitch of an earth. For some of us, anyway. How do you like it?

FRANKIE *begins to speak loudly in his own language, half Finnish, half gibberish. He walks toward the audience, gesturing excitedly, shouting. He stops suddenly, then walks off in silence.*

WATCHER 1: What'd he say?

WATCHER 2: Fuck the bank.

13.

One GIRL, *alone on stage. She hesitantly begins to sing.*

GIRL: I have a boyfriend Fatty
      He comes from Cincinatti
      With 48 toes and a pickle on his nose
      And this is the way my story . . . goes.
      One day while I was walking
      I heard my boyfriend talking
      To a pretty little girl with a strawberry curl
      And this is what he said to her
      I L. O. V. E. love you
      I K. I . . .
          She exits.

14.

A WOMAN *at a pay phone, on the street.*

WOMAN: *[on phone]* You want your medicine, you're gonna have to come down and see a doctor . . . I tried, dammit. They wouldn't give it to me . . . I said everything you told me. This black bitch of a nurse fills out this long goddamn form, and then I told her your leg all swelled up and you couldn't come to the hospital. "Put her in a cab" she says. I said "Where'm I gonna get the money for a cab?" She says "Whyn't you take some of your dope money and put your momma in a cab?" I hit her with her own goddamn telephone. Blood was dripping down her nasty face. They called the security guard, threw me outta there. Everybody in the 'mergency room was staring. That guard's gonna remember me. I was screaming. He hadda drag me through the door . . .

At a goddamn payphone. Look, Ma, I gotta see somebody, and then I'm coming home . . . I'll *be* there. Tomorrow, we'll go down to the hospital. We'll take a cab. But I ain't going in there. That black bitch'll have my ass. You gotta go in there by yourself.

The WOMAN *hangs up the phone. In the distance, the* MAN WITH THE STRAW HAT *appears. He sings, loudly and energetically.*

MAN WITH A STRAW HAT:

It makes no difference, anywhere you go
Cause I got something, want you to know

I got ants, in my pants, baby for you!
Anytime I come, and feel your charms
It makes my feelings, just get all wrong
Cause I got ants, in my pants, baby for you!

15.

A BLIND MAN *appears. He wears dark glasses. He moves hesitantly forward, his stick tapping in front of him.*

NARRATOR: *[offstage]* A blind man walks down the railroad tracks, stick tapping the ties. The track tells him where to go, but makes him slow, careful. In his pocket, he's got a Browning automatic. Blind man with a pistol. Old tracks, no train's run over them for years. Now the ties become rotten, crumbling. The rails twist, run into tall grass, and stop.

BLIND MAN: Little bitch! She's playing with the squirrels. GET OVER HERE! TRACK DIED! Goddamn government doesn't support the goddamn railroads, how's somebody gonna find his way across the goddamn country. Sweeeethearrrt!

  The LEAD GIRL *appears.*

LEAD GIRL: I caught one. A little creature to fight you for me. A gnat. Look! He's in the jar. Tonight when you're sleeping I'm gonna slip him up your nostril, and for seven years he'll drill little buzzholes in your brain, and you'll go nuts. Then you'll die. The doctors'll crack your skull open and the gnat'll be as big as a pigeon in there, with a mouth of copper and claws of iron.

BLIND MAN: Come closer, so I can hit you.

LEAD GIRL: You've been bad while I've been gone. Beating the bishop. Fly's open. Think so?

BLIND MAN: Shut up and take my hand. To the town. I want a doughnut. With sugar.

LEAD GIRL: No town. Just country. And a sign.

BLIND MAN: Read me.

LEAD GIRL: Ko-ko-mo. Ten miles.

BLIND MAN: Good. Good. I gotta talk to a man in Kokomo, right?

LEAD GIRL: I don't remember.

BLIND MAN: Yes you do. That's why I have the gun.

LEAD GIRL: Someone's coming! A hulking, stumbling woman, with huge breasts. She's blind, like you. She sniffs. She catches your stink on the wind. She's running this way, crazy with love!

BLIND MAN: Bad lie.

LEAD GIRL: Someone's coming. A man this time.

BLIND MAN: I hear him now. Do we need his money?

LEAD GIRL: Shhh, you big bear. Shhh. Be dumb.

> The FOREST RANGER enters.

LEAD GIRL: [to RANGER] This man's world is as dark as a dog's. Give us a penny.

RANGER: What are you two doing in here? You got a back-country permit?

LEAD GIRL: He's as perplexed as a sheep.

RANGER: You lead him around, right?

LEAD GIRL: Shhh. He'll get violent. Just to pretend he's sensitive to remarks like that. Actually, he doesn't give a shit.

RANGER: What remarks? He's blind, right? That ain't a bad thing to say if it's true.

The LEAD GIRL *moves close to the* BLIND MAN.

LEAD GIRL: You don't give a shit, do you, you dead hulk. You heaving bag of gristle. You dark tower, you. Ummm . . .

BLIND MAN: What's he look like? Handsome?

LEAD GIRL: The whites of his eyes are like the blue skin on a hard-boiled egg. His nose is like the . . .

RANGER: Look, you two. The fine's a hundred dollars. I'm trying to give you a break here. Just go back down to the ranger station at Point Lookout and . . .

BLIND MAN: POINT LOOKOUT?!

LEAD GIRL: *[to* RANGER*]* Now you insulted him.

BLIND MAN: You read Kokomo.

LEAD GIRL: Did I? I don't remember.

BLIND MAN: Little bitch.

LEAD GIRL: He's still here.

BLIND MAN: Is he now? Can he understand anything?

LEAD GIRL: Try him.

BLIND MAN: We are simple travellers, sir, through this dreary orchard of bones. Honest . . . honest . . .

LEAD GIRL: Working people.

BLIND MAN: Exactly.

RANGER: All right. I'm calling in a jeep and haul the two of you down to the highway. The fine's a hundred bucks.

BLIND MAN: You see? You see? The flames of hatred and stupidity burn day and night. Kiss him, and make him go away.

The LEAD GIRL *hesitates, then goes toward the* RANGER, *making a distorted ugly face at him, sticking out her tongue. Then, in a sexy voice . . .*

LEAD GIRL: Do you like me?

RANGER: Get away from me, you little slut.

The LEAD GIRL *goes back over to the* BLIND MAN.

LEAD GIRL: I'm not attractive today.

The BLIND MAN *grabs the* LEAD GIRL *by the arm, and steps toward the* RANGER.

BLIND MAN: Excuse her, sir. I'm taking her to school now. She's been playing hookey for weeks and weeks. Staying out late at night too, all by herself, looking into ponds in the forest. Listening to the fishes. Haven't you, honey? Don't be ashamed in front of the nice man.

LEAD GIRL: What nice man? He's another country-simple shitface. Shoot him, and let's get going. I'll stay real still. When something moves, it's him.

The BLIND MAN *draws his pistol. All three are motionless. Silence. A* WOMAN *steps into the scene, her back to us, staring at the other three performers. Another voice cries:*

ASSISTANT DIRECTOR: CUT!

16.

The FILM EXTRA, *with her back to us, remains. The* BLIND MAN, LEAD GIRL *and the* FOREST RANGER *walk off to their dressing rooms. The* ASSISTANT DIRECTOR *enters, shouting orders of various kinds to camera people and crew. A Donut Shop set is hauled on. The* ASSISTANT DIRECTOR *sets up the next scene to be shot. In it the* BLIND MAN *and the* LEAD GIRL *will approach a Donut Shop. As he does this, the* EXTRA *turns to the audience, while she's waiting to perform, and talks. Perhaps the film is "The Fumes of*

Life," *starring Mia Farrow and Sylvester Stallone. She talks about herself, her part in the film, what she thinks about the story and the stars. The* A.D. *gives her instructions: to stroll casually towards the Donut Shop. She's nervous. Her "Ready!" call comes, then "ACTION!" She proudly does her simple bit, and the* A.D., *perhaps satisfied with the scene and full of praise, perhaps angry and wanting a re-take, calls a break.*

ASSISTANT DIRECTOR: Ten minutes, everyone! And that *means* ten minutes . . .

The EXTRA *glances back at us a moment, and she's gone, along with everyone else.*

17.

A MAN *on crutches and his* GIRLFRIEND *enter. Street people. The* MAN *is unsteady, mumbling, having taken a few pills too many. One of his legs is clearly hurting. He wobbles forward on his crutches, needing her occasional support. His* GIRLFRIEND *is somewhat messed up herself, but she's together enough to keep them going. She does all the talking; comforting him, urging him on, treating him like a bad and stupid child. If she notices the audience it's to ask them for change, or to be annoyed by them.*

GIRL: Why you looking at my boyfriend like that? You got a problem, bitch?

He stops and, teetering on his crutches, gropes for a pack of Kools in his pocket. He fishes out the crumpled pack, but drops it. The cigarettes fall all over the floor.

His GIRLFRIEND *picks them up, finds an unbroken one for each of them, lights them up.*

GIRL: There. Now ain't that nice?

They move off slowly, smoking, her arm around his waist, her talking in his ear, step by step . . .

18.

A bell rings. We see once again the silent row of "Fascination" players. Behind them, on her raised platform, the TEENAGE GIRL *who runs the game. She rings the bell again. While she speaks, between games, the players are distracted, their attention wandering . . .*

GIRL: We have a winner, we have a winner! Number 19. Seven tickets, any prize, bottom row. Known from the rock-bound coast of Maine to the sun-kissed shores of California, it's Fascination. Time for another game of Fascination. Time for another game of Fascination. *[rings bell]* Roll 'em up! Roll 'em up! And the first ball is out.

The game begins, and the players become attentive, focused in their varying ways. The GIRL *picks up the phone and resumes her conversation with a* GIRLFRIEND *while the players play. She has one eye on the game, and when a winning number comes up, her* GIRLFRIEND *has to "Hold on."*

GIRL: *[rings bell]* We have a winner! *[and continuing . . .]*

She repeats her spiel, word for word, except for a new winning number. A new game begins, and this time, as she talks on the phone, she notices something among the players. She comes down off her platform and approaches a MAN *at the end of the row.*

GIRL: Excuse me. If you're not playing the game you'll have to vacate that seat. We got people waiting.

The MAN *doesn't answer her, but looks confused, and remains seated.*

GIRL: *[cont.]* Look, we got a policy. No dime, no hanging around, understand. I don't make the rules. Look, you . . .

She notices that a winner has hit, rushes back to her platform, makes her spiel again, interrupting it occasionally with "Hang on's" to the friend on the phone. Finally a new game begins, and she can resume her interrupted phone conversation. But once again she looks down, and sees the MAN *who's not playing, still in his seat.*

GIRL: HEY, YOU! MOVE OUT!

Suddenly, all the Fascination players get up and exit. The GIRL *looks at them going, then grabs the phone again.*

GIRL: *[into phone]* Just hang on a moment. I'll be right back . . .

She's gone.

19.

One PERFORMER *stands stage center. An* ANNOUNCER *appears, and repeats the introduction given before.*

ANNOUNCER: *[pointing to* PERFORMER*]* The laws of this person's existence are hideously simple. He [She] is permitted to suffer, and commanded to amuse.

The ANNOUNCER *is gone. Music. Another "Clown Show:" another desperate attempt by a* PERFORMER *to please the audience, using the barest minimum of words and/or props. This time the* PERFORMER, *improvising one comic, frightening or foolish thing after another, manages to continue until the music ends. He [She] takes a tentative and nervous bow, and walks off.*

20.

A café. At a table, the MAN *we've seen earlier with the lantern and the bell. He opens a newspaper, reads, laughs to himself. He has a coffee cup in front of him. Music plays. In the background, elegant couples dance. The* MAN *reaches for his cup, and as he does so, his hand begins to shake. The cup rattles in the saucer. It is only with a great and painful effort of will that he succeeds in controlling the trembling enough to bring the cup to his lips and take a sip. Some coffee spills.*

With some shaking still present, he sets the cup down. He looks about to make sure no one has noticed his weakness. He regains his air of dignity, and again he reads his paper.

One of the elegant dancing couples stops dancing. They turn to face each other. They begin to slap each other across the face, viciously, loudly, and very realistically. A WOMAN *enters the scene, walks up to the* MAN WITH SHAKING HANDS, *and taps him on the shoulder. He puts down his newspaper, stands, faces her, and they too begin to slap each other, in a strong rhythm, each blow striking home. Someone begins to sob. The hitting continues.*

21.

Music. Couples do their particular version of the '60s dance known as "The Stroll," sweeping up and back through the space on parallel lines, moving toward and then away from the audience . . .

    Come let's stroll, stroll across the floor
    Come let's stroll, stroll across the floor
    Then turn around, baby, let's stroll some
       more . . .
    [and the music continuing . . .]

At the far end of the path created by the "Strollers," an OLD MAN *sits. He stares out at the doings before him, and occasionally laughs, a heavy, nasty cackle. In front of him, at the floor at his feet, the legless* LEROY SMILES, *the Crab Man.* LEROY *begins to move forward with the music, between the line of Strollers, propelling himself angrily forward on his hands, his movements punctuated with harsh rasping breaths. He arrives, with great effort, at the point closest to the audience. Here he stops, his breath coming hard, his face twisted with the effort. Up and back, on either side of him, the dancers swirl.*

22.

A Tattoo Parlor, and a TATTOOIST *at work on a* CUSTOMER. *Also, a* MAN *slumped in a chair in a corner, a girl,* ROOTHIE, *doing her toenails and a* WOMAN CUSTOMER *who waits her turn, singing to herself. Buzz of the needle.*

CUSTOMER: . . . one of the best body men in the state till I fucked up this hand. Look at it. Thing won't even close . . .

I been married, once. I give her the goddamn house, all the furniture. Most of it was damn near new. I didn't want nothing. Then I figured first time ain't my mistake, second time would be. What's the use buying a cow when you can get the calf? Ninety-nine percent of goddamn women they all over you. Shack up with 'em two three at a time. You get tired of 'em, leave. Shit, if you can't get along, piss on it. Keep gas in the car, and a hundred dollar bill taped up in the spare. That's the way I believe in it . . .

Say I'm just somewhere, waiting for a tree to fall on me, and she walks on up. Now I got an ass pocket full of money, and we get a fifth. So next thing you know, she say "hey, let's go someplace." So we get in the car. Next thing we think about is where, but we don't think about it till we're on the highway doing seventy. Well, you're going, and you figure, after this next drink you'll figure out something, and by that time the empty flies out the window . . .

The MAN *in the chair in the corner laughs moronically.*

CUSTOMER: Hey, I'm no alcoholic, man. I can take it or leave it. But I always take it . . .

The CUSTOMER *laughs, and the Man in the corner laughs again. The Tattooist lays down his needle.*

TATTOOIST: *[to* CUSTOMER*]* Excuse me.

The TATTOOIST *approaches the audience.*

TATTOOIST: You must be eighteen, and sober. Females must be previously tattooed. I don't do firsts on women. It's bad luck.

    The TATTOOIST *returns to his customer. Buzz of the needle resumes.*

MAN IN CORNER: Everybody here is fucked up.

    The WOMAN CUSTOMER *approaches the* TATTOOIST *as he's working.*

WOMAN CUSTOMER: Whatcha got?

TATTOOIST: *[to* CUSTOMER*]* Excuse me. *[to* WOMAN CUSTOMER*]* This guy's getting a cross, on fire. And underneath, his name and social security number. So's he won't forget it. Right, Tony?

WOMAN CUSTOMER: That's stupid.

CUSTOMER: *[*TONY*]* Yeah? You get messed up enough, you forget everything. I don't want that to happen to me again. It's inconvenient.

TATTOOIST: You want that? Your name and number?

WOMAN CUSTOMER: Nah. That's stupid.

TATTOOIST: Look in the book. Roothie, show the kid the book.

    ROOTHIE *gets up, and leads the* WOMAN *to the book of tattoo designs. The* WOMAN *looks through it.*

WOMAN CUSTOMER: I want this one. Right over my tit.

ROOTHIE: Can't you read? That one's got a big X through it.

WOMAN CUSTOMER: I don't care. I want it.

ROOTHIE: Sorry. He don't do that one no more.

TATTOOIST: *[to* CUSTOMER*]* You're done. Don't touch it. Don't scratch it. Let it set a minute and I'll clean it with some alcohol. *[to* WOMAN CUSTOMER*]* Next.

    The CUSTOMER *leaves the tattooing chair, and takes a*

seat along one side of the room. The WOMAN *takes his place, bringing the book with her. She shows it to the* TATTOOIST.

WOMAN CUSTOMER: I want that one.

TATTOOIST: Roothie told you. I don't do that one no more.

MAN IN CORNER: EVERYBODY HERE IS FUCKED UP!

ROOTHIE: [MAN IN CORNER] Feed the dogs . . . FEED THE DOGS!

The TATTOOIST *begins work on the* WOMAN, *and she begins to tell him a story in a quiet voice as the needle buzzes away. The* MAN IN THE CORNER *slowly gets up, and crosses the room. As he does so, all fall silent, and become quite still. He exits. For a moment, silence and stillness, and then, as from a great distance, the howling of dogs . . .*

23.

An OLD MAN, *seated, and a* YOUNG WOMAN *standing alongside him. They sing the Dance Call. In another space, a couple slowly turns to the music.*

OLD MAN AND YOUNG WOMAN:
> Two little sisters form a ring
> Now you're born and now you swing
>
> Clothes all off and your toes are curled
> Monkey jumps through that hole in the world
>
> Eat ice cream, drink soda water
> Some old man gonna lose his daughter

> Drink soda water, eat ice cream
> Some young girl gonna lose her dream
>
> Girls and boys walk the same old trail
> Same old possum walks the same old rail
>
> Huckleberry shuffle and the clothesline cling
> Peppermint twist and the grapevine swing
>
> Round they go and they go around . . .
> *[continuing, repeating]*

> *The* OLD MAN *stands and comes toward the audience,*
> *as the* GIRL *continues singing. He's smiling to himself . . .*

OLD MAN: *[to Audience]* Quit that hugging! . . Ain't you
ashamed . . . Heh, heh . . . That's better . . . . . . that's
right . . .

> *The* OLD MAN *is gone. The couple still turns slowly*
> *to the music.*

GIRL: *[still singing, more softly]*

> Round they go, and they go around
> Round they go, and they go around
> Round they go, and they go around . . .

24.

Music. FRANKIE THE FINN *appears, holding his head in*
his hands, mumbling to himself. His body jerks and
sways, his voice rising and falling in a language we can-
not understand.

The TEENAGE GIRL *who runs the Fascination game*
rushes across the stage, and makes a phone call to her
boyfriend: casual, sexy, self-possessed.

One of the performers who previously performed a "clown show" appears, focused on the audience, doing one hopeless, funny or pathetic routine after another.

The Dragging Dance, an angelic GIRL *dreaming on the back of a* MAN *who writhes and twists like a demon, moves forward and back in the space.*

The BOATMAN/MANDOLIN PLAYER *who rowed in to shore at the play's beginning appears, steps toward the audience, tunes his instrument and sings. All the events behind him continue.*

BOATMAN: I have a dog

His name is . . . Bill

He . . .

The BOATMAN *pauses uncertainly. He exits*

The MAN WITH SHAKING HANDS *enters, views the chaotic scene around him with sang-froid, and seats himself at his café table. He opens his newspaper, reads, laughs to himself. He lifts his coffee cup, and his hand trembles violently. The coffee spills.*

The TEENAGE GIRL *asks her boyfriend to "Hold on . . . I'll be right back" and she's gone.*

The Dragging Dance is gone.

The CLOWN/PERFORMER *is gone.*

FRANKIE THE FINN *stops mumbling, looks up, and walks rapidly offstage.*

The MAN WITH SHAKING HANDS *is alone. Silence.*

AMPLIFIED VOICE: Mr. *[last name of actor playing the* MAN WITH SHAKING HANDS*]*, Mr. *[first and last names of the actor playing the* MAN WITH SHAKING HANDS*]*. Please pick up the white courtesy telephone.

MAN WITH SHAKING HANDS: I'm not expecting any call. I know. Must be for somebody else with my name.

But I better check it out. *[goes to phone, picks it up]*
Hello . . . yes . . . This is _____ _____ . . .
Who is this? . . . IS THIS SOME KIND OF A JOKE?

25.

One MAN, *alone onstage. He sings, and dances to illus-
trate . . .*

MAN: You put your right foot in,
       you take your right foot out
       You put your right foot in,
       and you shake it all about
       You do the hokey-pokey
       and you turn yourself around
       That's what it's all about!

       You put your left foot in,
       you take your left foot out
       You put your left foot in,
       and you shake it all about
       You do the hokey-pokey . . .
       and you turn yourself around . . .
       That's what it's all about!

       You put your whole self in,
       you take your whole self out
       You put your whole self in . . .
       and you shake it all about!
       You do the hokey-pokey

and you turn yourself around
That's what . . .

The MAN *pauses uncertainly, and exits.*

26.

A motel room somewhere. A MAN *sits in a chair. Some distance away from him, a woman unpacks groceries from a shopping bag onto a table.*

WOMAN: . . . box of Fab, fifty extra-strength Tylenol, Tampax, jar of Vaseline, box of these Mr. Salty pretzels, carton of Merit one hundreds, four bananas, your two beers, Nescafé, creamed spinach, creamed carrots, and this other jar of mush. That's it . . .

Hey, it's not like we're gonna be here forever. Half this shit's gonna go in the backseat tomorrow, be all over the carpet . . . I got this newspaper at the checkout. Listen to this: this one-legged guy had a pet beaver, and it ate his wooden leg off while he was sleeping. Next morning he went to stand up, an' he just fell over.

The MAN *in the chair remains silent, barely acknowledging her presence, his expression unchanged.*

Seems like you and me, we're doing life on the installment plan . . . ten days now and fifteen days there, and ten days later. Is she asleep in there?

The MAN *barely nods. The* WOMAN *goes into the next room. From offstage, we hear her begin to sing quietly Sam Cooke's "Bring It On Home."*

WOMAN: If you ever, change your mind
About leaving . . .
The WOMAN *emerges, walks slowly toward the* MAN.
[singing softly] . . . leaving me behind
Bring it to me, bring all your sweet loving,
Bring it on home to me.

You know I'll always, be your slave
Till I'm buried, buried in my grave
Ah, bring it to me, . . .

The WOMAN *moves next to the seated* MAN, *and puts
her arm around him. He leans his head on her breast.*
[singing softly] . . . bring all your sweet loving,
Bring it on home to me.

27.

An OLDER MAN *comes toward the audience. In the distance, the couple from the previous scene remain.*

OLDER MAN: When you get up sixty, seventy miles an
hour, you figger what the hell am I doing down
inside this boxcar? You can't sit down, an' you can't
lay down, and you're lucky if you can stand.
Always bouncing 'bout three foot off the floor. Ain't
a goddamn thing to hang onto. No wonder I got
arthritis. It ain't from the war, it's from the fucking
boxcars.
One time I'm with Hatcheck Murphy, an' we
were going over the hump, only we didn't know we

was going that way. Colder'n hell. I had a T-shirt
on, but I had a bottle of hot peppers. I drank the
juice off of those peppers, only thing that kept me
alive. I was walking the car the whole time, snow
blowing in all over the place. Everything outside
was white. I said "Lord, where the hell am I at?"

Murphy had him a tokay blanket. He drank the
bottle, an' then after awhile, I swear to God, he just
lights his cigarette, gets up, and walks out the door.
That sonofabitch was doing about sixty mile an
hour. I don't know whatever happened to him.

Ain't that something?

28.

The BOATMAN/MANDOLINST *from the opening scene,
rowing once again. With a beatific smile on his face, he
pulls away from shore. He rows smoothly. Beside him
stands a young* GIRL. *She sings, in a very slow rhythm.*

GIRL: Row, row, row your boat
      Gently down the stream
      Merrily, merrily, merrily, merrily
      Life is but a dream

      Row, row, row your boat
      Gently down the stream
      Merrily, merrily,merrily, merrily
      Life is but a dream

      The entire company joins the BOATMAN *and the* GIRL,

forming a group around them. Except the BOATMAN, *all sing, with some doo-wop harmony and back-up, the Harptone's 1950s "Life is But a Dream." Beautiful and slow.*

ALL: Life is but a dream, it's what you make it
       Always try to give, don't ever take it
       Life has its music, life has its songs of love

       Life is but a dream, and I dream of you
       Strange as it seems, all night I see you
       I'm trying to tell you, just what you mean to me

       Life is but a dream, and we can live it
       We can make a love, none to compare with
       Will you take part in, my life, my love—
       That is my dream—
       Life is but a dream . . .

As the song fades away, the MAN WITH SHAKING HANDS *comes forward from the group. In a language we cannot understand, he begins to explain the song, the performance, his own. . . . He falters, considers. Then, with a shrug and a smile, he falls silent and returns to the group. The* BOATMAN *begins once again to row, smoothly and steadily. The lights fade.*

END OF PLAY

Bill Sadler, Melissa Hurst , Eric Loeb, and Saun Ellis in
rehearsal for *Dark Ride*

LEN JENKIN

Len Jenkin is the author of over twenty plays, including *Kitty Hawk, The Death and Life of Jesse James, Grand American Exhibition, Mission, Gogol: A Mystery Play, Kid Twist,* and *The Five of Us.* The plays in this volume, *Limbo Tales, Dark Ride, My Uncle Sam, American Notes,* and *Poor Folk's Pleasure* were written in the 1980s. More recent plays include *Pilgrims of the Night* (1991) and *Careless Love* (1993), and several very free adaptations that stand as plays in themselves: *Candide* (from the Voltaire), *A Soldier's Tale* (from Stravinsky and Ramuz, with the Flying Karamazov Brothers), and *A Country Doctor* (from Franz Kafka's short story).

Jenkin describes himself as "delighted" to also have the opportunity to create two plays for children, both adaptations of novels: *Ramona Quimby* (from Beverly Cleary's novels) and *The Invisible Man* (from the novel by H.G. Wells).

He also writes for the movies, television, and the printed page. He is the author of the novel *New Jerusalem,* published, to critical acclaim, by Sun & Moon Press in 1986.

He has received a Guggenheim fellowship, four National Endowment for the Arts Fellowships, three OBIE awards, a Rockefeller Foundation Playwrighting Fellowship, and numerous other awards. He has also been nominated for a TV Emmy. And recently he served as the American representative (with his play *Poor Folk's Pleasure*) at the Toga International Arts Festival in Japan. He also was selected for an international exchange by USIA and the Russian Theater Worker's Union in Moscow.

Len Jenkin lives in New York City, where he teaches in the Dramatic Writing Program at New York University.

SUN & MOON CLASSICS

Sun & Moon Classics is a publicly supported nonprofit program to publish new editions and translations or republications of outstanding world literature of the late-nineteenth and twentieth centuries. Through its publication of living authors as well as great masters of the century, the series attempts to redefine what usually is meant by the idea of a "classic" by dehistorizing the concept and embracing a new, ever-changing literary canon.

Organized by The Contemporary Arts Educational Project, Inc., a non-profit corporation, and published by its program, Sun & Moon Press, the series is made possible, in part, by grants and individual contributions.

This book was made possible, in part, through a matching grant from the National Endowment for the Arts, from the California Arts Council, through an organizational grant from the Andrew W. Mellon Foundation, and through contributions from the following individuals.

Charles Altieri (Seattle, Washington)
John Arden (Galway, Ireland)
Dennis Barone (West Hartford, Connecticut)
Jonathan Baumbach (Brooklyn, New York)
Bill Berkson (Bolinas, California)
Steve Benson (Berkeley, California)
Sherry Bernstein (New York, New York)
Bill Corbett (Boston, Massachusetts)
Robert Crosson (Los Angeles, California)
Tina Darragh and P. Inman (Greenbelt, Maryland)
Fielding Dawson (New York, New York)
Christopher Dewdney (Toronto, Canada)
Philip Dunne (Malibu, California)
George Economou (Norman, Oklahoma)
Elaine Equi and Jerome Sala (New York, New York)
Richard Elman (Stonybrook, New York)
Lawrence Ferlinghetti (San Francisco, California)
Richard Foreman (New York, New York)
Howard N. Fox (Los Angeles, California)
Jerry Fox (Aventura, Florida)
In Memoriam: Rose Fox
Melvyn Freilicher (San Diego, California)
Peter Glassgold (Brooklyn, New York)
Perla and Amiram V. Karney (Bel Air, California)
Fred Haines (Los Angeles, California)

Fanny Howe (La Jolla, California)
Harold Jaffe (San Diego, California)
Ira S. Jaffe (Albuquerque, New Mexico)
Alex Katz (New York, New York)
Tom LaFarge (New York, New York)
Michael Lally (Santa Monica, California)
Norman Lavers (Jonesboro, Arkansas)
Jerome Lawrence (Malibu, California)
Herbert Lust (Greenwich, Connecticut)
Norman MacAffee (New York, New York)
Rosemary Macchiavelli (Washington, D.C.)
In Memoriam: John Mandanis
Toby Olson (Philadelphia, Pennsylvania)
Maggie O'Sullivan (Hebden Bridge, England)
Rochelle Owens (Norman, Oklahoma)
Marjorie and Joseph Perloff (Pacific Palisades, California)
Dennis Phillips (Culver City, California)
David Reed (New York, New York)
Ishmael Reed (Oakland, California)
Janet Rodney (Santa Fe, New Mexico)
Dr. Marvin and Ruth Sackner (Miami Beach, Florida)
Floyd Salas (Berkeley, California)
Tom Savage (New York, New York)
Leslie Scalapino (Oakland, California)
James Sherry (New York, New York)
Aaron Shurin (San Francisco, California)
Charles Simic (Strafford, New Hampshire)
Gilbert Sorrentino (Stanford, Connecticut)
Catharine R. Stimpson (Staten Island, New York)
John Taggart (Newburg, Pennsylvania)
Nathaniel Tarn (Tesuque, New Mexico)
Fiona Templeton (New York, New York)
Mitch Tuchman (Los Angeles, California)
Anne Walter (Carnac, France)
Arnold Wesker (Hay on Wye, England)

If you would like to be a contributor to this series, please send your tax-deductible contribution to The Contemporary Arts Educational Project, Inc., a non-profit corporation, 6026 Wilshire Boulevard, Los Angeles, California 90036.

*First edition
** Revised edition